Workers and Change in China

Strikes, protests, and riots by Chinese workers have been rising over the past decade. The state has addressed a number of grievances, yet has also come down increasingly hard on civil society groups pushing for reform. Why are these two seemingly clashing developments occurring simultaneously? Manfred Elfstrom uses extensive fieldwork and statistical analysis to examine both the causes and consequences of protest. The book adopts a holistic approach, encompassing national trends in worker–state relations, local policymaking processes, and the dilemmas of individual officials and activists. Instead of taking sides in the old debate over whether non-democracies like China are on the verge of collapse or have instead found ways of maintaining their power indefinitely, it explores the daily evolution of autocratic rule. While providing a uniquely comprehensive picture of change in China, this important study proposes a new model of bottom-up change within authoritarian systems more generally.

MANFRED ELFSTROM is Assistant Professor in the Department of Economics, Philosophy, and Political Science, The University of British Columbia, Okanagan.

Cambridge Studies in Contentious Politics

General Editor

Doug McAdam *Stanford University and Center for Advanced Study in the Behavioral Sciences*

Editors

Mark Beissinger *Princeton University*
Donatella della Porta *Scuola Normale Superiore*
Jack A. Goldstone *George Mason University*
Michael Hanagan *Vassar College*
Holly J. McCammon *Vanderbilt University*
David S. Meyer *University of California, Irvine*
Sarah Soule *Stanford University*
Suzanne Staggenborg *University of Pittsburgh*
Sidney Tarrow *Cornell University*
Charles Tilly (d. 2008) *Columbia University*
Elisabeth J. Wood *Yale University*
Deborah Yashar *Princeton University*

(continued after index)

Workers and Change in China

Resistance, Repression, Responsiveness

MANFRED ELFSTROM
The University of British Columbia, Okanagan

CAMBRIDGE
UNIVERSITY PRESS

CAMBRIDGE
UNIVERSITY PRESS

Shaftesbury Road, Cambridge CB2 8EA, United Kingdom

One Liberty Plaza, 20th Floor, New York, NY 10006, USA

477 Williamstown Road, Port Melbourne, VIC 3207, Australia

314–321, 3rd Floor, Plot 3, Splendor Forum, Jasola District Centre, New Delhi – 110025, India

103 Penang Road, #05–06/07, Visioncrest Commercial, Singapore 238467

Cambridge University Press is part of Cambridge University Press & Assessment, a department of the University of Cambridge.

We share the University's mission to contribute to society through the pursuit of education, learning and research at the highest international levels of excellence.

www.cambridge.org
Information on this title: www.cambridge.org/9781108926348

DOI: 10.1017/9781108923286

First published 2021
First paperback edition 2022

A catalogue record for this publication is available from the British Library

ISBN   978-1-108-83110-9   Hardback
ISBN   978-1-108-92634-8   Paperback

To my parents

Contents

Figures

Maps

Tables

Acknowledgments

Like any book, this one has gone through countless revisions that have tacked back and forth, with sentences, paragraphs, and whole chapters added, tweaked, cut, and added back again. But a few key drafts stand out from the blur of edits. Each benefited from a different circle of people. The first draft was my doctoral dissertation. This draft would not have been possible without the support of a truly outstanding dissertation committee at Cornell University. Each of the committee members deserves separate recognition. My advisor, Valerie Bunce, guided me through my research and writing process with thorough, constructive feedback, a broad comparative approach, dry humor, and just the right amount of structure. I could not have asked for a better mentor and model. Eli Friedman, a friend from before I began my doctoral studies, added a fresh sociological perspective, a crucial sniff test of claims about Chinese workers, and someone to talk to who shared my commitment to the labor movement. Andrew Mertha raised thought-provoking questions about my cases and what they meant, used his extensive experience to help me navigate fieldwork in China, and in several important instances, offered a sympathetic ear when I encountered frustrations along the way. Finally, Sidney Tarrow pushed me to clarify my claims, draw out the mechanisms involved, and root everything in the rich tradition of contentious politics scholarship. There were others beyond my committee who played crucial roles, too. Jeremy Wallace, my outside reader, provided useful feedback, especially regarding my statistical work, while Sarosh Kuruvilla, my advisor when I began my graduate studies at Cornell's ILR School, introduced me to important qualitative research skills, helped me interpret my research through an industrial relations lens and develop my thinking about the Chinese workplace and qualitative research and, through writing a paper together with me that was eventually published in *Industrial and Labor Relations Review*, showed me the ropes of academic publishing. And David Patel was an indispensable guide to social science methodologies in general. My final years of field trips and dissertation writing were done not in Ithaca but rather Vancouver, where the Institute of Asian Research at The University of British Columbia (UBC) generously allowed me to use a desk, gave me access to the UBC library, and welcomed me into its vibrant community of faculty and students. For this, I am grateful to Timothy Cheek, Pittman Potter, Christopher Rea, Tsering Shakya, and Yves Tiberghien.

The second major draft of the manuscript transformed a fairly dissertation-y dissertation into something approaching a book. This draft benefited from a China Public Policy Postdoctoral Fellowship at Harvard University's Ash Center for Democratic Governance and Innovation. There, I enjoyed the now-unimaginable luxury of just researching and writing with few other responsibilities. I was surrounded by a group of outstanding faculty and staff, especially the Ash Center's director, Anthony Saich, as well as Edward Cunningham, Jessica Eykholt, Kaori Urayama, and Odd Arne Westad. Rebecca Zhang provided assistance with updating my quantitative data. My friend Arunabh Ghosh offered thoughtful advice about the writing process. And I was also able to share ideas with a wonderful cohort of fellow post-docs: Chen Huirong, Lee Chengpang, Li Junpeng, Li Yao, and Sara Newland. Of particular benefit to the manuscript was a book workshop organized at the Center. In addition to several of the aforementioned Ash Center faculty and post-docs, the workshop participants included Joseph Fewsmith, Mary Gallagher, Elizabeth Perry, Emmanuel Teitelbaum, Saul Wilson, and Christine Wong, each of whom added something unique. Over the course of an intense day of discussion, I came to understand my argument as concerning an extended process of change, starting at the shop floor and extending to the halls of power, rather than a one-off claim of cause and effect.

My third and final draft was written in a very different place: sunny Los Angeles, California. As a Postdoctoral Scholar and Teaching Fellow at the University of Southern California's (USC) School of International Relations, I had the space to refine my manuscript still further. I am extremely grateful to the faculty there who briefly made me a part of their circle, especially Brett Carter, Erin Baggott Carter, Clayton Dube, Jacques Hymans, Patrick James, David Kang, Wayne Sandholtz, and most of all, Saori Katada and Stan Rosen. My students at USC, meanwhile, helped me refine my thinking about China in several ways through classes I taught on topics that I mistakenly believed to be unrelated to my book manuscript – Chinese foreign policy and Asian security issues – but instead yielded surprising insights. Joshua Meyer-Gutbrod offered very useful advice on my first chapter and overall framing at this point. My third draft was further polished here in Kelowna, British Columbia, where I live at the time of this writing. I am grateful to all my new colleagues at The University of British Columbia, Okanagan for the warm welcome and support they have given me, especially Thomas Heilke, Maxime Héroux-Legault, Andrew Irvine, Adam Jones, Jim Rochlin, and Helen Yanacopulos.

Several other institutions and individuals have contributed directly to the project. My dissertation was supported by a National Science Foundation Doctoral Dissertation Research Improvement Grant (Award #142194), a Lee Teng-Hui Fellowship in World Affairs, a Hu Shih Memorial Award, a Sage Fellowship, two International Research Travel Grants from the Mario Einaudi Center for International Studies, and an ILR School International Travel Grant. While conducting my initial fieldwork, I also benefited from several days spent at the Universities Service Centre for China Studies at the Chinese University of Hong Kong, where I dug into their vast collection of local government almanacs and police manuals. The School of Labor Economics at the Capital University of Economics and Business in Beijing generously acted as my academic host during part of my research. And funding from the Ash Center allowed me to return to China for follow-up interviews. I am grateful that *China Quarterly*, the *British Journal of Industrial Relations*, and their respective publishers, Cambridge University Press and John Wiley & Sons Ltd., gave me permission to use portions of articles I published in their journals (parts of my *CQ* article appear in Chapter 6; parts of my *BJIR* article, in Chapters 3–5). Finally, this book would not be possible if Robert Dreesen, Senior Editor at Cambridge University Press, had not taken an interest in the project and, together with Assistant Editor Erika Walsh, steered it along to completion. I also appreciate the feedback I received from my three anonymous reviewers. The production team led by Robert Judkins got the manuscript in publishable shape. Randi Hacker gave the book an expert final copy edit. Each of these institutions and individuals added a vital ingredient.

A broader group of people also shaped the manuscript more indirectly. Through undergraduate studies at Oberlin College and my graduate studies at Columbia University's School of International and Public Affairs (SIPA), I grew in my understanding of politics, art, and social justice under the guidance of people like Thomas Bernstein, Marc Blecher, Johnny Coleman, Li Kai, Liu Fang, Ma Qiusha, Andrew Nathan, John Pearson, Leonard Smith, and Steve Volk. Marc Blecher, in particular, generously read many papers of mine long after I left Oberlin, including some that evolved into chapters of this book. Deborah Cocco and Carl Jacobson were like a second set of parents during my two-year Oberlin Shansi Fellowship in rural China after college, a time that left a lasting impression on me and, ultimately, on this project. Labor academics in China, including Chang Kai, Liu Cheng, Meng Quan, Shen Tongxian, Shen Yuan, Wen Xiaoyi, and above all others, Wang Kan, contributed to the book through their discussions with me and the suggestions they made. Before reentering academia, I was active for several years in the non-profit world with groups supporting workers' rights and improved grassroots governance in China. I am deeply grateful for all I learned from Liu Yawei at the Carter Center; Li Qiang at China Labor Watch; Bama Athreya, Jeffrey Becker, Brian Campbell, Yulan Duggan, Aaron Halegua, Alan Howard, Kevin Lin, Eva Seidelman, Trina Tocco, and others I worked with at the International Labor

Rights Forum; and activists like Sun Aijing and the late Earl Brown, both at the Solidarity Center, and Ellen David Friedman, retired from the National Education Association and now social justice activist-at-large. My interviewees for the project – workers, businesspeople, officials – generously shared their time with me and trusted me to accurately capture their worlds. I hope my book proves worthy of that trust. Maybe most of all, China's committed labor activists, as friends and comrades and interviewees, provided me with insights and inspiration. However, given the current political climate in the country, it sadly would not be wise to list them by name here. Hopefully, in the future, I can give them the credit they richly deserve.

Last but most important, I am indebted to my friends and family. If I tried to list all the dear friends – in the United States, China, and elsewhere – who have helped me think about my purpose as an academic and global citizen and have, in different ways, contributed to the book, I would undoubtedly come up short. Rather than attempt such a list, I will simply say that these people know who they are. Particular note should be made, though, of my fellow graduate students at Cornell University's ILR School and in its Department of Government who discussed my work with me. These include Elizabeth Acorn, Joseph Bazler, Steffen Blings, Christopher Cairns, Sun-wook Chung, Sebastian Dettman, Todd Dickey, Lin Fu, Mark Gough, Isaac Kardon, Wendy Leutert, Martijn Mos, Elizabeth Plantan, Samir Sonti, Bradley Weinberg, and Hao Zhang, among others. My parents, Susan and Tove, to whom this book is dedicated, and my sisters, Miriam and Madelene, showed love and support throughout my research – as did my in-laws, Kathie, David, and Rhiannen. My sons, Rowan and Luca, were born at different stages of this project. Writing done after a night spent walking babies to sleep is perhaps not the finest writing but these boys gave me a perspective on life and work that has been absolutely invaluable. Finally, my wife, Freya, gave me encouragement and lent me a sympathetic ear even when our lives were at their busiest. She also carefully reviewed several drafts of the manuscript with a critical eye. Intentionally or not, Freya pushed me to continually return my writing to what really matters: what ordinary people are doing to change their lives.

This book is the product of all these influences. But I am solely responsible for any mistakes in it, and I and look forward to others' critiques of my work. If journalism is the "first draft of history," then the social sciences are the second and not necessarily more accurate draft. Many more drafts by many others will be required to fully tell the story of China's workers and the change they are bringing to their country.

Introduction

They had clocked punishingly long hours – eleven a day, six days a week, more during peak production periods – and been verbally and physically abused, eaten disgusting cafeteria food lacking the nutrition needed to sustain them, and slept fifteen people to a room in sweltering summers. Their earnings before overtime had been the local legal minimum at the time, no more, no less: US$54 per month. Fees for housing and meals, which totaled $30 per month, were deducted from this. There was little money left over to buy clothes and toiletries, let alone send home to help a sibling get through school or an ailing parent get medical care. Managers, who had come under scrutiny from foreign clients brandishing corporate codes of conduct, had put forward a plan to increase the number of rest days per month. However, the condition for this seeming generosity was that more overtime had to be worked on weekdays. Because weekday overtime paid less than weekend overtime, earnings were cut by another $12. Then, when payday arrived, even this reduced salary was inexplicably delayed.

These mounting challenges did not make the plight of thousands of workers at two shoe factories, Xing Ang and Xing Xiong, unusual. In fact, even with the wage cut and delay, conditions at the plants, located near a rare strip of parkland in the dusty boomtown of Dongguan in southern China and operated by the Taiwanese firm Stella International Holdings Ltd., were better than many other, similar operations. What distinguished the workers was what they did about their circumstances. In April 2004, 4,000 people at Xing Ang and 1,000 at Xing Xiong went on strike. Their actions quickly escalated. Several hundred workers raided production lines and company offices, using work tools to smash machinery and computers and spraying the spaces using fire extinguishers torn from the walls. Pantries were raided for food. Windows were knocked out. Workers attacked the dining halls and guard houses, too, and flipped cars belonging to management.

Although police had not intervened in a much smaller protest at another Stella plant the previous month, this time authorities felt forced to get involved. It took Public Security, aided by thirty factory guards, three hours to restore order. Afterward, the police detained dozens of the workers, eventually charging ten of them – apparently on the basis of their identification as trouble-makers by management, rather than on any concrete evidence of wrongdoing – with "intentional destruction of property." Authorities set a trial date, and it seemed that although the company had sustained substantial losses from the disruption, it had come out on top again.

But things did not end there. Labor groups based outside mainland China, including the International Confederation of Free Trade Unions (now the International Trade Union Confederation), Clean Clothes Campaign, China Labour Bulletin, and China Labor Watch placed intense pressure on the Chinese government and on the multinational brands sourcing from Stella, urging leniency. Moreover, the renowned human rights lawyer Gao Zhisheng agreed to take the accused workers' case. In a stirring speech, Gao declared that the roots of the riot stretched back to "the fact that our society today permits and encourages ... gross and inhuman exploitation of ... workers that has reached truly reactionary proportions." Official Chinese media covered the case, too. The final result: although the workers were initially convicted, they were acquitted on appeal. They could fight another day.

In 2015, 1,000 employees at Xing Ang once more took to the streets and were joined by hundreds of comrades at Xing Xiong. Much was the same as before. Workers blocked roads and a local labor nongovernmental organiza-tion (NGO) offered its services. However, there were important differences. The cause this time was not Dickensian working conditions but an issue that would have seemed a mere detail in 2004, namely the factory's failure to make required contributions to a housing fund for certain employees. Workers were now also coordinating online and posting social media updates on the evolving situation – along with photos and videos – in real time. Footage from the scene captured laughing protesters surrounding company vehicles.

The Chinese state was also better prepared. Photos of the 2015 protest showed hundreds of riot cops lined up in neat formation. After their initial road-blocking, employees were effectively "kettled" within the factory grounds. K-9 units were deployed. Workers were bitten by the dogs. Lawyer Gao, who gave the dramatic defense in 2004, had long since disappeared into prison, then been released, then disappeared again, punished for his work defending religious dissidents. Foreign groups had less political room to advo-cate for the strikers, and multinational social compacts had been scaled back. The local NGO that offered its services was prevented from continuing to meet with the workers. Though posts about the incident could be found on websites hosted abroad, a scan of China's main search engine, Baidu, generated no news results for the 2015 confrontation whatsoever, presumably due to censorship.

Labor's options had seemingly been significantly reduced since the last showdown.

However, authorities had also become more willing to meet workers half-way. The fact that Dongguan's minimum wage – now nearly three times what it was in 2004 – was no longer a factor in the incident reflected not only China's rising inflation, but also a better enforcement of basic labor laws. Doubtless under pressure from the government to do its part to maintain social stability, Stella quickly conceded to employee demands, paying the workers their housing subsidy in cash. Later, when the factory shut down, management went above and beyond what was required by law and generously compensated those who had lost their jobs, avoiding another standoff. Thus, from another perspective, labor was in a much better position than before.[1]

For the Stella employees, the situation had changed substantially over the decade-plus separating the two incidents. However, the change had gone in two clashing directions: if labor had become more empowered, the state had developed a greater capacity for repression *and* a greater capacity for responsiveness. New opportunities for workers were mixed with new constraints.

The Stella story is indicative of changes in China's workplaces more generally. From the beginning of the twenty-first century through the mid-aughts, workers from all over China, but especially in the country's southeast where Xing Ang and Xing Xiong are located, began taking to the streets in growing numbers. The first Stella strike was, as noted, fairly unusual when it occurred. However, by 2015, the year of the second strike, the Hong Kong–based advocacy group China Labour Bulletin (CLB) was counting an astonishing 2,774 work stoppages occurring across the country (China Labour Bulletin 2019). This was only slightly less than the number (3,036 strikes) reported by the International Labour Organization for all of eastern and western Europe and Israel the same year (ILO 2018). Comparisons with the United States are more difficult, as the United States only tracks incidents involving more than 1,000 participants. But whereas the US Department of Labor recorded a mere

---

[1] This narrative is based on a number of sources. My description of the 2004 strike incorporates information from advocacy groups, blogs, and news articles (China Labour Bulletin 2007; Gough 2004; J. Tang 2004; Zhao 2004). The mention of physical and verbal abuse, in particular, is grounded in an account that reported that protesters demanded an end to "beatings and insults" (J. Tang 2004). There is some lack of clarity on how much the workers earned after overtime. The wages in USD are based on the exchange rate at the time. For a report on Gao Zhisheng's defense of the arrested workers, see China Labour Bulletin (2005b). My description of the 2015 strike and subsequent factory closure is backed by similar reports (China Labor Watch 2015; China Labour Bulletin 2016b; D. Tang 2015; C. H. Wong 2015). There is some disagreement between managers and workers about how many employees protested in 2015 (China Labor Watch 2015; China Labour Bulletin 2016b; D. Tang 2015; C. H. Wong 2015). Full disclosure: as an intern at one of the organizations mentioned, I helped in a minor way with international support for the workers arrested following the 2004 strike.

twelve stoppages with that many people in 2015, CLB recorded eighty-three (BLS 2016). Given that CLB estimated that their dataset only captured 5–10 percent of the total number of incidents occurring at any given time (China Labour Bulletin 2016a), Chinese labor unrest may, therefore, have been up to ten times more intense than Europe's and seventy times more intense than America's.[2] Scholars began to describe China as an "emerging epicenter of world labor unrest" (Silver and Zhang 2009. Global trade union conferences invited speakers from China. Once an object of foreign pity, the focus of sweatshop exposés and anguished editorials about the dangers of free trade, Chinese workers gradually came to be seen in some circles as inspired militants worthy of emulation.

Alongside this popular mobilization, Chinese governance also evolved. The country as a whole spent much more on its internal security forces. In fact, it spent more on them than it did on national defense. It trained the forces better. It invested in new forms of surveillance, both human and technological. It put through new regulations on civil society groups and their supporters from abroad. This was most pronounced in the places with the most unrest. However, authorities – both in Beijing and in China's provinces and cities, especially, again, those with more conflicts – also passed new labor laws that increased the penalties for employers who violated workers' rights. They pushed China's hidebound official trade union to engage workers in fresh ways and to advocate more effectively on workers' behalf, such as by sometimes holding real elections for enterprise-level union chairs, trying out practices that came close to approximating the collective bargaining of other countries, and devoting union funds to rights litigation. Labor arbitration panels and courts were meanwhile made more accessible to employee-plaintiffs. High-level politicians also publicly expressed sympathy for the people left behind by the country's breakneck growth. For a period, China's leaders publicly advocated a "people first" policy rooted in an allegedly more balanced "scientific concept of development" that was supposed to reduce inequality and usher in a "harmonious society." The state at once ruthlessly confronted its working class and went out of its way to appease it.

These clashing policy alterations are not only substantively important to the lives of over a billion people but are also intriguing from a social science standpoint. They confound academic analyses of authoritarian political systems as either moving inexorably toward liberal democracy or as resolutely immune to the political trends of the post–Cold War era. The changes observed in Chinese industrial relations should also push us to move beyond a narrow

---

[2] The trend in the last couple of years has been somewhat murkier. However, despite the loss of one of CLB's main information sources, a pair of Chinese bloggers who were detained in 2016 (and only released in 2017 and 2020), and the group's rollout of a new, more restrictive sampling technique, it managed to document 1,702 incidents in 2018 (China Labour Bulletin 2017a, 2017b).

focus on social movement origins to a study of the complex results that movements bring with them. For the study of Chinese contentious politics, in particular, a growing area of scholarship, the scale of what has happened in the country's workplaces offers new opportunities for methodological innovation. Most importantly, the experiences of the Stella workers and their counterparts in other parts of China ought to direct our attention away from static political models and toward a more process-oriented approach to the understanding of what ordinary people can accomplish – and the ways things backfire for them – in challenging environments.

A PROCESS-ORIENTED APPROACH

My purpose in this book is to trace the full process of change occurring in Chinese labor politics, from start to finish – or at least as far as it has progressed up to this point. According to McAdam, Tarrow, and Tilly (2001, 27), "Processes are frequently recurring causal chains, sequences, and combinations of mechanisms." Figure 1.1 maps my process and its mechanisms. I start with the forms and causes of contention in the first place. Specifically, I analyze *recipes for resistance*. These are clusters of industrial sectors and worker demographics that are associated with contrasting forms of contention, namely contained, boundary-spanning, or transgressive. My purpose here is not to generate a general model of Chinese labor mobilization but to post hoc identify different combinations of structural "ingredients" that come together to ultimately place very different pressures on officials. Next, I explain how resistance in its various forms works through bureaucratic incentives to affect policy. Officials are all disciplined by China's cadre promotion system to demonstrate competence in the face of rising unrest. But the precise nature of the challenge faced by authorities is important. And each arm of the local state swings into action in its own way. Distinct *regional models of control* result. Where resistance occurs at a moderate level and takes a contained or, at most, boundary-spanning form, the model is *orthodox*; where the resistance occurs at a high

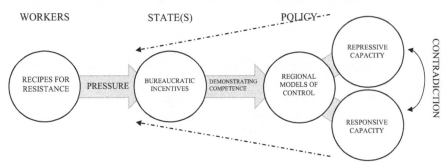

FIGURE 1.1 The process of change.

level and takes a boundary-spanning or even transgressive form, the model is *risk-taking*. I then show how, as it wrestles with labor and develops these diverse subnational models, the state is overall acquiring both more *repressive capacity* and more *responsive capacity* – at the same time. These dynamics may be shaped to a limited degree by the agendas of particular influential Chinese politicians at both the regional and central level. But in the final analysis, I posit that the politicians are responding to what is happening on the ground. I finish by arguing that the impact of rising workplace discontent is not limited to workplace governance, but is partly responsible for the lurching, uneven political development we have witnessed in China in recent decades. If the Chinese state has shown remarkable adaptability in how it has reacted to workers to date, it has also been *warped* – twisted out of shape but not broken – by its encounters with challenges from below, and it will likely face more contradictions going forward. Although the book does not set out to identify universal laws of protest and policy, I suggest that similar dynamics can be found in other post-state socialist authoritarian regimes, which cover an important swath of the world. China's experience offers a useful guide to a distinctive pattern of transformation, shared perhaps by many other countries, that defies easy categorization and prediction, but amounts to significant change all the same. In the remainder of this chapter, I will expand on each of these points in turn and provide an outline of subsequent chapters.

RECIPES FOR RESISTANCE

Before we examine the consequences of worker resistance, we must first explore its forms and causes. We have to clarify what we mean by "resistance" in the first place: the variety of kinds of conflict that are encompassed by the term. McAdam, Tarrow, and Tilly (2001) contrast contained and transgressive contention. O'Brien (2003), meanwhile, identifies an intermediary "boundary-spanning" type of protest as existing in the Chinese context, which employs semiroutinized contentious repertoires and successfully appeals to segments of officialdom. Contained resistance by Chinese labor means making minimal, legal claims; resorting to formal state channels; and/or not creating any organizations beyond the shop floor. Boundary-spanning resistance aims for *more*, irrespective of legal minimums; uses a wide range of tactics, from strikes to protests to riots; and may involve loose associations of workers or legally oriented NGOs in a minor capacity. Finally, truly transgressive resistance involves demands for *much more* and for institutional reforms, engages in cross-workplace and even cross-provincial strikes, and draws on movement-oriented NGOs or groups like leftist students. Nationally, growth in strikes, protests, and riots is overtaking formally adjudicated employment disputes, and the claims appearing in incidents are becoming more aggressive, even as NGOs, including movement-oriented ones, are proliferating (though they have been set back in the last couple of years). Evidence of this shift can be found in the differences between the first and second Stella strikes: minimal requests giving way to more ambitious calls for improved conditions, spontaneous protest supplanted by a disciplined strike, and autonomous action (albeit later supported by outside groups and a lawyer) replaced by (brief) coordination with an NGO interested in helping with the dispute. The escalation is more pronounced when certain factors are present. Light manufacturing, construction, and transportation account for most strikes, protests, and riots. Areas with large concentrations of migrant workers also see more of these actions. The proliferation of NGOs follows a similar pattern. In contrast, high-tech, high-skilled industries and local workers yield more contained activism. These "recipes for resistance" – "recipes" in the sense of combinations of "ingredients" that yield different (or similar) results – explain spatial variation in the intensity of contention – and in the pressure felt by officials.

BUREAUCRATIC INCENTIVES

The state's concern over unrest is transmitted down to local authorities and horizontally across different ministries in the form of bureaucratic incentives for local cadres to demonstrate to their superiors that they are on top of things. Thus, it is likely that, following the protests at Xing Ang and Xing Xiong, Dongguan authorities were on the phone with officials in the provincial capital, Guangzhou, and maybe Beijing, seeking to reassure them that order would soon be restored. Mechanisms for promoting and punishing officials based on objective criteria have been the subject of increased empirical analysis over the past decade, particularly in the realm of economic management, with scholars showing how officials, usually at the provincial level, compete for the attention of their principals by delivering higher GDP growth or revenue collection – or, failing this, by faking the same with cooked account books (Landry 2008; Lü and Landry 2014; Shih, Adolph, and Liu 2012; Wallace 2016). My interest is in how the same sorts of incentives function with regard to worker protest. Strong work has already been done on the topic of accountability for stability maintenance more generally (e.g., Lee and Zhang 2013; J. Wang 2015, 2017; Y. Wang and Minzner 2013). I am especially indebted to Heurlin's (2016) demonstration of how petitioning waves driven by land confiscation and housing demolition have reshaped national policies. But my interest is in how these incentives can also backfire, as different arms and levels of the state – townships versus provinces, police versus courts – each do what they know best, revealing not just the state's flexibility in the face of popular discontent – Heurlin's focus – but its tendency to undermine its own efforts. Bureaucratic incentives, when tripped by unrest, speed the electric charge of dissent through the system, but with clashing results at various points.

REGIONAL MODELS OF CONTROL

The first results of the interaction of conflict and bureaucratic incentives are distinct *regional models of control.* The state's reaction to the unrest in Dongguan and in the broader region where the Stella strikes occurred was different from the reaction observed further up China's coast or inland. Officials in areas with contained resistance have every reason to keep managing affairs as they always have: creative approaches to labor relations policy could inadvertently introduce more intense conflict. The default in such places is thus *orthodoxy.* Legislators pass incremental laws. Police carefully monitor workplaces. The judiciary quietly mediates disputes. Branches of the party-controlled trade union hand out welfare benefits and try to meet contract quotas. However, officials in areas with high levels of unrest, especially places where dissent takes a boundary-spanning and even transgressive form – like Dongguan and its province, Guangdong – do not have the same luxury. They might not realistically be able to fully restore order. But such officials must at least demonstrate to their superiors that they are doing everything in their power to calm the situation down. This means *risk-taking.* Whether through coordination or entirely autonomously, each arm of government experiments in the ways it can. Laws are shaken up by local legislatures. Police beat and detain activists. Trade unions start to genuinely negotiate with employers. There is obviously a downside to shaking up governance in this manner. What if things escalate? But there is less to lose than doing so when the situation is calm. The different bundles of policies adopted by different local governments congeal into contrasting models.[3] Other scholars, such as Hurst (2009) and Lee (2007), have examined geographic variation in Chinese state reactions to protests by different groups of state-owned enterprises workers and to state workers versus migrant workers during a previous wave of conflict. However, whereas the implied chain of reaction in their analyses leads from local economic structures to government policies to worker protests (or, in Hurst's work, more accurately, from economic structures to both protests *and* policies), mine points in somewhat the opposite direction. Recipes of resistance cause particular patterns of resistance that generate particular local approaches to governance. Figure 1.2 "zooms" in on the first section of Figure 1.1 to capture these dynamics.

INCREASED STATE REPRESSIVE AND RESPONSIVE CAPACITY

Although each region comes up with its own way of trying to control workers, more labor resistance means more state *repressive capacity* and more state *responsive capacity* overall. As Slater (2010) puts it, social conflict can "build"

---

[3] Here, I expand the analysis of an article I published in the *British Journal of Industrial Relations* (Elfstrom 2019c).

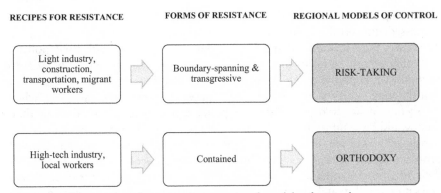

FIGURE 1.2 From recipes for resistance to regional models of control.

the state in the same way that interstate wars do. I noted at the outset of this chapter that what the workers at Stella International experienced during their second industrial action was not uncommon: tougher, better trained and equipped police coupled with a greater ability on the part of authorities to overcome the objections of powerful local employers and deliver meaningful concessions. Broad statistical patterns can be observed. More unrest in a given place is correlated with an expansion of anti-riot forces, even when factors such as economic development are controlled for. Greater conflict is also correlated with places allowing employees to win more in the legal system – or at least have the benefit of more split decisions – although such openings also encourage more conflict, in turn.[4] Overall, with each wave of worker protest, the government builds up its ability to coerce labor and increases its nimbleness when it comes to addressing the demands of different social groups. It is empowered along two dimensions.

BOTTOM-UP VERSUS TOP-DOWN CHANGE

This is a story of bottom-up change. But there are complications to the story. First, as the arrows pointing backward from state capacity to recipes of resistance in Figure 1.1 indicate, we must keep feedback effects in mind. Labor's future options are affected by the changes in governance that workers have previously wrought. Regional models of control become self-reinforcing to some extent: orthodox approaches to governance encourage contained forms of resistance. But when some shift in the economy causes unrest to rise, orthodoxy becomes unworkable – on the ground and when it comes to the government's internal politics. And, again, there is no reason to introduce

---

[4] This builds on an article published in *China Quarterly* (see Elfstrom 2019b).

risk-taking in the midst of calm. Second, the role of local elite politics must be addressed. Powerful regional leaders with idiosyncratic agendas can make a difference, both in terms of spurring or dampening unrest with their policies and, of course, in terms of their reactions to unrest. They have the potential to be a powerful confounding variable. For example, it may have been significant that the tough party secretary Hu Chunhua was in power in Guangdong when the second Stella strike happened: the police probably took a harder line than they would have under his predecessor, Wang Yang. However, reformists and hardliners alike only direct their energies to labor issues when labor presents a problem. When workplaces are calm, dynamic leaders of whatever stripe focus their attention on other areas of policy. The decisions of politicians in provinces and cities are ultimately more barometers than drivers of what is happening in the streets. Third and similarly, at a national level, China has gone through periods marked by greater reliance on repressive versus responsive capacity. Such shifts cannot help but affect worker resistance. This book covers events in both the Hu Jintao-Wen Jiabao and Xi Jinping administrations. The latter government has been marked so far by the much tougher line it has taken toward civil society, including labor organizations. Thus, the first Stella strike occurred at the outset of the Hu-Wen period in power; the second, under Xi. This may have played some role in how the two clashes played out. Tightening like that which has occurred recently cannot help but affect activism. But changes, even dramatic ones like those under Xi, should not obscure the considerable continuity that exists between different governments in Beijing. Labor organizers were targeted under Hu and Wen, too, as they were under Jiang Zemin before them, and small but meaningful concessions have been made to labor under Xi. Overall, the increase in repressive and responsive capacity described above continues despite turnovers at different levels of government, even if the precise balance between deployment of one tool or the other alters.

STATE WARPING

The Chinese state's dual strengthening might turn out to be a net gain for authorities, albeit one earned via intense instability. If this turns out to be the case, then China will fit Slater's (2010) argument of contention-driven capacity-building nicely. The People's Republic will furthermore mesh well with Crouch's (1996) analysis of how, in Malaysia, repression and responsiveness have played "mutually supporting" roles in sustaining autocratic rule (or, at least, a hybrid regime). It will also echo Kerkvliet's (2010) findings about the Vietnamese government's willingness to bend to the demands of workers, farmers, and entrepreneurs, while simultaneously coming down hard on activists it believes present a serious threat to its rule, a phenomenon that leads Kerkvliet, building off Crouch, to describe the country as possessing a "responsive-repressive state." And China will be yet another example of what

Heydeman and Leenders (2013), based on conditions in Syria and Iran, dub "recombinant authoritarianism," meaning the successful reordering and reconfiguring of a variety of institutions in seemingly clashing ways to meet popular challenges (although the focus of their study is economic institutions, not repression and responsiveness). However, there are strong reasons to believe that growing in two clashing ways will prove unsustainable over the long haul.

Strengthening in this way can, first, come at the expense of other state priorities. Repressive and responsive capacity are just two of the many forms of state capacity that exist, after all. Almond and Powell (1966, chap. 7) list several others: extractive capacity (Slater's focus), distributive capacity (the state's ability to redirect the gains of economic development), and symbolic capacity (the ability to build buy-in for the state's mission). Despite China's remarkable economic growth since the beginning of reform and opening, it still has budget constraints. Money directed to riot equipment is money not spent on healthcare or education (distributive capacity). As domestic security outlays have skyrocketed, welfare expenditures have only inched upward, despite a widespread acknowledgment that more of a social safety net is necessary to deal with a greying population, encourage domestic consumption, and reduce China's wealth divide. China's previous Hu Jintao-Wen Jiabao administration did more for expanding the Chinese welfare state than the current government (Gao, Yang, and Zhai 2019; Howell and Duckett 2019). This stasis hurts the country's symbolic capacity: What is the "China Dream" without housing and healthcare? A repressive-responsive state defers difficult commitments.

Moreover, enhanced repressive and responsive capacity do not build a strong class coalition for Chinese Communist Party (CCP) rule. Rattled by unrest, the CCP in some ways resembles the Asian and African "counterrevolutionary parties" described by Slater and Smith (2016, 1472), which have mounted "collective and reactive efforts to defend the status quo and its varied range of dominant elites against a credible threat to overturn them from below." But different from the most effective of these groups, e.g., the ruling parties of Malaysia and Singapore in Asia and Botswana and Apartheid-era South Africa in Slater and Smith's analysis, China has not assembled a powerful mass or elite coalition around it. Repression against labor undercuts the possibility of working-class support. Meanwhile, the responsive gestures made by authorities to date have not been enough to counterbalance the repression for workers – but have been enough to strain the CCP's alliance with business groups. For years, China assiduously courted "red capitalists," welcoming them into the Party, adapting various institutions to fit their needs, and reframing the CCP's mission as broadening the "middle stratum" rather than serving as an instrument of proletarian power (Dickson 2003; Goodman 2014; K. S. Tsai 2006, 2007). New labor laws and more even-handed arbitration panels and courts set back these efforts.

Finally, coordinating the growth of repressive and responsive capacity will be difficult. China may be steadily developing along these two lines, but as

I noted above in my discussion of national elite politics, it has up to now relied *more* on one tool for a period, then on the other, then circled back to the first, with the current Xi Jinping administration primarily using repression to resolve challenges. These adjustments may be carefully directed by authorities. Crouch (1996, 7) writes of Malaysia: "At times the government has been inclined to resort to authoritarian measures, while at other times it has adopted a relatively liberal attitude. Nevertheless, these oscillations have taken place within a limited range and do not fundamentally change the nature of the political system." However, while China's oscillations have also not been wild, they have not been perfectly calibrated, either. In fact, the country's shifts in policy have sometimes canceled out rather than reinforced each other. As Minzner (2018, 33) perceptively writes,

Over the past three decades, a pattern has developed. Individual leaders sponsor reforms to address latent governance problems. Doors open. Citizens start to use them to participate politically .... At that point, central Party authorities get nervous ... Reforms are smothered, activists are detained. For precisely this reason, China has remained in a one-step forward, one-step-back dance since the 1990s ...

Workers are driving state capacity building. They are doing so in two diametrically opposed ways. And given the difficulty of managing this dual empowerment, political development takes a staggered, imbalanced form that ultimately warps the state.

MOVING BEYOND TRANSITOLOGY AND RESILIENCE

As already indicated above, the argument of this book builds upon and challenges important existing research. Scholarship on authoritarian regimes has a long, distinguished history in political science and sociology (e.g., Linz 2000; Montesquieu 1990; Moore 1966). But it has tended to swing between extremes. For a period in the 1980s and early 1990s, spurred on by excitement around the "Third Wave" of political liberalization, a "transitology" paradigm dominated these disciplines (e.g., Huntington 1991; for a review, see Art 2012). This paradigm treated dictatorships as only a way station on the road to democracy, with research, therefore, focused on the terms of their destruction, such as "pacted" handovers of power versus violent revolutions (e.g., O'Donnell and Schmitter 1986). The most controversial work along these lines was, of course, Fukuyama's (1992) *The End of History and the Last Man*, which posited capitalist democracy as the natural endpoint for all states. There were at least two problems, however. One was that many new democracies, such as Russia's, after rocky starts, began to move in a decidedly more authoritarian direction. The other was the remarkable staying power of nondemocratic governments, including several of the successor states of the Soviet Union, as well as, most glaringly, China. In the popular press, the imminent fall of the CCP was repeatedly predicted in the years immediately following the

Tiananmen Square Massacre (a late but especially influential contribution to this literature was G. G. Chang 2002). And academics enumerated the reasons that a transition was likely *sometime* in the future (Gilley 2004). Yet, the Party prospered. A better paradigm was needed.

The issues with the transitology paradigm have given rise to an alternative approach focused on "authoritarian resilience." This has shifted scholars' attention to the variety of mechanisms that autocrats possess for maintaining control, including limited experiments with elections and other forms of power-sharing (Gandhi and Przeworski 2007; Levitsky and Way 2010; Magaloni 2006; Svolik 2009, 2012), powerful secret police (Bellin 2004; Greitens 2016), and the careful collection and control of information (Gehlbach, Sonin, and Svolik 2016; Wintrobe 1998). The new paradigm has also led to a proliferation of more fine-grained typologies of non-democracy (Collier and Levitsky 1997; Diamond 2002; Geddes, Wright, and Frantz 2014; Levitsky and Way 2010; Svolik 2012; Weeks 2012). Along these lines, in China studies, researchers have generated a vast body of research on sources of regime stability, including everything from restrictions on urbanization (Wallace 2014) to the selective doling out of state benefits (Wright 2010), to high-tech censorship (King, Pan, and Roberts 2013; Roberts 2018), to co-opted civil society groups (Hildebrandt 2013; Mattingly 2020), to grievance monitoring via the petitioning system (Xi Chen 2012; Dimitrov 2015; Heurlin 2016) and controlled protests (Xi Chen 2012; Y. Li 2019a, 2019b; Lorentzen 2013, 2017), to institutions like the National People's Congress and village voting (Manion 2006; Truex 2016) to improved systems for leadership succession (Nathan 2003). New terms have meanwhile been applied to the CCP's practices, such as "responsive authoritarianism" (Heurlin 2016), "contentious authoritarianism" (Xi Chen 2012), "authoritarian deliberation" (B. He and Warren 2011), "consultative authoritarianism" (Teets 2014), and "consultative Leninism" (Tsang 2009). The implication is remarkable flexibility.

Neither the transitology nor resilience approach is entirely satisfying. The shortcomings of transitology are obvious: it does not do a good job of explaining non-transitions, such as China's. The resilience turn has, on the whole, yielded a much more nuanced picture of nondemocratic rule. But taken too far, it risks producing an equally dogmatic picture as that generated by earlier work, one in which autocrats are assumed to always act in optimal ways to preserve their rule, or, at the most extreme, to be master puppeteers fully in charge of their fates. Borrowing terms from software programming, any seeming "bug" is thought to be a "feature" whose purpose only awaits explanation. More importantly, both the transitology and resilience paradigms, by focusing exclusively on the binary of stability versus collapse, obscure the considerable change that can occur within a shell of regime continuity. They are static snapshots of complex states.

In contrast, this book is interested in authoritarian *evolution*. It thus extends many early studies of how governance evolved in the Soviet Union and other post-revolutionary state-socialist countries (e.g., Bunce 1980; Ekiert 1996; Johnson 1970a), as well as research like that of Finkel, Gelbach, and Olson (2015) on Tsarist Russia. At the same time, the book adds to the findings of China scholars like Ang (2016), Heilmann and Perry (2011), Fewsmith (2011), and Whiting (2001) concerning Beijing's ability to continually adjust to challenges – while echoing some of their doubts about the sustainability of the precise adjustments made. Although questions concerning regime longevity inevitably undergird any study of dictatorship to some degree, my primary interest is in alterations occurring in the here and now. And my focus is on the role popular pressures play in generating these alterations.

UNDERSTANDING MOVEMENT OUTCOMES, NOT JUST CAUSES

If scholarship on authoritarianism has tended to overly concern itself with long-term outcomes, social movement scholars have, instead, traditionally been more interested in the causes of movement formation, not the effect of movements. In particular, research has highlighted the roles played by political opportunities, mobilizing structures, and issue framing in facilitating collective action (McAdam 1999; McAdam, McCarthy, and Zald 1996; Tarrow 1998), as well as the protest repertoires developed in the process (e.g., Tilly 2006). Nonetheless, there is a growing body of work concerning protest results. Up to now, this scholarship has mostly been about liberal democracies, especially the United States (e.g., Amenta and Halfmann 2000; Davenport 2015; Ganz 2009; Gillion 2013; Giugni 2007; Giugni, McAdam, and Tilly 1999; Giugni and Yamasaki 2009; Piven and Cloward 1977; Tarrow 2012, chap. 9; Wasow 2020). Similar investigations of outcomes under authoritarianism are rare (for discussions of this gap, see Amenta et al. 2010; Tarrow 2008). And to the extent that such dynamics are studied, researchers have generally focused, again, on the prospects for regime change (e.g., Bunce and Wolchik 2011; Chenoweth and Stephan 2011). Scholarship has also been more concerned with hybrid regimes like Vladimir Putin's Russia today or Mexico under the Institutional Revolutionary Party, rather than full autocracies (e.g., Robertson 2011; Trejo 2012). Here, I look at an extended process of movement-driven alteration in day-to-day governance in an environment seemingly extremely inhospitable to popular pressures.

EXPANDING THE STUDY OF CHINESE CONTENTIOUS POLITICS

Research on Chinese contentious politics has arguably gone further than most in exploring the routine impact of grassroots mobilization outside of democracies. Scholars have, for example, identified a type of "rightful resistance" that uses official rhetoric to drive a wedge between local and higher-level authorities (O'Brien and Li 2006), as well as "troublemaking" tactics that can draw a positive response from the government by at once being disruptive and staying

within certain well-established boundaries (Xi Chen 2012). This protest reper-
toire has been traced to patterns of contention in imperial China (Hung 2011;
Perry 2002, 2010). In the realm of labor mobilization, specifically, Fu (2016,
2018) demonstrates how "disguised collective action" and "mobilizing without
the masses" can win concessions. Scholars have also examined how successful
Chinese activists draw on broad social networks (Cai 2010) and the services of
journalists and policy entrepreneurs, including sympathetic local officials and
leaders of "mass organizations" like the China Disabled Persons Federation to
open the policy process (Xi Chen and Xu 2011; Mertha 2008). Insider and
outsider tactics have thus been found to be mutually reinforcing (Steinhardt and
Wu 2016). For the most part, this research has taken a case study approach, but
there are several great surveys of trends in Chinese unrest (C.-J. J. Chen 2018;
Goebel 2019; Y. Li 2019a, 2019b; Ong and Goebel 2012; Steinhardt 2013;
Tong and Lei 2014; Wright 2018; for a review, see Elfstrom and Li 2019).
Moreover, while scholars have tended to focus on the determinants of wins and
losses in individual confrontations between citizens and the state, there have
also been important works probing the broader, systemic effects of activism.
For example, Bernstein and Lü (2003) trace changes in rural tax policy during
the Hu Jintao and Wen Jiabao administrations back to a massive wave of
peasant protests over the previous decade, an analysis built upon by Heurlin
(2016). Outside protest studies per se, scholars have shown how Chinese NGOs
focused on the environment, AIDS, and other issues have forced the government to accommodate them (e.g., Teets 2014). In this book, I extend this
important, trends- and results-oriented line of inquiry. I turn to my methods
and data next.

METHODOLOGY AND DATA SOURCES

The book combines multiple levels and forms of analysis. At one level, by
focusing only on China, this is a "holistic case study," i.e., a project aimed at
capturing a particular, important situation – the world's largest country, largest
authoritarian regime, and largest working class – from every angle. Wherever
possible, I, therefore, try to triangulate information, drawing on statistics,
interviews, and government texts to capture the same phenomena (Jick 1979;
Tarrow 2010). As a holistic study, the book is located somewhere between a
"configurative-ideographic study," which allows its case to speak for itself on
its own terms, and a "disciplined-configurative study," which uses a case to
inquire into – if not exactly test – broader processes prevalent around the world
(Eckstein 1992, 136–43; Yin 2003, chap. 2). I make my strongest claims about
China. But in conclusion, I raise the possibility that similar phenomena might
be observed in other authoritarian states, especially other post-state socialist
authoritarian states.

At another level, this is what Yin (2003, 42–46) calls an "embedded case
study," because, within China, I examine how different patterns of contention

TABLE 1.1 *Most similar cases*

	Jiangsu	Guangdong
GDP	2	1
Exports	2	1
Total Investment by Foreign Enterprises	1	2
Number of Migrant Workers	4	1
Number of SOEs	4	2

Above: Jiangsu and Guangdong ranked relative to all of China's thirty-one provinces, directly administered cities, and autonomous regions.
Source: *China Statistical Yearbook 2014.*

yield different models of control in different regions (i.e., in different cases "embedded" in the broader Chinese case). Here, I am building on a rich body of work that has already been conducted on regional variation in the country's worker politics. For example, Lee (2007) has contrasted the struggles of state sector workers in the northeastern "rustbelt" with those of workers in the southeastern "sunbelt." Hurst (2009), focusing on SOE workers, meanwhile describes four regional political economies: the Northeast, North-Central, Central Coast and Upper Changjiang (with provincial capitals forming a fifth category of sorts). Blecher (2010), responding to Lee (2007), distinguishes between a "highly globalized" southeastern "sunbelt," a "barely globalized" northeastern "rustbelt" and a "broadly 'reformed' but only partially globalized and still largely domestically-oriented" class of areas such as the city of Tianjin. And Friedman (2017) compares the "extra-legal precarity" of teachers in Beijing migrant schools with the "market discipline" of their Guangzhou counterparts. Where I differ from these studies is that I consciously choose places for analysis that are as similar as possible with the exception of their worker resistance (on such "most similar" designs, see George, Bennett, and Bennet 2004, chap. 4; Przeworski and Teune 1970).

My two main regions are Jiangsu's portion of the Yangtze River Delta and Guangdong's portion of the Pearl River Delta. The provinces involved are not, of course, carbon copies of each other, but they are arguably more alike than any other two provinces with regard to the variables typically treated as important in studies of Chinese labor issues: economic growth, integration into the global economy, state sector presence, and migrant worker density. In Table 1.1, Jiangsu and Guangdong are ranked relative to all of China's thirty-one provinces, directly administered cities and autonomous regions with regard to these variables. Note that the provinces are never more than three notches apart in the rankings, and, on three of the five measures used, they trade first and second place. However, although both Jiangsu and Guangdong are relatively contentious, they still differ with regard to their frequency and forms of worker resistance – and consequently, I argue, with regard to their approaches to governing workplaces. Residual differences in industrial sectors and worker demographics account for the regions' contrast in militancy but do not determine state responses, meaning they do not fundamentally confound the protest-policy relationship.

Additionally, I use a brief, shadow case study of the directly administered (i.e., provincial level) city of Chongqing and its dynamic successive leaders Wang Yang and Bo Xilai to examine whether local political elites impact labor politics in an important way. If any place lent itself to policy innovation and if any individuals were most likely to try out new approaches to workplace governance it would arguably be this city and these politicians in the mid-2000s (on this form of "most likely" case selection, see Eckstein 1992, chap. 4; Gerring 2008). Chongqing is an up-and-coming metropolis. Wang and Bo for a period led, respectively, the liberal and left-populist wings of the CCP, both of which have a keen – but different – interest in labor policy reform. I further explore the role of elite politics through an examination of the shift in the repressive-responsive balance nationally between the Hu-Wen and Xi administrations. This shadow case, though, is just that – a shadow of the much more in-depth investigations I conduct in Jiangsu and Guangdong.

At yet another level, my book attempts a large-N analysis of the average relationship between resistance, on the one hand, and repressive and responsive capacity, on the other. Case studies are excellent for identifying processes (Checkel 2008; George, Bennett, and Bennet 2004; Slater and Ziblatt 2013) but they are not well suited for understanding average trends. Thus, I break China down into as many statistical "observations" as possible, examining correlations between strike rates (resistance) and both spending on the para-military People's Armed Police (repressive capacity) and pro-worker or split decisions in formally adjudicated employment disputes (responsive capacity) at the provincial level over the course of a decade (31 provinces × 10 years = 310 observations or enough to find patterns but only important ones) (on multiplying observations, see King, Keohane, and Verba 1994). If in the case study analysis, I choose main cases that are as similar as possible, in the large-N analysis I statistically control for as many potential confounders as possible: economic vitality, urbanization, penetration by the official trade union, etc. I also check for reverse causality using lagged dependent variables and instrumenting on past values of the independent variable. The quantitative component of the book provides a rough sense of China's general trajectory amenable to a big-picture analysis – and projection into the future – that complements and extends the qualitative, comparative case study sections that make up the core of the work.

Data Sources

My data sources are varied. First of all, I rely on 152 interviews with 197 labor activists, workers, factory managers, government officials, and others

TABLE 1.2 *Interview characteristics*

Characteristics	Number	Percent
Total number of interviews	152	NA
Total number of interviewees	197	NA
Women	42	21.3
Workers	94	47.7
Labor activists	25	12.7
Government and trade union officials	25	12.7
Businesspeople	19	9.6
Academics and other experts	34	17.3
Interviews in Yangtze River Delta	51	33.6
Interviews in Pearl River Delta	39	25.7
Interviews elsewhere	62	40.8

conducted between 2011 and 2017. These interviews were all semi-structured, meaning that I came into them with certain questions I wanted to be answered but allowed the flow of conversation to determine the questions' order – and I engaged new topics as they were introduced (Bernard 2006, chap. 9). In general, I did not record my discussions but rather took quick, handwritten "jottings" that I later fleshed out in typed summaries (on jotting, see Emerson, Fretz, and Shaw 1995). A breakdown of the interviewees' characteristics is provided in Table 1.2, and a list of all the interviews is available in Appendix 1. This material is paired in my case studies with over 200 local government yearbooks, mostly from the Yangtze River Delta and the Pearl River Delta. These are glossy volumes recording an area's achievements. They are often given as gifts to visiting authorities from higher levels of government, and as such, they provide a unique window into the pressures felt by officials to impress their superiors. In one instance, I subject the yearbooks to automated content analysis.

Finally, in my statistical sections, I utilize China Strikes, a unique dataset that I have constructed, which includes geo-referenced information on 1,471 strikes, protests, and riots by Chinese officials between the years 2003 and 2012 – the full Hu Jintao-Wen Jiabao administration. In other words, this is a study primarily of the current protest wave, not previous ones, like the activism of the late 1990s and early 2000s; other data extend the analysis closer to the present in places. China Strikes is publicly available online, and visitors to its website can upload reports on incidents I have missed. Map 1.1 is based on a screenshot of the website's map of incidents. More details on this dataset and its strengths and limitations are provided in the next chapter. I match China Strikes with information from government statistical almanacs: China Statistical Yearbook, China Labour Statistical Yearbook, and China Trade

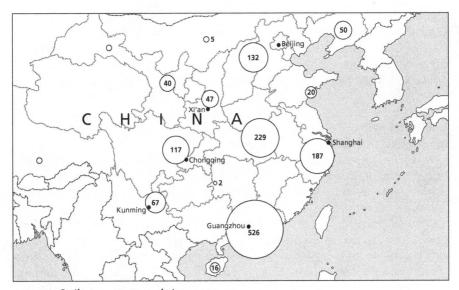

MAP 1.1 Strikes, protests, and riots 2003–12.
Source: China Strikes (2017), accessible at https://chinastrikes.crowdmap.com/.

Unions Yearbook for the full period of 2003–12, and the Financial Statistics of Cities and Counties through 2009 (*Quanguo dishixian caizheng tongji ziliao* or *difang caizheng tongji ziliao*) (for a list of all the government sources I draw upon, see Appendix 2). These different sources complement each other and provide a broad picture of China's changes – from the very bottom to the very top of the country's political system.

ORGANIZATION OF THE BOOK

The book's organization follows the contentious process outlined above: from changes at the shop floor level to the interaction between labor protests and elite politics. In the next chapter, after reviewing some key characteristics of Chinese industrial relations and the existing research on work in China, I document the different *forms* of Chinese worker resistance today and the *recipes for resistance* that seem to generate them. Then, in Chapter 3, I switch my focus to the way unrest works through bureaucratic incentives to have the *effects* that it does, introducing my two case study regions in the process. Chapters 4 and 5 then dig deeper into the case studies to capture specific regional models of control that are the result of particular levels and forms of resistance: an orthodox approach to managing conflict characterized by pre-emption, caution, and nudging, in Jiangsu's Yangtze River Delta (Chapter 4) and a risk-taking approach characterized by the reaction, experimentation, and crackdowns in Guangdong's Pearl River Delta (Chapter 5). In Chapter 6, I use statistical analysis to show how, on average, increased resistance (as captured by the *China Strikes* data) is yielding increased repressive and responsive capacity nationally, as measured, again, by more spending on the paramilitary police and more pro-worker or split decisions in mediation, arbitration, and court. Chapter 7 addresses the issue of elite politics and its impact (or lack thereof) on worker-state interactions, focusing on Chongqing and its powerful leaders, as well as an analysis of what has changed – and what has not – since the beginning of the Xi Jinping administration. I finish the book with a conclusion (Chapter 8) that focuses on the implications of these findings for China's long-term political development, while situating my work in the broader context of workers and states more generally, especially in post-state socialist authoritarian settings.

The Chinese case shows that grassroots-driven change can occur in unlikely places. However, it cautions that that change means both new openings and new challenges for everyone involved. Workers win more official solicitousness to their claims but at the cost of new hurdles to organizing. Authorities develop new powers to crush and co-opt, but set up new contradictions for themselves in the future. Labor is gradually altering governance from below – but it is doing so in a circuitous, ambiguous manner. People like the Stella employees who went on strike in Dongguan and the police and other government agents who confronted and cajoled them are navigating a different world from that of just a few years before. It is at once a world of their own creation and one filled with great uncertainty.

2

Recipes for Resistance

Before we can examine the *consequences* of China's rising worker resistance, we must explore the *recipes for resistance* that drive it. Why and how Chinese labor mobilizes have already been the focus of a rich body of literature. In this chapter, I will first very briefly summarize the key characteristics of Chinese industrial relations and then review the scholarship that has been conducted to date, emphasizing how perspectives on workers in China have changed over time, from pessimism to guarded optimism and back again, while highlighting certain key themes in the research, such as extreme exploitation, workplace arrangements that facilitate and frustrate organizing, the unique constraints and opportunities of migrant workers, and concerns over informal and flexible work. Then, I will introduce a fresh typology of different forms of activism distinguished by the varying level of pressure that they bring to bear on the state. Specifically, I will identify certain combinations of demands, tactics, and organizations as contained, boundary-spanning, or transgressive. Next, I will provide evidence that boundary-spanning and transgressive mobilization are on the rise. Strikes, protests, and riots are increasing more quickly than formally adjudicated employment disputes; workers are claiming more than the bare minimum of what Chinese law guarantees them, and new organizations, such as movement-oriented labor NGOs and leftist student networks, are entering the fray. As I will explain, these phenomena are concentrated in certain parts of the country. Moreover, they are correlated with particular sectors, namely light industry, construction, and transportation, and with the presence of migrant workers. These findings highlight the continued relevance of many arguments made previously by other scholars, while also complicating those arguments. Light industry and transportation are sectors that are both exploitative and yet, at the same time, facilitate organizing. Construction and, to a lesser extent, transportation protests show how, given the right conditions, informality need not be a barrier to mobilizing. And the (current) dominance of migrant workers in activism suggests that the constraints on migrant collective action are not as insurmountable as once imagined. These inductively derived recipes for resistance must be kept in mind as confounding variables when we attempt to trace the connections between protest and policy. But more fundamentally, they mark the beginning of a contentious process that extends from shop floors all the way to the halls of state power. They are the base upon which worker action and superstructural change are built. But let us first start with the basics: the key characteristics of Chinese industrial relations.

KEY CHARACTERISTICS OF CHINESE INDUSTRIAL RELATIONS

Chinese industrial relations have three distinguishing characteristics. First, although more than 60 percent of China's GDP growth comes from the private sector, and private enterprises account for over 80 percent of the country's employment, the state sector still plays an important role (Xinhua 2018). In the past, under state socialism, the most coveted jobs were in state-owned enterprises (SOEs), followed by collective enterprises managed by lower levels of the government (Bian 1994). In SOEs, "work units" (*danwei*) provided a range of benefits, from childcare to housing, and constituted worlds unto themselves (Lü and Perry 1997; Saich 2016). The private sector barely existed (almost all the remainder of employment was taken up by agriculture). Now, SOEs are constantly in the firing line of economic reformers but dominate crucial sectors. In fact, they are playing an increasingly crucial role in the government of China's current Communist Party Secretary and president, Xi Jinping, especially when it comes to foreign policy. Second, Chinese citizens' access to social services is managed by a household registration (*hukou*) system that effectively restricts everything from schooling for a person's children to pension payouts based on the place where that person's parents were registered when they were born. There have been important tweaks to the system over time. With "reform and opening," rigid controls on the mobility of labor were relaxed, allowing people with rural household registration to work in the new urban private sector. Until 2003, these individuals, often called "peasant workers" (*nongmin gong*), could be arrested and sent home if they lacked the proper paperwork. But following a high-profile death in police detention that year, this "custody and repatriation" policy was abolished (for a discussion of this case, see Hand 2006). Some areas have made further efforts to grant urban status to residents in peri-urban areas or to extend education to migrant children. In general, though, Chan and Buckingham's (2008) analysis from a decade ago continues to ring true: the hukou system is "potent and intact." Finally, China has a single, Communist Party-controlled trade union federation, the All-China Federation of Trade Unions (ACFTU). Although its roots lie in radical 1920s organizing (Perry 1993), the ACFTU today sees itself as first and foremost "a bridge and a link between the Party and masses of workers," and the 2001 Trade Union Law states that, in the event of a work stoppage, "the trade union shall assist the enterprise or institution in properly dealing with the matter so as to help restore the normal order of production and other work as soon as possible" (ACFTU 2006; Trade Union Law of the People's Republic of China 2001). In the 1950s and again in the 1980s, the union's leadership made bids for greater autonomy, but these were firmly shut down by the Party's leadership (China Labour Bulletin 2009a; Pringle 2011, 29–32, 62–65; Sheehan 1998, chap. 2). The right to strike was removed from the Chinese Constitution in 1982, following the tumultuous Cultural Revolution and as the country marketized. Striking is not formally prohibited (T. Feng 2011; B. Taylor, Chang, and Li 2003, 33). But the ACFTU does not organize strikes. All collective actions are thus wildcats. With these key points in mind, we can now review research about Chinese labor from recent decades.

CHANGING PERSPECTIVES ON LABOR IN CHINA

Research on Chinese labor issues has gone through several overlapping phases. Mao-era industrial relations were understood as relatively static, at least from the late 1950s onward, marked by scarcity, political campaigns, and clientelistic bonds between workers and managers – but also allowing some channels for worker input in firm decisions. Walder (1988) called this system "communist neo-traditionalism," while Andreas (2019) has more recently dubbed it "participatory paternalism" (with the Cultural Revolution years marking a radical exception). From the mid-1990s to early 2000s, scholars such as Chang (1995, 455) analyzed how market reforms, by weakening state economic plans, were rapidly constituting "laborers" and "enterprises" or "managers" as distinct actors with more obviously clashing interests and clashing conceptions of rights, rather than as similar cogs in the same nationwide production drives, thus making labor laws increasingly central to labor relations (see also B. Taylor, Chang, and Li 2003). The uncertain status of migrant workers also began to draw attention (Solinger 1999). Concern grew that these people had become second-class citizens (P. Alexander and Chan 2004; Solinger 1999; for a more recent reflection on this theme, see Xiong 2008). Academics and activists highlighted the abysmal conditions in the sweatshops where migrants were often employed, along with scattered reports of worker resistance there (e.g., A. Chan 2001; Liu 2003). Discussions also developed over what role the ACFTU might come to play (e.g., Ng and Warner 1998). In particular, would the union develop in a state corporatist direction (A. Chan 1993; Unger and Chan 1995) or become entirely a non entity? After an extended hibernation, the system appeared to be in flux.

These themes were developed further by researchers in the early to mid- to late-2000s. In particular, they focused on the restructuring of Chinese state-owned enterprises (SOEs) and the subsequent layoffs and impoverishment of millions of their workers starting in 1998 (for an overview, see Hassard et al. 2007). Scholars documented how SOE employees took to the streets in massive protests, making powerful claims rooted in a "socialist social contract" (Au and Bai 2010; Cai 2006; Feng Chen 2000; Hurst 2009; Hurst and O'Brien 2002; Lee 2007; Weston 2004; Yu 2010). But barriers to more effective collective action were also emphasized: competition between workers spurred by foreign direct investment (Gallagher 2002, 2005), fragmentation induced by different alternative job opportunities and managerial prerogatives (Cai 2006; although novel manager-employee alliances were also found, see K.-C. Lin 2009), wariness of the repercussions of cross-factory organizing (Cai 2002; Lee 2007), local governments' weak fiscal capacity to make concessions (Hurst 2009), and a younger generation in thrall to the state's new market ideology (Blecher 2002). Despite early discussions, the union and related institutions, such as Staff and Workers' Representative Congresses (SWRCs), were seen to play a minimal role (if any) (but on SWRCs, see Estlund 2013; X. Zhu and Chan 2005). Here was a group that had lost everything, had gone from "master to mendicant," in Solinger's (2004) words – not without spirited resistance, but with little in the way of institutional support and little hope for the future.

At the same time that they tracked the decline of SOE employees, researchers began to analyze the conditions of migrant workers in greater depth. Scholars went into their factories and documented the shocking abuses there, as well as the different ways in which people were disciplined into their new roles, physically and psychologically, and constrained by gendered networks of people from the same hometown (Lee 1998; Pun 2005; Sargeson 1999). The fallback option for migrants of returning to farms maintained in the interior, where social reproduction occurred, where the elderly were cared for and children raised while parents labored in the cities, was viewed as dampening protest (Lee 2007, chap. 6). Some structures, such as a new dormitory labor regime in which employees were housed on the grounds of production facilities, were seen more as double-edged swords, facilitating both corporate surveillance *and* worker solidarity (Pun and Smith 2007). However, whereas state sector workers at least possessed a fiery class consciousness inherited from the rhetoric of the government's state socialist past, migrants seemed captives of a narrow individual rights mentality born of the country's new emphasis on the rule of law and their own experiences with discrimination (Lee 2002, 2007) – although some scholars also recognized that the same workers who drew upon the law in increasing numbers could be quite clear-eyed and even cynical about it (Gallagher 2006). The NGOs that were beginning to take root in the southeast to serve migrants outside the aegis of the ACFTU were seen as reinforcing this legalistic tendency, limiting themselves to labor law training and *pro bono* advocacy (or advocacy for a small fee) in court or haggling with employers in the shadow of the law (Franceschini 2014; Halegua 2008; Lee and Shen 2011). Migrant workers not only endured brutal exploitation but lacked the ideological tools and local bases of support to push back. Their only recourse was bringing their cases before the state's preferred forums.

A more optimistic tone developed among observers of Chinese labor in the late 2000s. This new outlook was spurred on by the mounting industrial actions across the country that were noted at the beginning of the previous chapter. Spectacular strikes captured special attention, such as one at a Honda auto parts supplier in Nanhai, Guangdong, in 2010, which shut down the company's entire Chinese supply chain and led to extended bargaining between employee representatives and management (Butollo and ten Brink 2012; Lyddon et al. 2015). These actions showed that migrants actually possessed a strong capacity for organization, one rooted in part in precisely those informal networks previously viewed as constraints, bolstered by a committed core of itinerant worker-activists (C. K.-C. Chan 2010; Leung 2015). A nascent class consciousness was furthermore detected in the group (C. K.-C. Chan and Pun 2009; whereas the formerly militant SOE employees came to be viewed as backward, reduced to everyday forms of resistance such as shirking, see J. Li 2012). More generally, scholars described Chinese workers of all types as increasingly offensive in their demands – no longer just calling for observation of old social contracts or legal minimums, but instead simply and brazenly claiming "more" (K. Chang and Brown 2013; Elfstrom and Kuruvilla 2014). Moreover, the trade union seemed to at last be emerging from its slumber to engage in modest but promising reforms (Feng Chen 2010; Howell 2008; Mingwei Liu 2010; Pringle 2011; Y. Zhu, Warner, and Feng 2011). There was even speculation that direct elections for the heads of enterprise-level unions might strengthen civil rights in China more generally (T. Feng 2009). Scholars no longer perceived labor NGOs as necessarily the narrow, ineffective institutions they were once portrayed as (Becker 2014, chap. 8; Feng Chen and Yang 2017; Franceschini 2016; Franceschini and Lin 2019; Froissart 2018; Fu 2016, 2018; Pringle 2017; Spires, Tao, and Chan 2014; Xu and Schmalz 2017; Zajak 2017). Although by no means universally (see, for example, the skepticism of Hui 2018), laws came to be seen as both a tool of state control *and* a cover for more subversive efforts – as well as a vulnerability for authorities (Gallagher 2017; Pun and Xu 2011). Labor, it appeared, was on the move, and making gains on multiple fronts.

At the time of this writing, pessimism has crept back into academic treatments of the world's largest working class (for a good review, see Kuruvilla 2018). The new government of Xi Jinping clearly takes a much dimmer view of civil society, including worker organizing, compared to its predecessor (Fu and Distelhorst 2018; Minzner 2018). Researchers are documenting a dramatic clampdown on labor NGOs, with organizations shut down entirely or forced to switch to more politically innocuous programming (Franceschini and Nesossi 2018). And the news seems to bring fresh stories of intimidation every day: prominent activists caught up in great sweeps and jailed, leftist students supporting workers disappearing from campuses. The trade union no longer appears to be going anywhere fast. Promising initiatives such as an organizing campaign directed at Wal-Mart workers appeared hollow on closer inspection (e.g., Blecher 2008; Unger, Beaumont, and Chan 2011). Now, seemingly wider-ranging reforms, such as sectoral collective bargaining agreements in places such as Wenling, or repeated, intensive negotiations at the Yantian port in Shenzhen, are being criticized as covers for managerial or state power (Pringle and Meng 2018; Wen 2015; Wen and Lin 2014) and genuine, worker-led bargaining is seen as a distant dream (C. K.-C. Chan and Hui 2013). The deepening precarity of employment in China is also raising new concerns (X. Feng 2019; Gallagher, Lee, and Kuruvilla 2011; Lee 2016; Swider 2015; H. Zhang and Friedman 2019). And the slowing economy threatens to under-cut gains made by labor, leading workers to defensively "strike to survive" (Fan 2018). At best, workers and the state seem to have arrived at a stalemate or, in the words of E. Friedman (2014b), an "insurgency trap," featuring high levels of contention but little institutional development. There are yet darker prognoses. Chinese labor relations, according to Howell and Pringle (2018, 15), have continually shifted between different "shades of authoritarianism," but if the immediately previous one was relatively flexible, this one is "encapsulating" – marked by a "stronger shade" that is "less open to influences external to the Party" and "ruthlessly intent on regime survival," with few benefits for workers.

Throughout these ups and downs, Chinese workers – their conditions, their responses – have generally been the dependent variable of interest in scholarship, echoing the broader social movements literature described in the first chapter. There are exceptions, of course. Research on the SOE activism of the late 1990s and early 2000s shows how unrest spurred the state to dramatically build out its social safety net, introducing new unemployment insurance and job retraining schemes, to a degree that even rivaled other states going through similar transitions (Cai 2010, chap. 8; Hurst 2009; for a comparative perspective, see Solinger 2009). Worker protest has also been credited with spurring the enactment of a new Labor Contract Law in 2008 and other legislation, such as a Labor Dispute Mediation and Arbitration Law and Employment Promotion Law the same year (K. Chang 2009; Estlund 2017; Gallagher 2017; L. Zhang 2015, chap. 7). And trade union reforms, in particular, are generally attributed to pressure from below (C. K.-C. Chan and Hui 2013; E. Friedman 2014b; Howell 2008; Pringle 2011; Pringle and Meng 2018; K. Wang and Elfstrom 2017). There has also been interesting research on the outcomes of individual disputes (Yujeong Yang and Chen 2019). However, these exceptions aside, and especially in recent years, as pessimism has deepened, the emphasis has been on how workers are stymied and channeled by authorities – not on how they, in turn, stymie and channel government policies. Labor, then, is a group to be explained, not itself part of an explanation for change in China.

In subsequent chapters, I will focus precisely on how workers are altering governance from below. However, my analysis in this chapter is very much indebted to the findings of previous scholarship on protest *causes* – even as it complicates this work in certain regards. Certain themes recur here. The first one is extreme exploitation of the sort discussed in early investigations of Chinese sweatshops (e.g., A. Chan 2001; Pun 2005). The second is particular workplace and labor market arrangements that facilitate or hinder collective action, such as the managerial power and different job opportunities noted as divisive by Cai (2006) or the dormitory regime identified as playing a dual role by Pun and Smith (2007). The third is discussions concerning informalization, flexibilization, and precaritization carried forward by scholars, including Lee (2016) and Swider (2015). And fourth and finally, there is the continually contested place of migrant workers in resistance. I will note my debts to previous work as they come up. However, before addressing protest causes, I will borrow from the general contentious politics literature to lay out my own typology of different forms of worker resistance in the Chinese context and introduce my *China Strikes* dataset in more detail (plus official figures) to provide an update on which forms of resistance are in the ascent and where they cluster.

CONTAINED, TRANSGRESSIVE, AND BOUNDARY-SPANNING RESISTANCE

The contentious politics literature provides a useful framework for distinguishing between different forms of resistance. For example, McAdam, Tarrow, and Tilly (2001, 7–8) contrast "contained" and "transgressive" contention. The former features "previously established actors employing well established means of claim making," whereas in the latter, "at least some parties to the conflict are newly self-identified political actors and/or ... at least some parties employ innovative collective action" (McAdam, Tarrow, and Tilly 2001, 7–8). Innovation, in turn, means adopting claims, objects of claims, or means "that are either unprecedented or forbidden within the regime in question" (McAdam, Tarrow, and Tilly 2001, 49). Thus, for instance, with regard to the tactics involved, the insider advocacy of African Americans before the Civil Rights movement took off constituted "contained" contention, whereas the innovative Montgomery bus boycott and lunch counter sit-ins constituted "transgressive" action (McAdam, Tarrow, and Tilly 2001, chap. 2). However, this typology just captures two extremes. Based on protest dynamics in China, O'Brien (2003) identifies a class of "boundary spanning contention" that fills the gap, in which the activism is "not prescribed or forbidden, but tolerated (even encouraged) by some officials, and not tolerated by others" (O'Brien 2003, 53). Arguably, the distinctions between these three categories – contained, transgressive, and boundary-spanning – ultimately come down to the distinct challenges they present to the objects of claims. Contained resistance is relatively easily handled; boundary-spanning resistance, less so; transgressive resistance, least of all.

In the Chinese context, contained, boundary-spanning, and transgressive resistance involve particular combinations of tactics, demands, and organizations. Let us start with contained resistance. *Tactics* that are relatively contained range from using the formal legal system to lodging complaints via China's unique system of letters and visits or petitioning offices (on petitioning, see Dimitrov 2015; Minzner 2006). Contained *demands*, meanwhile, hew closely to the state's own previous commitments and take the form of what O'Brien (1996) and O'Brien and Li (2006) call "rightful resistance." This sort of framing, in turn, contains considerable variation. For example, examining scores of complaint letters to mayors, Distelhorst and Fu (2019) identify three ideal types of "performing citizenship" in China: subjecthood, in which people present themselves as weak and beseech help from "benevolent rulers," socialist citizenship, which "appeals to the moral duties of officials to provide for collective welfare," and "authoritarian legal citizenship," focused on "formal legal commitments of the state." Finally, to be fully contained, resistance must not involve any formal *organizations* that can be perceived in any way as competing with the Party's monopoly on power and should not bring together people from different places or breach the walls of society's other various divisions (Perry 2008; Shue 1990). Staying within all these boundaries is no easy task.

In practice, most resistance takes a boundary-spanning form. There is always a gray zone in China between what is proscribed and what is tolerated. Here, informal norms come into play: officials may disregard laws prohibiting gatherings, for example, in the interests of preventing escalation (Y. Li 2019). Meanwhile, veteran "troublemakers" consciously make life difficult for local officials but hold back in crucial regards. Thus, Xi Chen (2012, 139–40) describes how villagers have blocked the entrances to government offices – but only some of the entrances and not others. Meanwhile, journalists and lawyers unsure of where the line between acceptable and unacceptable criticism lies tend to err on the side of caution (Xi Chen 2012; Y. Li 2019a, 2019b; Stern and O'Brien 2012). Of course, what is merely boundary-spanning today may be treated as transgressive tomorrow and vice versa. When petitioning via letter and visits to offices surge, this is alarming for authorities, who clamp down on even this approved channel (L. Li, Liu, and O'Brien 2012). Conversely, other, seemingly more confrontational tactics, such as street protests, may become something approaching "well-established" means of claim-making. A seemingly innocuous claim, grounded in the government's policies, might be quite challenging for elites to meet in practice, pitting officials against each other (O'Brien and Li 2006). Or an edgy claim may be couched in an anodyne manner that makes it less transgressive. Borders may shift, but one thing remains the same: to be boundary-spanning, activists must be modest in the structures they create, avoiding "linking up" (*chuanlian*) widely or associating with "illegal organizations."

Not all resistance stays contained nor does it conform to a simple definition of boundary-spanning. Sometimes, tactics take novel forms that the government does not know how to manage. The student protests in Tiananmen Square are the most obvious example. During these, authorities profoundly misjudged activists' intentions (and the reverse), leading to slaughter (Manion 1990). Consider, too, how Falun Gong practitioners suddenly surrounded Zhongnanhai, China's leadership compound, and engaged in a silent protest in 1999, catching officials off guard and spurring a harsh crackdown (Minzner 2018, 121–26; Saich 2015, 15). Lorentzen and Scoggins (2015) argue that claims that reflect a "rights consciousness" derived from changed values rather than changed government policy are especially destabilizing (read: transgressive). Thus, authorities have grappled with how to address the demands of China's new generation of feminists, as well as how to deal with advocates for the rights of lesbian, gay, bisexual, transsexual, and questioning (LGBTQ) citizens (Fincher 2018). Organizations such as the short-lived China Democracy Party or the Open Constitution Initiative unsurprisingly raise alarm bells. But so, too, do seemingly rule-abiding efforts by students to show support for janitors on campus or draw attention to sexual harassment by professors, as these also introduce "newly self-identified political actors" into the mix. Again, categories are fluid. Activism on LGBTQ issues may be normalized over a long period. The point here is, again, that everything depends on how threatening something is to the state and how well equipped the latter feels to deal with a challenge at a particular point.

DIFFERENT FORMS OF WORKER RESISTANCE

In the context of Chinese labor issues, we can observe all these forms of resistance in operation. As noted, categories are fluid. What was once considered disruptive may now be tolerated. Or the government may lose the capacity to handle certain kinds of conflicts that it once had under firm control. Authorities in certain parts of the country may feel more confident in managing industrial relations, including large-scale work stoppages. Others may panic over very little: a small gathering of construction workers that would be considered routine elsewhere. Nonetheless, in general, we can identify certain combinations of worker tactics, demands, and organizations (or the lack thereof) as contained, boundary-spanning, and transgressive.

Contained Worker Resistance

On the fully contained end of the spectrum, we find workers joining together to bring employment disputes to mediation, arbitration, and court. In the Chinese system, arbitration must precede litigation, and mediation, whether within enterprises or via the offices of neighborhood-level governments, is increasingly promoted as a semi-required precursor to arbitration (for good overviews of the full process, see Cooke 2008; Gallagher 2017, 85–89; B. Taylor, Chang, and Li 2003). Collective disputes, moreover, are often divided into individual cases (Gallagher 2017, 93). Contained *demands* hew close to bare legal requirements. For example, workers may call for the payment of the minimum wage or wage arrears or compensation for work-related injuries. *Organizations* beyond shop floor networks will be absent.

Boundary-Spanning Worker Resistance

Contained resistance may be enough to achieve modest aims. However, more is often needed to force employers to the bargaining table or really get the government's attention. Strikes, protests, and riots present a boundary-spanning alternative. These forms of contention may seem quite disruptive, but they have taken on a routinized form in many parts of the country. As the government has increasingly leaned into the "rule of law" (or rule *by* law), it has become more confident in dealing with purely legal claims. Boundary-spanning demands, in contrast, include calls for "more," especially higher wages, irrespective of what the law guarantees. These require more from authorities: new dispute resolution institutions or the reform of old ones, such as mediators or reformed trade union branches (but see Yujeong Yang and Chen 2019). The presence of more organization – fairly well-coordinated stoppages, the inclusion of labor lawyers and NGOs focused on legal support – is similarly boundary-spanning.

Transgressive Worker Resistance

When strikes are especially disciplined or involve multiple factories or even multiple cities and provinces, they become transgressive. Examples include recent national stoppages by crane operators, truck drivers, and delivery workers. Transgression also occurs when *much more* is demanded, and authorities are far from developing the forums to handle such claims *or* when various institutional reforms, such as changes to enterprise-level unions or local laws, are directly demanded. Finally, when labor NGOs become involved in strikes, as direct organizers or facilitators of bargaining sessions, that is, when they do not just provide legal advice – Feng Chen and Yang (2017) call such daring groups "movement-oriented labor NGOs" – this can cause the conflict to be treated as transgressive. Other networks, for example, ones involving leftist student activists or veterans of Cultural Revolution struggles, may have the same effect. Table 2.1 plots this typology of worker resistance. Note, again, that the classification of the contention as contained, boundary-spanning, or transgressive is ultimately the call of the object of pressure, i.e., the state.

TABLE 2.1 *Different forms of worker resistance*

	Contained	Boundary-spanning	Transgressive
Tactics	Litigation, petitioning	Strikes, protests, riots	Especially disciplined or cross-work site strikes
Demands	Legal minimums	Legal minimums, raises beyond minimums	Raises, union reforms, other new claims
Organizations	Only worksite networks	Legally oriented NGOs	Movement-oriented labor NGOs, other associations

CHANGING WORKER TACTICS

Documenting the extent of worker resistance of various sorts in China is difficult. This is especially true of activism that employs boundary-spanning and transgressive tactics. The country does not release official strike statistics. Therefore, to capture what is happening in the streets, I rely on an original, geo-referenced dataset I have assembled called *China Strikes*, which includes information on 1,471 strikes, protests, and riots by Chinese workers between 2003 and 2012. These years match the length of the Hu Jintao–Wen Jiabao administration, keeping elite politics relatively constant (subsequent chapters will draw heavily on fieldwork conducted during the subsequent Xi Jinping administration). The incidents that are featured in *China Strikes* are mostly drawn from my close reading of state media, foreign reporting, dissident websites, online bulletin boards, and social media. A research assistant has double-checked the completeness of the dataset using a fixed set of search terms and sites listed in Appendix 3. As noted in the previous chapter, China Labour Bulletin runs a similar strike mapping project that continues up to the present. It draws on the same sorts of materials, as well as interviews with Chinese workers conducted by the group's founder, Han Dongfang, on his Radio Free Asia program (the CLB project also includes more social media information). Although CLB has documented an impressive number of incidents, their project does not reach back before 2011. I have checked my dataset against CLB's for the years that the two sources overlap, adding any incidents CLB captured that I did not. My dataset is furthermore publicly available online and visitors to its website can upload reports on conflicts I might have missed. I have received half a dozen reports in this manner. Although I have not followed Cook and Weidmann's (2019) advice and included each underlying *report* as a separate observation, I have placed the full texts of all the reports on the website, so readers can make their own judgments about coding decisions. In sum, *China Strikes* is likely the most complete collection of information of its sort, at least for the period that it covers. However, it only represents a small sample of the total number of conflicts occurring in China's workplaces. In 2005, the last time official data on "mass incidents" were made public, 87,000 incidents of all types were reported, while a leak put the figure at 120,000 in 2008, and scholars have estimated that up to a third of these are employment-related disputes, meaning tens of thousands of such conflicts per year (C.-J. J. Chen 2009, 2018; Qin He 2014, 2; Tanner 2004; Wedeman 2009). One incident in China Strikes thus likely corresponds to hundreds in the larger "population" of contention. The dataset is, moreover, not a random sample of that population. Nonetheless, the geographic breadth of the dataset gives me confidence in it. Although the incidents *China Strikes* documents are concentrated on the coast, it captures conflicts across a remarkable swath of the country. Moreover, the timing of the incidents in the dataset is largely as one would expect, both within years and between years: more incidents every year in December, before China's Spring Festival, as migrant workers prepare to return home for the holidays and desperately try to recoup wage arrears, and fewer incidents during and immediately after Spring Festival; fewer before the 2008 financial crisis, then a spike during the crisis, followed by a steady climb from 2010 onward. Thus, although the dataset should not be subjected to overly fine-grained analysis, it gives a reliable picture of aggregate trends. Capturing activism using *contained tactics* is more straightforward. The Chinese government has, since the 1990s, compiled annual counts of employment disputes brought to mediation, arbitration, and court broken down by province. As I will show in Chapter 7, these counts are further divided into pro-worker, pro-business, and split outcomes, a useful distinction for understanding the impact of unrest on state responsiveness. Certain additional details would be useful, such as which types of cases are decided which way (collective vs individual cases, benefits vs pay cases, etc.). But for now, we are principally concerned with the rate at which activism is occurring. Figure 2.1 shows that both strikes, protests, and riots and formally adjudicated employment disputes have risen, but whereas the former started to table off after the financial crisis, the latter have only continued to skyrocket (more recent figures would show adjudicated disputes picking up again somewhat). China is experiencing a dramatic upsurge in workplace resistance of all sorts, yet boundary-spanning and transgressive tactics seem to have the edge. This should be alarming for authorities.

CHANGING WORKER DEMANDS

The *demands* that feature in Chinese worker resistance are also shifting. All the incidents in the *China Strikes* dataset for which demand information is available are carefully coded, something missing from early quantitative analyses of strikes (for a review, see Franzosi 1989; for an example of what could nonetheless be accomplished with the data available, see Shorter and Tilly 1971).

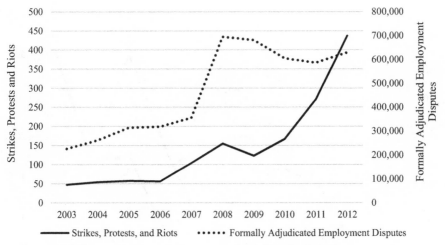

FIGURE 2.1 Strikes, protests, and riots versus formally adjudicated employment disputes.
Sources: *China Strikes* (2017) and *China Labour Statistical Yearbook* (2013).

The patterns are fairly clear. In 2003, only 4.3 percent of the conflicts presented in *China Strikes* featured calls for higher wages, as opposed to calls for the payment of wage arrears, for the payment of the local legal minimum wage, or for the cancelation of wage cuts, etc. However, aggressive wage demands featured in 29.9 percent of demonstrations in 2010 (before falling to 20.1 percent in 2012). Figure 2.2 tracks this trend. Other changes in demands include more agitation for humane work hours, for respect from managers, and for real collective bargaining (K. Chang and Brown 2013; Elfstrom and Kuruvilla 2014). From 2003 to 2006, *China Strikes* only showed at most one incident per year featuring calls for union reforms. Then, in 2007, there were two; in 2010 and 2011, three incidents per year. These are vanishingly small numbers compared to the total number of incidents in the dataset but represent an important change. Some calls for more representative unions, such as during the 2010 Honda strike, have captured international attention and spurred broad discussions within the ACFTU. Based on an earlier version of *China Strikes*, Sarosh Kuruvilla and I describe workers as going on the "offensive" (see again Elfstrom and Kuruvilla 2014). This description fits with Tilly's (1995) schema of different stages of mobilization, as well as Knowles' (1952) categorization of different forms of labor conflict. Of course, in general, worker claims may reflect more what is deemed acceptable at a given moment than what workers are actually most concerned about, as argued by Hyman (1989) in the British context. More "aggressive" activism may simply be a response to

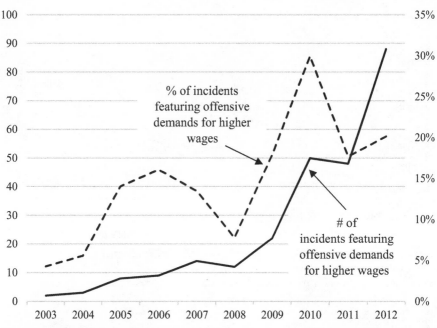

FIGURE 2.2 Demands for higher wages in strikes, protests, and riots.
Source: *China Strikes* (2017).

signals that the government is more open to advocacy framed in more purely interest-based terms. Conversely, as noted, strikers in the People's Republic today tend to couch even very ambitious demands as being about basic legal rights. They claim, for example, severance packages that go well beyond what the law guarantees, but do so chanting "return my blood and sweat money" and "protect my legal rights." Nonetheless, the general trend to date has been toward asking for more, regardless of the precise terms used or their deeper drivers. Like tactics, demands are shifting in a more boundary-spanning and transgressive direction.

CHANGING WORKER ORGANIZATIONS

Chinese worker resistance is also altering in terms of its *organizational* underpinnings. Chinese labor NGOs were once seen as focused on narrow, individualistic, legal rights and, in some cases, hampered by their dependence on donors in Hong Kong or further abroad (Franceschini 2014; E. Friedman 2009; Froissart 2011; Jennifer Hsu 2017; Lee and Shen 2011). Now, their contributions to strike organizing and, especially, poststrike negotiations are increasingly recognized (e.g., Feng Chen and Yang 2017; Franceschini 2016;

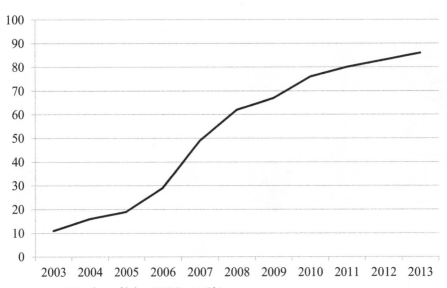

FIGURE 2.3 Number of labor NGOs in China.
Source: List of organizations and their founding dates provided to the author by China Labour Bulletin.

Franceschini and Lin 2019; Froissart 2018; Pringle 2017; Xu and Schmalz 2017; Zajak 2017). In an especially interesting take, Fu (2016, 2018) shows how such groups work behind the scenes to coach and coordinate multiple small, seemingly spontaneous confrontations in a dynamic she calls "disguised collective action" or "mobilizing without the masses." Spires, Tao, and Chan (2014) find that labor NGOs have developed strong boards and informal ties to officials, while putting down quite strong societal roots. Meanwhile, a growing group of students has in recent years thrown itself into labor advocacy, from undercover investigations of Coca-Cola bottling plants and the electronics supplier Foxconn to, more recently, rallying in support of strikers at the Jasic Technology Company (China Labor News Translations 2009a; Yuan Yang 2019). Finally, there are groups that are rarely considered in civil society studies, such as neo-Maoist networks of retired workers in the northeast and interior. One such organization tried to initiate trade union reforms in Xi'an (see China Labor News Translations 2010). These developments are difficult to document quantitatively. However, we can at least roughly track the increase in the *number of labor NGOs* that exist in China. Figure 2.3 shows this, based on a list of groups and their founding dates provided to me by China Labour Bulletin. At the very least, when it comes to the organizations involved, Chinese worker resistance is moving in a boundary-spanning direction. Like the new tactics and demands appearing, this is a challenge for the state.

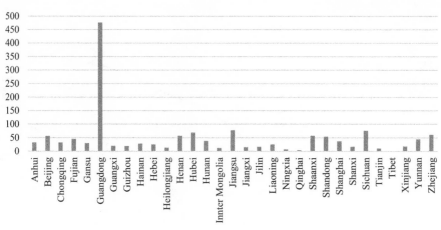

FIGURE 2.4 Strikes, protests, and riots per province.

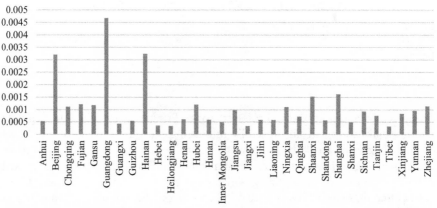

FIGURE 2.5 Average strikes per 10,000 people per province.

REGIONAL PATTERNS WORKER RESISTANCE

There are clear regional patterns in the forms of resistance employed by workers. In terms of incidents featuring *boundary-spanning* and *transgressive* tactics, the total number of strikes, protests, and riots over the period covered by *China Strikes*, Guangdong province is far and away the leader (see Figure 2.4), so much so that no other province gets more than 10 percent of Guangdong's total, although in terms of average annual incidents per 10,000 people there are a couple of provinces that are close runners-up (namely, Beijing and, unexpectedly, Hainan, where there have been a number of garment factory and taxi strikes in recent years) (Figure 2.5). The picture with regard to fully contained conflicts is very different. Both in terms of total numbers of

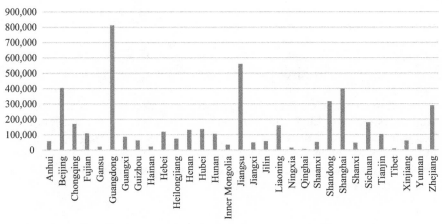

FIGURE 2.6 Total formally adjudicated employment disputes per province.

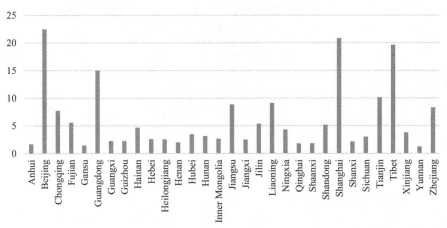

FIGURE 2.7 Average formally adjudicated employment disputes per 10,000 people per province.
Sources: *China Strikes* (2017) and *China Labour Statistical Yearbooks* (2004–13).

formally adjudicated disputes and their population-weighted averages, the distribution nationally is much more even (see Figures 2.6 and 2.7). Guangdong leads again in terms of total number of disputes, but it is followed closely– and in some years, overtaken – by Jiangsu. Moreover, although Guangdong ranks high in its per capita number of mediation, arbitration, and court cases, it is surpassed by both Beijing and Shanghai (as well as Tibet, but the statistics of this "autonomous region" are likely skewed by the fact that many of its labor incidents occur among workers from other places employed on infrastructure projects or in natural resource extraction, while the region's population count is based on its very small local population). Other high-ranking provinces include Jiangsu, Liaoning, Zhejiang, Tianjin, and Chongqing. Regarding worker *demands*, there is a fairly even spread between the Jiangsu-Shanghai-Zhejiang region (the greater Yangtze River Delta) and Guangdong (the Pearl River Delta) in numbers of strikes, protests, and riots featuring calls for the payment of wage arrears or the minimum wage or for the cancellation of wage cuts. However, Guangdong dominates calls for higher wages irrespective of legal minimums. Finally, labor NGOs, too, concentrate in Guangdong, although there are also significant pockets in Jiangsu, Shanghai, and, especially, Beijing. Clearly, there is considerable variation in both the level and form of worker resistance across China. I will next turn to the sectoral and demographic reasons for this spread.

RECIPES FOR RESISTANCE

What accounts for the dramatic regional variation in level and form of worker resistance? Answering this question requires briefly stepping down into the "hidden abode" of production described by Marx (1990, chap. 6). Here, I will focus on tactics, as these are easier to document systematically. According to China Strikes data, three economic sectors, in particular, are driving strikes, protests, and riots, that is, transgressive and boundary-spanning activism: light manufacturing, construction, and transportation with its sub-sectors of taxi drivers, and bus and truck drivers. In contrast, more high-tech, high-skilled jobs are associated with mobilization that stays contained. Also, those parts of the country with large migrant worker populations are likely to see the highest levels of strikes, protests, and riots; those with more local workers, litigation. Some of these factors, such as migrants and light manufacturing and construction, overlap so much that they are virtually indistinguishable. Others are distinct. But this all suggests that we ought to focus on *recipes for resistance*, in the sense of Ragin's (2008, 109) idea of "causal recipes" or "the causally relevant conditions that *combine* to produce a given outcome" (emphasis my own). Different recipes with different combinations of ingredients can lead to similar results. Here, I derive my recipes inductively, based on my dataset. I leave an overarching theory of the causes of worker action to others. The point is to have a rough set of conditions that can be looked out for in my subsequent analysis of the consequences of unrest.

Sectors with Transgressive and Boundary-Spanning Activism

Not all industries are equal in terms of the total volume of labor unrest or the form of unrest they experience. Table 2.2 lists the five economic sectors and sub-sectors that account for the most incidents in *China Strikes* dataset, that is,

TABLE 2.2 *Leading sectors for strikes, protests, and riots*

Sector	Number of incidents	Percent of total incidents
Construction	240	16
Taxi drivers	205	14
Electronics factories	177	12
Textile, apparel, shoes	148	10
Bus and truck drivers	124	8

that dominate in terms of transgressive or boundary-spanning tactics. They are: construction, taxi drivers, electronics factories, apparel and textiles manufacturers, and bus and truck drivers. If we collapse these categories somewhat, we find that two light industries (apparel and textiles) together account for 22 percent of all incidents; two transport sub-sectors (bus and truck drivers and taxi drivers), another 22 percent; and construction, 16 percent. Together, they make up 60 percent of all incidents. These broad groupings would account for even more if we added in other, smaller sub-sectors that can be grouped with light manufacturing: ceramics, furniture-making, etc.

Extreme exploitation of the sort analyzed in the research of the late 1990s and early 2000s likely explains part of this pattern (see again A. Chan 2001; Pun 2005). Light industry in China is characterized by what Lüthje (2012), in a useful survey, terms "corporate high-performance," "flexibilized mass production," and "low wage classic" employment regimes, in which people are pushed to the limit, with punishing work schedules, but are also gathered together in large numbers. For instance, in plants run by the Taiwanese-owned electronics assembly firm Foxconn, workers must meet the quick turnarounds demanded by the product launches of firms, such as Apple, Inc., sometimes working through the night for days on end (J. Chan and Pun 2010; J. Chan, Pun, and Selden 2013, 2020). In general, as Mosley (2011) has shown with global data, subcontracted production, such as that done by the Foxconns of the world, is more likely to be abusive than production associated with foreign direct investment, such as by a firm like Apple itself. And subcontracting is prevalent in light industry. Construction workers in China also labor under dangerous conditions. And driving a taxi, bus, or truck is grueling in a similar manner (Elfstrom 2019a).

However, exploitation is not enough of a driver on its own. Mining is also brutal work. However, although it was once a hotbed of organizing, it sees little activism today, except following mine accidents or closures (on the revolutionary history of the Anyuan mine, especially, see Perry 2012). Shop floor and labor market arrangements that bring workers together or give them powerful influence of the sort focused upon by "labor process" scholars (e.g., Braverman 1998; Burawoy 1979) and many researchers of Chinese labor, such as Cai

(2006) or Pun and Smith (2007), offer an additional layer of explanation. The sectors with the most transgressive and boundary-spanning activism are additionally organized in ways that physically bring workers together on a large scale (light industry) or, if they do not physically bring them together, function in a way that gives scattered workers considerable leverage if they act together (transportation). Foxconn's two plants in Shenzhen employ over 450,000 employees, who are housed in massive dormitories or in surrounding neighborhoods.[1] When more than 10,000-some cabbies in Chongqing went on strike, they tied up the city's roads with gridlock.

Interestingly, at least on a broad scale, it does not appear that precarious/flexible/informal work in and of itself dampens activism. This is despite the warnings of scholars, such as Lee (2016). Taxi drivers often labor under nesting employment relationships: teams of drivers under one "cab boss" (*che laoban*) and several cab bosses in one company (Elfstrom 2019a). Construction workers, in particular, are often employed at arms-length (Pun and Xu 2011; Swider 2015). There are, moreover, indications that the most indirect emerging forms of employment, such as mobile phone app-directed delivery workers, are also becoming hotbeds of contention (China Labour Bulletin 2018b). As Swider (2015) and Zhang and Friedman (2019) have argued, it may come down to how, exactly, these relations are structured. Regardless, unlike in, say, Russia, difficulty with attributing blame for wage arrears, etc., does not seem to be a barrier to activism in China (Javeline 2003).

Sectors with Contained Activism

Sectors and sub-sectors that are more capital-intensive and involve more highly skilled jobs are more likely to feature contained tactics. Ship-building only accounts for eight incidents in the *China Strikes* dataset or about half a percentage point; on the upper end, machinery and appliance factories account for fifty-four incidents or 3.7 percent. The increasingly high-tech auto sector is something of an outlier, as it does not rank high in the total number of street conflicts but tends to adopt strikes over other options when a conflict *does* arise (see Zipp and Blecher 2015). Here, though, the internal divisions between less skilled workers on limited contracts and long-term employees may be revealing: as in the state-owned enterprises of the Cultural Revolution, the exploited contract employees have often been the leaders of auto strikes (L. Zhang 2015). The reasons that such sub-sectors tend to otherwise feature more contained activism are unclear and could range from the knowledge of the law possessed by skilled workers to the relative lack of common cause felt by

---

[1] Although I use Foxconn here as an example of what light industry in China can look like in its most extreme form, that firm, in particular, has seen only middling levels of activism. This may be because of the company's extraordinary scale, which goes well beyond that of any other company, as well as its military-style management.

people who are isolated with their specialized equipment, to the competitive "games" that emerge in such settings (see Burawoy 1979). Certainly, the workforces involved are generally smaller than they are in light industry – or a city's taxi fleet. Regardless of the precise causes, the high value-added "peaks" of the Chinese economy are not generally where you will see disruption. They are sites of comparatively restrained advocacy.

Boundary-Spanning and Transgressive Migrant Workers

The other factor closely related to particular forms of contention is migrant worker density. In countries the world over, people have moved to rapidly industrializing areas in search of work, and these population flows have been politically consequential. Consider, for example, the great migration of African Americans from the south to midwestern and northeastern factories in the early twentieth century in the United States (Korstad and Lichtenstein 1988; McAdam 1999). The fact that employees in the textile mills and other enterprises of treaty ports in prerevolutionary China were largely from elsewhere meant that they formed native place associations for mutual aid, which provided a basis for organizing (Perry 1993). And the distance from families was a source of grievance for the protesting contract workers on the margins of SOE work units during the Cultural Revolution (Perry and Li 1997). Contrary to early analyses concerning migrant passivity, similar dynamics can be observed in China today.

China's resilient household registration system currently ensures that migrant workers live and work somewhere other than where their households are registered – and other than where their families are located, too. To some extent, this means that migrants' social reproduction is spread between the countryside, where their parents take care of their small children and state-guaranteed parcels of land provide some minimal support, and cities, where migrants earn most of their income (Lee 2007, 206–16). As noted, this dynamic was once viewed by scholars as serving to constrain activism. As Lee (2007, 216) argued, combined with migrants' "lived experience of power" in the countryside, where village authorities exercise near-feudal control, "the availability of farming and the vision of an eventual return to the countryside undermines migrant workers' willingness to sustain collective resistance." There was considerable truth to this observation in the past, and it still carries weight today.

But China's peculiar arrangement has always had a flip side that is more threatening for the regime. In cities, the day-to-day experience of migrants mirrors the social isolation that industrial relations scholars Kerr and Siegel (1954) argue is most conducive to militancy. Taking light industry, again, as an example, the group is housed in massive, company-run dormitories, such as the Foxconn ones described above (Pun 2016, chap. 5; Pun and Smith 2007). As noted, this is changing, as more and more young workers choose to live "off campus" in apartments in nearby urban villages (Siu 2015). But these villages are also worlds unto themselves and serve the same purposes for organizers (C. K.-C. Chan 2010, chap. 3; C. K.-C. Chan and Pun 2009; Chung and Unger 2013). Migrants have a physical base from which to mobilize.

The arrangements of local workers are, by comparison, easily penetrated by the state, even as locals enjoy more insider options than migrants. In old apartment blocks, neighborhood committees keep tabs on what people are doing (see Read 2012; the gated compounds of the new rich are different, see Tomba 2014). Authorities know who is related to whom and can use "relational repression" on dissidents (Deng and O'Brien 2013). At the same time, locals have more of a voice in political institutions (see, for example, Paik 2014). The same committees that monitor people can also serve as helpful intermediaries to the state (Read 2012), as can other organizations such as lineage halls, at least in parts of China (L. L. Tsai 2007). Locals have every reason to exercise contained contention at most, in other words. But shut out of these venues, migrants find it more natural to press their demands in the streets.

Moreover, the rural–urban divide is gradually changing, undermining the previous pacifying effect of migration. Land seizures by authorities in the countryside and peri-urban areas have cut off the agricultural fallback option for many migrant workers (Chuang 2015; on some of the more complicated ramifications of this, see Zhan 2017). The younger generation of migrants, in particular, who have little experience with tilling fields or patience for learning how to do so, increasingly see themselves as urbanites and wish to remain in cities (Frenkel and Yu 2015). At the very least, they are "doubly dis-embedded" (*shuangchong tuoqian*) from both rural and urban society (B. Huang 2014). Lu (2012, chaps. 7–8) shows that villages are emptying out of able-bodied workers, and the countryside's increasingly denuded soil is being farmed by a dwindling number of old people. In some ways, we are witnessing the birth, at last, of something quite different from the "socialist social contract" working class of Mao era and the hybrid rural–urban working class of early migration, namely a real proletariat. And that proletariat is beginning to behave as Marx predicted: staying and combining to fight where it works.

The SOE protests of the late 1990s and early 2000s documented by early studies of labor in China such as those of Cai (2006), Hurst (2009) or Lee (2007) showed how locals can take to the streets when necessary, but in general, nonlocals are now both the most likely to mobilize against their bosses *and* the most likely to choose extra-institutional channels to do so. Map 2.1 uses *China Strikes* data to illustrate how migrant worker populations correlate with more strikes, protests, and riots at the subprovincial level, in Guangdong's portion of the Pearl River Delta. If we run a basic negative binomial regression[2]

---

[2] A negative binomial regression is the type of model generally preferred when the outcome of interest is a count of the number of times something occurs. See Zwilling (2013).

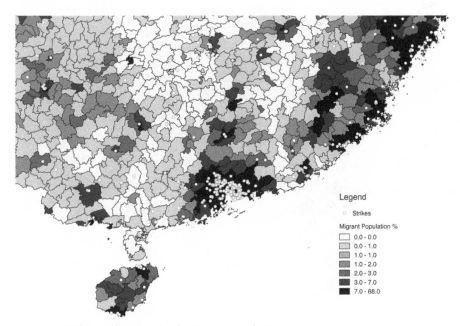

MAP 2.1 Strikes and county-level migrant populations.
Sources: China Strikes (2017) and the 2010 Census. Strikes are from the full period of 2003 to 2012 and their markings overlap in contentious hotspots.

with controls for urbanization and provincial population, we find that the percentage of a province's residents who are migrants is positively and significantly correlated with strike activity. In contrast, migrant percentage is *negatively* correlated with the number of formally adjudicated employment disputes that occur in a province (albeit it at a low level of statistical significance). The percentage of a province's workers employed in state-owned enterprises, meanwhile, has no significant relationship to strike rates *and* a negative relationship with formal disputes (see Table 2.3). Nonlocals drive today's worker militancy – and they drive it in a boundary-spanning or transgressive direction.

SUMMARY

Chinese industrial relations have three key characteristics: a largely private economy with a strong state sector, the *hukou* system that divides local workers from migrants, and a party-controlled trade union federation. Within this context, scholars have built up a rich body of research on why and how Chinese workers mobilize. This literature has moved from a pessimistic appraisal of the opportunities available to labor to a more optimistic appraisal and back again. In contrast, my book builds on a narrower but still significant

TABLE 2.3 *Provincial-level correlates of strikes, protests, and riots*

	Strikes (Migrant workers)	Strikes (SOE workers)	Disputes (Migrant workers)	Disputes (SOE workers)
GDP (log)	1.340***	1.476***	0.603***	0.527***
	(0.158)	(0.156)	(0.0501)	(0.0495)
Percent migrant	0.0209***		−0.00573*	
	(0.00676)		(0.00317)	
Percent SOE workers		0.00490		−0.0550***
		(0.0518)		(0.0196)
Population	0.000162***	0.000160***	0.000169***	0.000123***
	(0.0000469)	(0.0000493)	(0.0000231)	(0.0000266)
Percent urban	−0.0129***	−0.00670	0.00584***	0.0103***
	(0.00456)	(0.00607)	(0.00169)	(0.00257)
Constant	−12.62***	−14.02***	−4.505***	−3.521***
	(1.404)	(1.449)	(0.467)	(0.482)
N	310	310	310	310

Negative binomial regression. Standard errors in parentheses. ***$P < 0.01$, **$P < 0.05$, *$P < 0.10$.
Sources: *China Statistical Yearbooks* (2004–13) and *China Strikes* (2017).

strand of scholarship concerning the political *impact* of what workers are doing. Yet, before we explore this topic in depth, we must first identify the different forms resistance can take and revisit how those forms are rising or falling along with the possible reasons why. To this end, I have categorized resistance from low to high in terms of the challenge it presents to authorities: as contained (low), boundary-spanning (medium), or transgressive (high). Contained activism uses formal government channels to pursue legally defined rights of workers and it features little in the way of worker organization beyond shop floor networks. Boundary-spanning activism, in contrast, includes strikes, protest, and riots, may reach beyond bare legal minimums to demand *more*, without reference to the law, and can draw on the services of legally oriented labor NGOs. Finally, transgressive activism features well-coordinated strikes that can span workplaces or regions, features aggressive demands that can encompass institutional reforms, and involves more movement-oriented NGOs or other associations, such as those made up of leftist students. I have offered evidence that strikes, protests, and riots are rising more quickly than formally adjudicated employment disputes, that demands for *more* are growing (although they have slowed in the most recent years), and that labor organizations are proliferating. Particular economic sectors and sub-sectors – light industry, construction, taxi drivers, and bus and truck drivers – account for most boundary-spanning and transgressive action, and migrants are more likely than locals to take this route. These findings contribute to ongoing discussions among scholars about extreme exploitation, shop floor and labor market structures that foster or impede collective action, the impact of increasingly informal and flexible work arrangements, and, especially, the changing role of migrant workers. Recipes for resistance, not any single factor, provide the best understanding of how Chinese labor contention is rising and how its different forms have concentrated in different parts of the country. They also provide a concrete, workaday starting point for our broader process of contention. In the next chapter, we turn to the ways in which contention works through bureaucratic incentives to affect state policy.

3

Bureaucratic Incentives

The previous chapter focused on the *causes* of different *forms* of worker resistance. Specifically, I reviewed the existing scholarship on Chinese labor unrest and provided fresh evidence, in the shape of a new dataset and government statistics, that resistance in China is not only rising but also increasingly boundary-spanning or transgressive in nature. Moreover, I showed that, owing to particular local combinations of sectors and worker demographics – recipes for resistance – this dynamic is more evident in some parts of the country than others. Now, I begin an extended exploration of the *consequences* of resistance for the state. It should not be controversial to argue that the quantitative and qualitative shift in contention underway places tremendous pressure on authorities, especially in those areas where the shift is most pronounced. To make such a claim begs the question, though, of *how*, exactly, that pressure is exerted. This chapter is devoted to this "how" question. Answering it requires a less monolithic understanding of "the state." In particular, it demands an approach that acknowledges that, at the end of the day, decisions about ruling China's contentious workplaces are not made by some abstract "regime" but instead by individual planners in the great gated government compounds of provincial capitals. Or by cadres from the official trade union pulled from their lunches to calm disputes. Or by tired cops on the beat in dusty industrial parks. These people and the institutions in which they are embedded all face bureaucratic incentives, transmitted down from Beijing, to take worker resistance seriously, but they react differently, based on the levels and arms of the government to which they belong, as well as the form of resistance they face. The result of the officials' combined efforts, as we will explore in greater detail in subsequent chapters, is a proliferation of distinct regional models of control – and ultimately increased repressive and responsive capacity nationally. However, before we discuss such effects, we must first trace the basic process that gets us to them.

In this chapter, as in the previous one, I begin by reviewing the research that has already been conducted on the topic, in this case, research on what is called the "cadre promotion system" and how it pushes officials to meet certain benchmarks, including "stability maintenance." Building off of this research and drawing on official documents, news reports, and interviews I have conducted, I then explain how cadres are charged with carrying out particular plans of action in the event of large-scale workplace incidents and are evaluated on their management of industrial conflict more generally. Those who wish to rise in the ranks have strong reasons to go all out to contain dissent, but so do muddlers who simply wish to be left alone. I note the nuances in the system, too, such as how growth is weighed against stability in evaluations, as well as outright flaws in the system, such as how officials can stay safely within narrow jurisdictional boundaries, hide problems, pass the blame for unrest to outsiders, and kick the can down the road to their successors. But I argue that China's bureaucracy is set up in a way that nonetheless generally incentivizes officials to demonstrate competence in social control to their superiors.

These dynamics are illustrated with a brief sketch of the change in Jiangsu's portion of the Yangtze River Delta (YRD) and Guangdong's portion of the Pearl River Delta (PRD), regions I explore separately and in much more depth in the next two chapters. Specifically, I demonstrate that there is a greater turnover of cadres in the organs responsible for maintaining stability in the tumultuous PRD than in the relatively quiescent YRD, which indicates the way contention both creates opportunities for officials to prove themselves and rise in the hierarchy and threatens nonperformers with demotion or firing. Moreover, the public security sections of provincial and municipal government yearbooks – volumes that trumpet local achievements and are given as gifts to higher-level officials – have gradually devoted more attention to labor issues in the PRD compared to the YRD as worker resistance has grown in the former relative to the latter. This I take to indicate that, given the level of contention on the region's shop floors, authorities in the PRD feel a stronger need to prove themselves to higher-level leaders in the arena of industrial relations management.

What does it mean for an official to prove themselves, though, beyond talking a lot about an issue in yearbooks? In a situation of intense conflict – high levels of incidents of a boundary-spanning or transgressive sort – each arm of the government is spurred into action, whether in a coordinated or autonomous manner. There is less to lose by adopting bold measures. Police crack down forcefully. Unions reform. Judiciaries act more solicitously toward workers. These reactions congeal into distinct regional models of social control in contentious places as compared to less contentious places. Specifically, the former areas are characterized by risk-taking in governance; the latter, by orthodoxy. In subsequent chapters, I examine the PRD and YRD as examples of each, respectively. Then, moving beyond these models of control, I explore the average impact of resistance on state capacity. But in this chapter, again, I focus on the bureaucratic incentives that, combined with unrest, help get us there.

EXISTING RESEARCH ON BUREAUCRATIC INCENTIVES

To understand the bottom-up change in governance in China, we need a theory that is attuned to broad policy trends but that refuses to treat the Chinese government as a monolith. Such a theory must, first of all, acknowledge the state as something independent enough to be acted upon – not the "committee for managing the common affairs of the whole bourgeoisie" polemically described by Marx and Engels in *The Communist Manifesto*, but rather the state described by Marx in *Capital* as shaped by various pressures, including those emanating from the social reformers (whose factory investigations Marx liberally quotes) (Marx 1990; Marx and Engels 1848). But we must go further. As Migdal (2001, 22) perceptively writes: "In brief, the state is a contradictory entity that acts against itself. To understand domination, then, demands two levels of analysis, one that recognizes the corporate, unified dimension of the state – its wholeness – expressed in its image, and one that dismantles that wholeness in favor of examining the reinforcing and contradictory practices and alliances of its disparate parts." If protest shapes policy, it does so by challenging the state in both its "wholeness" *and* its "disparate parts." I argue that the parts care about dissent in the first place primarily because of the priority placed on social harmony by the whole. Without that prioritization, protests would mostly be experienced as a nuisance, disrupting day-to-day management but not portending anything bigger. But the whole's response to contention is ultimately an aggregation of the responses of its parts, which, as Migdal notes, can pull in multiple directions. The connecting mechanisms are bureaucratic incentives.

Thankfully, I am not reinventing the wheel here. China's bureaucratic incentives are the subject of a growing body of scholarship. In particular, research has focused on the pressure exerted on authorities' behavior by what is called the "cadre promotion" system or, borrowing from the Soviet experience, the *nomenklatura* system. As Brodsgaard (2012, 76) states, "personnel policy is the heart of power" in any Leninist structure. In the view of Bell (2015), the Communist Party's elaborate vetting of candidates for higher offices is what makes China a "meritocratic" state worthy of emulation. There is good reason to be skeptical of such arguments (see Nathan 2015). Regardless, the system clearly serves another, distinct purpose: it allows the Chinese government to be remarkably decentralized while remaining firmly under Party control (Landry 2008). In the words of Landry (2008, 57), "Leading local cadres may well have extensive prerogatives, but their ability to govern depends ultimately not on the locality in which they serve, lying instead in the hands of higher-ranking Party officials positioned above (and outside) these localities." Put differently, the system rewards effectiveness, but only effectiveness that serves Beijing's objectives. At the same time, the system's output reshapes the center's options.

How the System Works

The basic mechanics of the cadre promotion system are well established. As of 1998, what are called China's "cadres" numbered 40.5 million and included both Party members and nonmembers, with Party members making up 38 percent (Brodsgaard 2012, 73). Cadres comprise everyone from mayors to professors, but the individuals ultimately responsible for managing worker unrest – officials at the city and provincial levels, including those in "mass organizations," such as the ACFTU – rank among the 508,025 "leading cadres" or even more select 2,562 "high level cadres" (Brodsgaard 2012). Party members make up a larger proportion of leading and high-level cadres. Since the onset of Reform and Opening, the CCP has tried to rationalize its management of such people (Manion 1985). Rising leaders are regularly evaluated by a succession of committees: within their own work unit, by the unit above theirs, by the Organization Department at the next level, and via "individual recommendations" (Manion 1985, 226–32). From the 1990s onward, the Party has exerted more, not less control over this process relative to government agencies (Brodsgaard 2006). Under the previous Hu-Wen administration, in an effort to foster intra-Party democracy and clamp down on corruption, the CCP briefly pushed the "democratic recommendation" of candidates for certain offices and semi-competitive elections at Party Congresses (Zeng 2016). However, these initiatives have been hampered by the nonbinding nature of recommendations, the rotation of cadres between localities and functional departments, and excessive control by the Organization Department (Zeng 2016). Personal connections and votes aside, performance with regard to key benchmarks is still paramount.

Social Stability as a Benchmark

According to existing research, cadres are evaluated based on a range of criteria. Landry (2008, 82–85), for instance, highlights a China Urban Development Research Committee collection of a full thirty-three benchmarks used to rank cities and their officials' performance. But not all of these are equal. Some benchmarks are formally designated "one vote vetoes" (*yi piao foujue*), meaning failure on these items cancels out any other achievements by an official. In general, officials deem economic targets to be especially important. Those surveyed by Liu, Hou, and Tou (2013) consistently rank investment as their most critical goal; however, Shih, Adolph, and Liu (2012) suggest growth has little real effect on promotion; and Wallace (2016) shows that economic statistics are frequently fudged.[1] But cadres are not just in an economic race. Their accomplishments and failures in other arenas can also advance or doom their careers, and social stability is one of the other main benchmarks for evaluating officials. The 2005 National Petition Regulation and a 2008 Party decision regarding "strengthening the implementation of integrated public security management," among other documents, establish that if a major "social disturbance" occurs in a given jurisdiction, "the hierarchy of leaders responsible for that jurisdiction will all be subject to the 'one veto rule,'" depriving "officials of bonuses, promotions, and the eligibility of the unit to compete for organizational honors" (Lee and Zhang 2013, 14853–54). Any other accomplishments will be disregarded. Along these lines, Y. Wang and Minzner (2013, 352) write that officials face "increasingly tough career sanctions whenever outbreaks of citizen petitioning occur within their jurisdictions" (petitioning being the practice, again, of aggrieved citizens bringing their complaints to a system of Letters and Visits Offices with branches at every level of government, including central offices in Beijing, see Minzner 2006).[2] Heurlin (2016) thus finds that petitioning around land and housing issues in the late 1990s and early 2000s correlated with provincial adoption of policy changes in these particular areas. Openly ranking regions by their petition numbers has since been discontinued, as this practice created incentives for local officials to abuse petitioners and cover-up discontent (Interview POS #1 BJ 03-15-2017). Nonetheless, the prospect of mass petitioning, as well as other forms of protest, hangs heavy over Chinese bureaucrats. Providing powerful evidence of this pressure, J. Chen, Pan, and Xu (2016) conducted a field experiment, making online requests for social support to local governments and found that requests that include a threat of collective action or of contacting officials' superiors are more likely to receive meaningful responses. Distelhorst and Hou (2017) conducted a similar experiment using the "Mayor's Mailbox" system. Given this general imperative to maintain stability, cadres seeking promotion are anxious to demonstrate their capacity to manage labor unrest effectively.

PROTOCOLS FOR HANDLING UNREST

There are basic protocols that local officials are expected to follow when confronted with worker resistance. These are freely available online via government websites. The documents give step-by-step instructions on bringing order. For example, a "contingency plan" put together by the personnel bureau of Shaoyang in Hunan stipulates that persons "on duty" at the bureau should

---

[1] For a fascinating history of statistical work in the People's Republic of China, see Ghosh (2020).
[2] On the other hand, high conflict numbers can be used to argue for more local "stability maintenance" funds (see Lee and Zhang 2013). Acquiring such funds may, of course, affect cadre promotion, too.

arrive on the scene no more than thirty minutes after the start of "mass incidents," including "illegal collective strikes" (*feifa jiti bagong*), report the details of the situation to County Party Committee, form an onsite emergency command center, coordinate with public security to control the site, and engage protesters person-to-person and hear their opinions (People's Government of Shaoyang 2014). After the situation has quieted down, the plan says, the responsible officials should follow up to make sure that any commitments made to protesters are honored, so that people do not feel that the government "makes false promises" and therefore escalate the conflict (People's Government of Shaoyang 2014). Another document, this one put out by the Beijing Commission of Housing and Urban–Rural Development and directed at incidents involving migrant construction workers, in particular, mandates the establishment of a "Beijing City Migrant Construction Worker Mass Incident Emergency Response Leading Small Group" responsible for coming up with plans for handling incidents and conducting incident response training (Beijing Commission of Housing and Urban-Rural Development 2013). In the event of a "major" protest, that is, one involving sixty to one hundred people and some danger of personal or property damage, the Leading Small Group must ensure that the city building authority, the Ministry of Human Resources and Social Security, the Beijing Federation of Trade Unions, and the Public Security Bureau all arrive at the scene and perform their allotted tasks (the union is given the vaguest directives: "supporting" the other departments in "doing good migrant worker work") (Beijing Commission of Housing and Urban-Rural Development 2013). Protests are given different color codes depending on their proximity to major political meetings in the city and other factors (Beijing Commission of Housing and Urban-Rural Development 2013). Personal responsibilities are also clarified in these documents. For instance, a document from Fuxin City, in Liaoning Province, the site of many labor conflicts in the early 2000s, specifies that the head of Human Resources and Social Security in the city must chair its "Stability Maintenance Work Leading Small Group" and that the vice chairs are the vice-head of Human Resources and Social Security, along with the head of Discipline and Inspection and the chief of the municipal trade union (Fuxin City Bureau of Human Resources and Social Security 2017). Sometimes, materials like this include the names of the particular people holding these positions. In principle, it should be clear who should do what when resistance occurs.

EVIDENCE FROM INTERVIEWS REGARDING OFFICIAL ACCOUNTABILITY FOR INSTABILITY

Interviews I conducted across China – in Beijing, Tianjin, Shanghai, Guangdong, and Jiangsu – emphasized that the cadre obligations detailed in these sorts of protocols have real teeth. For example, someone formerly employed by Shanghai's petitioning office explained to me: "If there is a large number of petitioning cases somewhere, this hurts the career prospects of the officials there. Mass protests, especially those that get out of control [are particularly detrimental to cadres' prospects]. Quantitative analysis is conducted on these kinds of cases ... Risk assessments are made" (Interview POS #2 March 2017). Similarly, according to a researcher at a government think tank in Nanjing:

> The government is always concerned about stability. It is especially concerned around events like this summer's Youth Olympics. Or when there have been big protests in Guangdong, it pays careful attention, let alone when something happens nearby, like in Shanghai. It is afraid of things spreading. We write up risk assessments. When really big things happen, reports must be made to the central government and it will respond ... The central government will have certain topics every year that it wants attention paid to. We will send our reports on that straight to the central government. It grades reports, giving them good, medium, bad scores, etc. It usually wants to give places a bit of face, so what it will do is say these two places did excellent work and say the third place did alright. That way it is clear that the third place needs to improve its report but it doesn't criticize that place directly. (Interview 37)

The indirect criticism the researcher described sounds relatively mild. However, the same person said to me at another point, "Officials are judged as much or more on stability as they are on economic development. It doesn't matter how much you grow the economy; if you have many big incidents, that cancels out your economic achievements" (Interview 52). A leader in Jiangsu's provincial labor bureau furthermore told me directly that labor unrest could constitute a "one vote veto" (Interview 113). Although sometimes couched in polite terms, the pressure on cadres appears to be quite serious. At its most dramatic, it can be career-changing.

CAREER PENALTIES FOR OFFICIALS

Local officials can sometimes pay a heavy price for not anticipating or for mishandling major conflicts. News reports provide evidence of this. And they are likely just the tip of the iceberg. The most dramatic example in recent years is the fate of Xinjiang Party Secretary Wang Lequan. In July 2009, in Xinjiang's capital, Urumqi, peaceful protests by Uighurs, the dominant ethnic group of the "special autonomous region," led to violent clashes between Uighurs and security forces, leaving scores dead, and sparking a round of counter-demonstrations and violence by Han Chinese a couple of days afterward (see Human Rights Watch 2009b). After a remarkable fifteen years in power, Secretary Wang was demoted to deputy head of the province's Politics and Law Committee the next year (Branigan 2010). Punishments can also be observed following less large-scale but nonetheless high-profile incidents. For example, when three people self-immolated in protest against housing demolitions in Yihuang County, Jiangxi Province, the county chief and party secretary were both fired (Xinhua 2010). This accountability extends to labor disputes. For instance, during the high tide of SOE worker activism in the early 2000s, protests in Liaoyang City resulted in not only the arrests of organizers, but also the detention of corrupt officials and the demotion of the city's police chief (Eckholm 2002, 2003). Similarly, when workers employed by the state-owned Longmay Mining Holding Group protested substantial wage arrears in Heilongjiang Province in 2016, the province's governor, who had inflamed the situation by claiming that workers had not been "shortchanged a single cent," was forced to publicly apologize (The Economist 2016). Riots by migrant workers in the Zengcheng District of Guangzhou in 2011 led the city's authorities to sack senior Zengcheng officials (Y. Zhang 2011). Even incidents that *threaten* to unleash labor unrest also draw reprisals against leaders deemed responsible. Thus, following a deadly factory explosion in Kunshan, Jiangsu Province, both the city's party secretary and mayor were removed and the deputy provincial governor was handed an administrative punishment (Reuters 2014). Other examples could be cited. The point is that, whatever the frequency of such sanctions, they hang over officials as a possibility, incentivizing conformance with central government mandates.

ACCOUNTABILITY FOR MUDDLERS

For many cadres, rising in the ranks is not a goal.[3] Instead, they hope to just muddle through. In his autobiography, a noted ACFTU reformer complains that "some union cadres lack a spirit of forging ahead and passion for their work" (he also criticizes the narrow focus on quantitative achievements of union go-getters, see W. Chen 2012, 56–57). Why is this? As Juan Wang (2015, 15) argues in her study of village governance, "the technical complexity and uncertainty of the work performance assessment system" means that very few cadres are "motivated toward *optimal* performance" (emphasis added). Moreover, being assigned a job by superiors can lead to indifference as surely as it can lead to an eagerness to please the same superiors. A recent article in a Chinese trade union journal reports that over 80 percent of prefecture-level union chiefs surveyed hold their positions because "the next level up arranged it" and they "had no choice in the matter" (*bu gan bu xing*), leaving only a tiny minority claiming an "interest in the work itself" (Y. Liu 2014, 13–14). The authors argue this generates severe bureaucratism. Finally, cadres above a certain rank are rotated around their provinces and around the country and are constantly handed new challenges as tests (P. T. Y. Cheung 1998). Promotion thus means potentially uprooting one's family and, at the very least, spending more time in the office. In contrast, the outer reaches of the

---

[3] I am grateful to Joseph Fewsmith for first bringing this issue to my attention.

bureaucracy can move at a comfortingly slow pace. And officials left there are surrounded by their community. Some relish this situation. Why give it up?

Nonetheless, there are inducements for even muddlers to take stability seriously. The village officials studied by Juan Wang (2015) may not pursue "optimal performance" but they are deeply concerned about avoiding penalties from superiors for protests that occur in their jurisdictions. Usually, these penalties do not take the form of the demotions, firings, and detentions noted above, but they nonetheless hurt. Wang documents officials being suspended without pay, receiving fines of fifty to five hundred RMB, and having to pay the costs of catching villagers who travel to petition higher levels of government (J. Wang 2015, 6). Lee and Zhang (2013, 1493–94) report that bonuses paid out to officials who manage stability well can account for up to a third of their salaries. Missing those bonuses for poor performance amounts to a real blow. Moreover, there are plenty of opportunities for cadres to lose face in their circles. For instance, an official in Tianjin's labor bureau described an intimidating group evaluation process to me:

There's a city-level mediation group that will grade districts. The districts must report to it ... Everyone takes this issue seriously (*zhongshi*). Why do officials care? Every year, the city will review their reports. The officials from different places will just have to sit there and not be able to say anything while the city notes where they have done well or badly. This puts a lot of pressure on people. (Interview 49)

It was not clear to me from this description whether or not the Tianjin officials would actually be demoted for doing badly, but they would certainly be placed in an awkward position. If muddlers do not feel as much pressure to achieve harmony as their coworkers striving for promotion, they are not altogether free from pressure, either. They, too, have inducements, just negative ones. Everyone must make at least some token effort toward maintaining stability.

NUANCES IN THE SYSTEM

If the system incentivizes officials to take unrest seriously, it does not always do so in a rigid manner. Stability is, again, balanced by other concerns. Formally, protests can "veto" economic growth, but economic growth can also "veto" protests. Bulman (2016) conducted a fascinating analysis of otherwise similar local governments on different sides of the Jiangsu-Anhui line, showing how the former are subject to more economic performance pressures from their superiors; the latter, more stability maintenance pressures. Priorities change over time, as well. An official in the Shanghai petitioning bureau explained, "Today, the focus is on urbanization, and cadres are evaluated more on this. There's an emphasis on social management. The evaluation is more holistic now. Lots of factors are considered together" (Interview POS #1 BJ March 2017). Because localities have ceased to be publicly ranked according to their annual number of petitions, the official continued,

It is now unclear how petitioning numbers will be used by [officials'] superiors. Local officials will always feel bad if there are many petitions in their areas. But they won't know for sure what the effect will be on them. They may think: "Perhaps lots of petitions are just a result of fast development [and therefore not necessarily perceived by superiors as negative]." (Interview POS #1 BJ March 2017)

Moreover, *how officials respond* to instability may be as important as *how much* instability occurs on their watch. In the words of a trade union leader at an SOE in Nanjing, "People know if you have had disputes. But disputes can happen anywhere, so officials are not blamed for having something happen in their area of responsibility. The question is how they react. If they are very cold (*leng jing*) about things and don't seem to care, then this will be a problem" (Interview 27). A protest does not automatically mean a loss of promotion or even embarrassment for officials. At its most sophisticated, the system balances different goals and gives cadres a sympathetic hearing – but not without ensuring that they *are* taking action.

FLAWS IN THE SYSTEM

The system also has clear flaws. Jurisdictional boundaries hinder accountability. After criticizing a neighboring city's practices, for example, a union leader in Shenzhen said to me, "But I am just a railroad policeman. Do you know what that means? It means I am only responsible for my section of the track" (Interview 101). As in other countries, cross-city coordination on security efforts, in particular, is weak. A labor activist, also in Shenzhen, thus commented to me, "Mostly, they just don't want you to cause problems in their area. When I left Shenzhen for Dongguan, the Shenzhen people didn't care anymore what I did. There's a very strong district-level bias" (Interview 79). A policeman in Zhongshan confirmed this: "We don't usually cross boundaries. Whoever is responsible for an area handles problems in that area" (Group Discussion 61). This is obviously not always the case. The experiences of activists who are hounded from province to province (Interview 73) or whose family members in other parts of the country are visited by state security (Interviews 12, 78) speak to growing harmonization of surveillance and intimidation. Yet, such harmonization may still be the exception and a more siloed approach to the rule. The result is a spatial shuffling of contention rather than resolution.

More importantly, accountability within the system can break down through the manipulation of reporting and the blocking of higher levels of government from accessing an area and acquiring information about events on the ground. Asked about faked petitioning figures, the former Shanghai petitioning official I interviewed replied simply, "Yes, this happens" (Interview POS #2 March 2017). Obviously, when the numbers relied upon by superiors to evaluate cadres are not real, then promotions, demotions, and penalties cannot be doled out in a rational manner. Blocking access is equally serious. Speaking of a major 2014 Dongguan shoe factory strike, a Beijing researcher said:

At first, the Dongguan authorities ... refused entrance to provincial-level officials, including from the trade union, demanding certain documents before they would receive them. Once higher level officials started to take the incident really seriously, though, Dongguan itself paid for police from neighboring cities and even from other provinces to come help – gave each a stipend, covered their housing, etc. ... They also brought out the People's Armed Police, though they did not have permission for this. (Interview 23)

In this particular case, the strategy did not work. Officials were not able to maintain complete control of the volatile situation and others had to become involved eventually. But the case shows how much accountability depends on transparency, which is often lacking.

By attributing problems to others, local authorities can furthermore escape punishment. For instance, regarding the Dongguan shoe strike, the researcher also said that the city

was ultimately evaluated positively for its handling of the incident. They were hardline in their handling of things. For example, they tapped the phones of all the workers. And they broke a lot of rules. Originally, the social security issue [which had sparked the strike] was partially their fault, as they'd given the company permission to not pay out; and when workers were told about this, it made the situation even worse. But in the end, the authorities could blame NGOs. (Interview 23)

No one with real responsibility was held to account. The deeper lessons from a conflict may therefore never be absorbed and the wrong signals may be sent to officials.

There can also be strong temptations for cadres to "kick the can down the road." In the words of an instructor I interviewed at the Central Party School, "How municipalities respond depends on the leader. Some just pay people off to settle things. Others know that this will encourage more protests and don't want to pass on the problem to future leaders" (Interview 115). Lee and Zhang (2013, 1485–86) describe the former approach as "paying for peace" and see it as ultimately transforming the state into a "marketplace where gamesmanship ... between officials and citizens determines the price of stability." According to a former leader of the Guangzhou Federation of Trade Unions, "Chinese people are very good at using the opportunities provided by the government's anxiety about stability. *Beigong shiying* – the government is like a drunk person who sees the reflection of a bow in his alcohol and thinks it's a snake" (Interview 62). The opposite problem also exists: officials feel incentivized to overreact to incidents, breaking the law, abusing citizens, and inflaming the situation further (D. L. Yang 2017). Either way, fundamental issues are either left to fester unresolved or are exacerbated.

These are all serious flaws, but they are not fatal. It may be possible for an official to stay safely within his or her jurisdiction, pushing contention elsewhere; manipulate reports, temporarily block access by high levels of government, and shift blame; or irresponsibly pay people off and magnify the problems for the next generation of officials. But there are redundancies built into the system. For example, the Nanjing government researcher cited above explained to me,

When a particular big labor incident occurs, maybe everything should be handled through the Ministry of Human Resources and Social Security, as it is in its jurisdiction. But [if the ministry does nothing] other departments ... will go around it, and report directly up the chain. Functional departments will send information to the provincial government when maybe the city or county government would prefer that things stay [closer to home] ... Our own research department often reports things straight to the provincial authorities, skipping levels. (Interview 37)

An incident here or there can be covered up or attributed to someone else, but it is obvious to everyone if an area is roiling with contention. And the people responsible will be found. Despite imperfections in the way China's bureaucratic incentives work, they generally push individuals in different parts of the system to try to show that they are "on top of things."

ILLUSTRATING THE PROCESS WITH COMPARATIVE REGIONAL CASES

To illustrate in rough terms this process of worker resistance leading to official demonstrations of competence, I will now turn to two regions that will be the focus of subsequent chapters of the book: Jiangsu's portion of the Yangtze River Delta (YRD) and Guangdong's portion of the Pearl River Delta (PRD). As noted in Chapter 1, these regions are arguably more alike than any other two parts of China, at least with regard to factors typically treated as important in studies of Chinese labor issues and examined in Chapter 2, such as migrant workers and state-owned enterprises. This allows us to zero in on the two deltas' contrasting reactions to labor unrest, while holding other factors more or less constant (Przeworski and Teune 1970). In Chapters 5 and 6, I will explore the implications of the remaining discrepancies between the YRD and PRD in terms of their dominant sectors and worker demographics, and I will examine the qualitative differences in governance that can be observed between the regions, that is, their different models of control.

Diverging Patterns of Worker Resistance

Although the Yangtze River Delta and Pearl River Delta governments vary little in their prioritization of stability, the challenges they face in terms of labor resistance have diverged over time. Figure 3.1 tracks the total number of

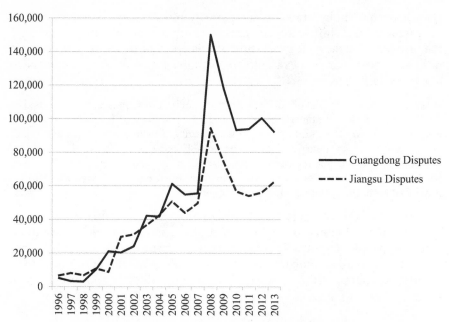

FIGURE 3.1 Formally adjudicated employment disputes in Jiangsu and Guangdong.
Source: *China Labour Statistical Yearbooks* (1997–2013).

formally adjudicated employment disputes accepted for formal mediation, arbitration, and court appearances in Jiangsu and Guangdong between 1996 and 2013. In other words, it shows a change in contained activism. As I will explain in the next chapters, contention generally takes a contained form or, at most, a boundary-spanning form in the YRD and runs the gamut from contained to boundary-spanning to transgressive forms in the PRD. This difference, in turn, profoundly shapes the different models of control deployed by the two regions' governments. For now, though, I focus only on differences in contained contention, as this is easier to track over a long period, owing to the existence of official dispute data from the 1990s. This analytical decision means that the variation discussed here understates, if anything, the contrast between the two regions. As seen in Figure 3.1, levels of conflict in the YRD and PRD only really began to follow distinct trajectories around 2006–7. The regions then both experienced spikes in conflict in 2008 during the financial crisis – but to very different degrees – and have remained on different tracks ever since, with the PRD typically experiencing 40 percent more disputes annually than its northern counterpart. The YRD and PRD now seem to be converging somewhat again, but they are still very much on different tracks.

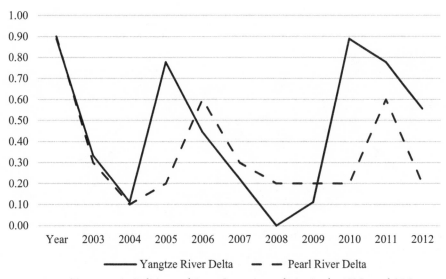

FIGURE 3.2 Turnover in Politics and Law Committee chairs in the YRD and PRD (percent).
Source: Municipal yearbooks of Changzhou, Huai'an, Nanjing, Nantong, Suzhou, Taizhou, Wuxi, Zhenjiang, Dongguan, Foshan, Guangzhou, Huizhou, Jiangmen, Shenzhen, Zhaoqing, Zhongshan, and Zhuhai, between 2003 and 2012.

Diverging Patterns of Cadre Turnover

The divergence in resistance between the two deltas means different career pressures for local officials. Although anecdotes of official accountability for instability are common, patterns are hard to precisely identify. However, an approximate sense of the tumult that unrest introduces into official promotion can be obtained by observing the membership of the Politics and Law Committees (also translated as Political-Legal Affairs Committees) of local Communist Party branches, as documented in municipal yearbooks. Aside from the Ministry of Public Security, these Committees are the organs most directly responsible for social stability in a given jurisdiction (and their chairs often concurrently serve as heads of Public Security). The turnover rates in the membership of the Committees in the Yangtze River Delta and Pearl River Delta offer interesting contrasts. They follow similar overall trends. For example, immediately following the financial crisis, when millions of workers lost their jobs and thousands took to the streets, there was great churn in membership in both the YRD and PRD, before both returned to normal. But when it comes to the chairs of the Committees, turnover in the relatively quiescent YRD has consistently been lower than that in the more contentious PRD, as shown in Figure 3.2, which tracks membership changes with regard to

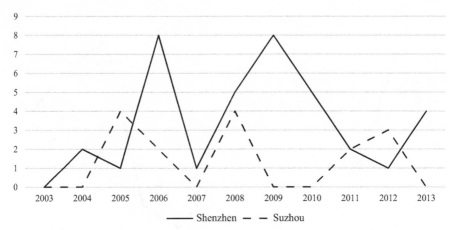

FIGURE 3.3 Turnover in all Politics and Law Committee members in Suzhou versus Shenzhen.
Source: Municipal yearbooks from Shenzhen and Suzhou, between 2003 and 2012.

the Committees of a selection of cities from each region: in the YRD, Changzhou, Huai'an, Nanjing, Nantong, Suzhou, Taizhou, Wuxi, and Zhenjiang (a city west of Nanjing, not to be confused with Zhejiang Province); in the PRD, Dongguan, Foshan, Guangzhou, Huizhou, Jiangmen, Shenzhen, Zhaoqing, Zhongshan, and Zhuhai. Data on Committee members other than chairs are not published for all cities in the YRD and PRD. However, they are available for both Suzhou (YRD) and Shenzhen (PRD). These cities moreover make for a good comparison because they are both the wealthiest in their respective provinces and are both tech manufacturing hubs. As shown in Figure 3.3, Shenzhen, in the tumultuous PRD, has seen much wider jumps in terms of total Committee membership than Suzhou, in the relatively quiescent YRD. This is not to say that these officials are necessarily fired or hired based solely on counts of unrest. Many other factors come into play, from elite connections to professional backgrounds. But more protest means *less* space for official bench warming and *fresh inducements* for ambitious leaders to elbow their way into various forums and make their mark. Contentious places have livelier bureaucratic politics; quiescent places, more elite stability. If officials everywhere are eager to demonstrate to their superiors that they take stability seriously, the liveliness of cities like Shenzhen makes officials in such places anxious to demonstrate that they are attentive to the specific causes of instability in their jurisdictions.

Demonstrating Concern for Stability in General in the YRD and PRD

Authorities in both the Yangtze River Delta and Pearl River Delta seem to be eager to prove to higher levels of government that they take instability in general seriously. This is evident in their local government yearbooks. These glossy volumes, complete with pictures of political meetings and inspections of various industries and advertisements for local firms, are published every year in all localities and trumpet local accomplishments, while trying to place a positive spin on local difficulties. They are handed out to visiting delegations from the central government and other localities. As such, yearbooks offer a unique window into what officials feel they must demonstrate to receive positive assessments of their performance. The Politics and Law sections of yearbooks from both deltas place a heavy emphasis on resolving "mass incidents" (as explained in the previous chapter, a euphemism for popular protest of various forms). This emphasis is often conveyed in quantitative terms. Nantong in Jiangsu, for example, claims in its yearbook that it resolved "325 mass incidents" in 2009 (Nantong Yearbook 2006, 165). The Guangdong provincial yearbook reports a drop in such incidents of 17.1 percent in 2012 (Guangdong Yearbook 2013, 166–67). Guangdong's Nanhai meanwhile says it reduced petitioning to Beijing in 2010 by 61 percent (Nanhai Yearbook 2011, 181). Shenzhen says it resolved 78,600 disputes and 419 mass incidents in 2009 (Shenzhen Yearbook 2010, 162). Dongguan takes credit for handling 224 mass incidents and dealing with 260 "different kinds of destabilizing factors" (*gelei bu wending yinsu*) in 2011 (Dongguan Yearbook 2012, 179). Shantou writes of a drop in petitioning of 66.5 percent, as well as effective responses to, in particular, "instances of instability" started by a death at the hands of a security guard in Chenghai and a protest over Japanese claims to the Diaoyu Islands by over 1,000 retired soldiers in 2012 (Shantou Yearbook 2013, 249–50). The yardsticks clearly vary from report to report. Is it the absolute number of incidents that matters? The number of "serious" incidents? The percentage drop in incidents? Or the percentage successfully resolved? One gets the distinct impression that the most flattering measure for a given local government is the one publicized! Regardless, the goal is to convey measurable progress toward full harmony – and to dispel any doubts others, especially people in higher levels of government, might have about local control.[4]

In addition to quantifiable achievements in stability maintenance, both Jiangsu and Guangdong local governments frequently highlight their responses to specific challenges. Zhongshan, for instance, reports "perfecting emergency plans" to deal with such difficulties as a movement described as "one million people marching countrywide" (*quanguo baiwan ren sanbu xingdong*), local

---

[4] The yearbooks' frequent resorting to numbers should be familiar to scholars of state socialist systems and their successors. It also echoes the findings of O'Brien and Li (1999) concerning "selective policy implementation" in rural China: what can be enumerated is given priority over more amorphous state priorities. Beijing would presumably find claims of a place being entirely conflict-free unbelievable. Thus, continuous improvement is the next best thing. Documenting improvement has an additional benefit: you can always improve more the next year, but you cannot improve on a perfect record.

citizens' participation in the international "Kony 2012" awareness-raising campaign regarding Lord's Resistance Army atrocities in Central Africa, and "other illegal assembly actions" (Zhongshan Yearbook 2013, 116). Nanjing reports "sternly striking against enemy forces' destructive activities" and establishing "no evil cult districts" (*wu xiejiao diqu*, referring to the Falun Gong), with the aim of maintaining "national security and social stability" (Nanjing Yearbook 2011, 394–95). Wuxi says that it cracked five cases involving national security in 2010 and "deepened" its struggle against the Falun Gong and other "superstitious" organizations, arresting twenty-six related people (Wuxi Yearbook 2011, 112). Special events such as the sixtieth anniversary of the founding of the People's Republic, the Shanghai World Fair, and the annual "two meetings" of the National People's Congress and Chinese People's Political Consultative Committee are noted as a focus of politics and law work (e.g., Changzhou Yearbook 2013, 89; Dongguan Yearbook 2012, 179; Nantong Yearbook 2006, 165; Nanhai Yearbook 2011, 181). Zhenjiang reports that it strengthened its surveillance over the course of a laundry list of "sensitive" dates: March 12, April 24, May 1, and June 4 (Zhenjiang Yearbook 2010, 95). Some of the implied threats seem absurdly inflated (e.g., the Kony 2012 campaign). Yet, the message of such reporting seems to be: "We take nothing for granted. Stability is our top priority." How then do things change when labor unrest, in particular, rises? Is there a difference in what officials emphasize?

Diverging Concern with Labor Issues in Particular

More worker resistance means more anxiety on the part of officials to prove that they are doing something about workplace problems, that they are "on top of things." This is evident from the public security sections of the same yearbooks discussed above. These sections, typically located within the broader Politics and Law sections, detail accomplishments in terms of routine policing but also, given the politicized nature of China's police, stability maintenance. I conducted an automated content analysis of the yearbooks of the same cities from the YRD and PRD used in the official turnover investigation above, plus the Jiangsu and Guangdong provincial yearbooks, for the years 2004–13, the most recent years for which a complete selection of volumes is available, for a total of two hundred yearbooks (10 yearbooks × 2 deltas × 10 years = 200). By "automated content analysis" here I simply mean that I instructed a computer program to search for certain phrases and calculate the percentage of text devoted to those phrases (I use percentages rather than a simple count of the number of times a phrase appears because some yearbook writers are wordier than others). Specifically, based on my hand-coding of a smaller selection of yearbooks and using the program Yoshikoder, I created a dictionary of words relating to labor issues (e.g., "workers," "wage arrears," "jobless"), corporations (e.g., "enterprise," "company," "work unit"), social conflict more generally (e.g., "protest," "political incident," "unstable"), policing innovation (e.g., "informationalization," "oversight," "risk analysis"), and routine policing ("drugs," "theft," etc.). Appendix 4 contains a complete list of the words. I then applied the dictionary to the 200 yearbooks, again using Yoshikoder. The results are displayed on the following pages. Figures 3.4 and 3.5 show fifth-order polynomial trend lines[5] for the counts of actual employment disputes in Guangdong and Jiangsu (based on the same data as Figure 3.1) beginning in 2004, a little before the time their numbers start to diverge, versus the percentages of yearbook public security section word counts devoted to labor issues in the PRD and YRD. Figures 3.6 and 3.7 present the percentages of words devoted to labor issues alongside the percentages devoted to other topics using linear trend lines for greater clarity. Labor issue percentages are displayed on the second vertical axis in the second set of figures. My purpose in creating these figures is to provide an intuitive, visual sense of how both worker resistance and anxiety to convey concern and on-top-of-things-ness with regard to resistance shift over time.

The patterns are conspicuous. From Figures 3.4 and 3.5, it clear that expressions of police concern about worker resistance in the two deltas started out at similar levels but diverged in much the same manner as actual employment disputes around 2006–7, breaking apart most in 2008. Interestingly, discussion of labor in the YRD seems to have caught back up to the PRD in recent years, while the regions' dispute numbers have remained dissimilar. Perhaps Guangdong's growing tumult has made Jiangsu officials concerned about the unrest in their own backyard, even if that unrest is less serious. Or perhaps a new national emphasis on stability maintenance has made yearbook language across regions converge. Nonetheless, the overall relationship between workplace conflict and security discussion is remarkably tight. Moreover, it is tighter for the increasingly high-unrest PRD than in the lower-unrest YRD. Specifically, in the PRD, there is a correlation of 0.62 between actual disputes and mentions of labor issues and 0.64 between disputes and writing about social conflict more generally, while in the YRD, the correlations are –0.25 and 0.11, respectively, that is, relatively low. Stability is an overriding imperative everywhere. But more activism has the effect of focusing state attention, as Heurlin (2016, chap. 2) has argued, and means more eagerness on the part of local authorities to appear to higher-ups to be doing something about instability and about labor issues in particular.

Nor are these the only patterns deserving of attention. Figures 3.6 and 3.7 reveal other interesting relationships. For example, in both regions, discussion of policing innovation has closely tracked discussion of general social conflict.

---

[5] Polynomial trend lines, as opposed to linear or logarithmic trend lines, are used to capture fluctuations in data. A fifth-order polynomial trend line can capture up to four rises or falls.

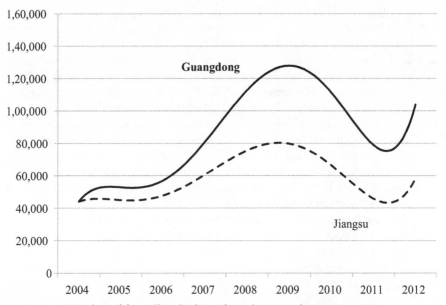

FIGURE 3.4 Number of formally adjudicated employment disputes.

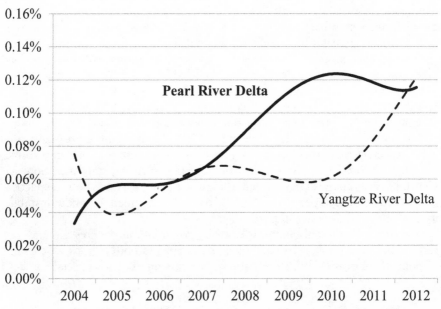

FIGURE 3.5 Percentages of words in public security sections of yearbooks devoted to labor.

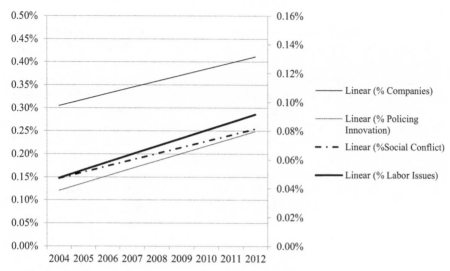

FIGURE 3.6 All issues in public security sections of yearbooks in YRD.

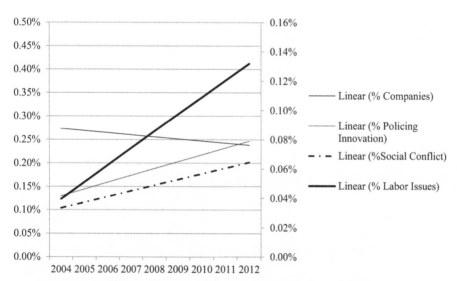

FIGURE 3.7 All issues in public security sections of yearbooks in the PRD.
Sources: Dispute data from *China Labour Statistical Yearbooks* (2005–13), all other data from municipal yearbooks of Changzhou, Huai'an, Nanjing, Nantong, Suzhou, Taizhou, Wuxi, Zhenjiang, Dongguan, Foshan, Guangzhou, Huizhou, Jiangmen, Shenzhen, Zhaoqing, Zhongshan, and Zhuhai, between 2005 and 2013.

This suggests that over the long term, unrest spurs an upgrading of the state's repressive capacity, anticipating an argument that I will make in Chapter 6. Similarly, previewing my point in the same chapter that protest drives authorities to increase their responsive capacity vis-à-vis labor and, consequently, downgrade the concerns of capital, the percentage of words dealing with companies has risen in yearbooks in the relatively low-unrest YRD along with mentions of labor issues, while in the higher unrest PRD, the percentage of words dealing with companies has gradually declined. This also fits with my description in the immediate next two chapters of the YRD as nudging capital into compliance with regulations via various inducements, formal and informal, and the PRD as acting more outright punitively toward abusive employers. In contrast to these dynamics, the proportion of words relating to routine policing has changed little in either delta. Ordinary crime, in other words, has not captured any more attention than in the past, or at least it has not featured any more in local governments' messaging to superiors. As they rise, instability and labor instability, especially, is where authorities' feel they need to prove themselves more.

The various patterns discussed here do not, of course, by themselves establish a causal relationship between protest and particular policies, let alone the direction of causality. But they show clear changes over time in state priorities or, at least, in what officials choose to advertise to the upper echelons of the state (via its yearbooks) as their priorities. As Heurlin (2016) argues, spikes in resistance send a more powerful "signal" than contention at a low boil. And "strong protest signals" from a particular social group "crowd out" weaker signals from other groups and place the issues of the former higher on the government's policy agenda. Regional authorities always care about stability. But as seen in the YRD-PRD comparison, they will attempt to demonstrate competence on "stability maintenance" more, and in particular with regard to industrial relations management, when they have more labor contention on their hands.

DIFFERENT ARMS OF THE GOVERNMENT TAKE ACTION

The analysis above has suggested how worker resistance pressures local officials to convince others that they are on top of things. But messaging aside, what do the officials actually *do*? Put differently, what policies do they enact? The natural instinct of local officials is to hang back and play things carefully, that is, to practice orthodoxy. Why rock the boat and risk introducing conflict where there is little or none? However, protest, especially protest that stretches beyond or spills out of accustomed channels, that is, boundary-spanning and transgressive contention, encourages cadre risk-taking. Authorities cannot necessarily hope to put the genie of conflict back in the bottle, but they can at least show they are responding with grit and creativity. Quiet measures will not be noticed by superiors; flashy measures, even if unsuccessful, might win praise. This means different things for different arms of the local state. Each may be logical on its own terms but together they illustrate, to quote Migdal (2001, 22) again, how the state can be a "contradictory entity that acts against itself." Below, I sketch what this means for two particular arms: the security apparatus and the official trade union.

Orthodoxy and Risk-Taking in the Security Apparatus

The state security apparatus has always played an important role in Chinese politics. It has figured in factional struggles at the very top of the regime (Guo 2012). But it has also, of course, kept a careful lookout for challenges from below. The fact that it is not divided into multiple competing branches cut off from society, as would be the case if coup-proofing was its primary aim, suggests that maintaining social stability is its dominant purpose (Greitens 2016). This has traditionally meant an overtly ideological approach to policing. Public security publications well into the late 1990s and early 2000s emphasize the need to safeguard the "people's democratic dictatorship" against a small group of "enemies" (Chinese Characteristics Study Group of the China Police Studies Association Basic Theory Specialists Association 1996). Several scholars, such as K. C. Wong (2012) and Trevaskes (2010) see a gradual shift underway toward less political and more "scientific" or "regularized" policing in China. Today, some policing manuals extol Western management practices and advocate "creativity" and "efficiency" (e.g., Z. Zhang 2007). But politics are never far removed. Thus, a book on neighborhood policing from 2003 explains how to monitor politically suspect individuals (*zhongdian ren*) (T. Wang 1997). And a volume concerning human rights and the police warns of efforts by foreign countries to use rights rhetoric and nongovernmental organizations to undermine the country (Cui and Cui 2000). One can thus imagine that orthodoxy for a local police force might mean keeping close tabs on possible sources of dissent and clamping down decisively at the first sign of protest, while risk-taking might entail a more hands-off, genuinely public order-oriented approach, characterized by low-violence crowd management and dispute resolution. But it seems more likely that the relationship between cruder forms of control and protest forms an inverted U-shape: cruder at low levels, then more sophisticated as police become used to handling conflicts, then crude again when things appear to be spiraling out of control and officials must demonstrate to their superiors that they are taking the situation seriously (slow-moving reforms are often invisible). Thus, we might mistakenly imagine a steady upward trajectory in police professionalism if we observe only areas with middling contention, but the true nature of the security apparatus becomes clearer when its back is against the wall. Then, it throws care aside.

Orthodoxy and Risk-Taking in the Trade Union System

Orthodoxy for the union means tending to old welfare functions and keeping on good terms with local elites. However, when resistance starts to rise, perhaps again because of union inaction, and especially when contention takes boundary-spanning and transgressive forms that existing state dispute resolution practices were not designed to handle, things change. The easiest response is pursuing quantitative targets set by union headquarters in Beijing: more collective contracts, or local rollouts of national campaigns, for example, to bring Fortune 500 companies on board, etc. These can – and are – advertised in yearbooks. But intense unrest demands more. Examples of gutsier ACFTU reforms intended to deal with intense conflict include the systematic provision of legal aid to workers (Pringle 2011, chap. 5); genuine if often short-lived experiments with collective bargaining at an enterprise level, involving elected worker-representatives (C. K.-C. Chan and Hui 2013; Pringle and Meng 2018); and sectoral bargaining initiatives, whereby new wages are set for an entire industry (E. Friedman 2014b; Mingwei Liu 2010; Wen 2015; Wen and Lin 2014). As noted in the previous chapter, even the most ambitious union initiatives have been found to be quite thin on close inspection. But their proliferation reflects the pressures that this branch of local government feels. Like the security apparatus, the ACFTU must show that it is ready to shake things up when challenges proliferate. The old ways are no longer enough.

MODELS OF CONTROL

As the different arms of local governments spring into action – not just the police and unions, but also courts and local legislatures and government-organized business councils – their policies congeal into distinct regional models of control. These may be the result of some coordinated plan by local authorities. Certainly, the protocols for handling unrest noted earlier in this chapter urge coordination. But models are just as likely clusters of semi-spontaneous reactions by the arms responding to the challenge of unrest in the ways they know how to respond. Clashing state reactions are therefore inevitable. Indeed, the more active each arm is, the more likely it is to act on its own initiative – and then have to negotiate its space with other arms. Thus, in his memoirs, a reformist former head of the Guangzhou Federation of Trade Unions, recalling his union's role in the 2010 Honda strikes, writes proudly of moving first, rather than waiting for other authorities to lead the way or, as he puts it, "not following the local party and government's ass into the enterprise" (*bu yao genzhe dangdi dangzhengde pigu jin qiye*), but also of having to then convince public security to hold off on intervening while the union advocated on behalf of the workers (W. Chen 2012, 80–82). At the same time as this leader was urging a peaceful resolution to the conflict, however, Guangdong Province was reportedly bringing in reserves of People's Armed Police in case they were needed for riot control (Lam 2010). Was this a carefully stitched together carrot and stick policy? It seems more like a series of decisions on the fly that ended up working out (the strike was resolved without violence and the union's actions, in particular, for a period, were held up as a guide for others, while the expanded paramilitary presence likely gave authorities peace of mind that things could not go too wrong). Regardless, though, as I will explain in the next two chapters, repeated instances like this mean that the PRD has – intentionally or not – evolved a distinct, risk-taking model of control characterized by reaction, experimentation, and crackdowns, which can be contrasted with the YRD's more orthodox model of preemption, caution, and nudging. I turn to the latter, less flashy case first, in Chapter 4.

SUMMARY

If there is a regime-level logic to the changes underway in China's workplaces, there is also a more mundane logic situated at the level of local governments and local officials undergirding it. Plans for responding to unrest are promulgated to all. Why do officials follow these plans and even go further and take their own initiative to craft new solutions to conflict? The cadre promotion system disciplines the country's vast bureaucratic apparatus into taking worker resistance seriously. Officials are promoted, demoted, fired, and fined based on their handling of instances of instability in their jurisdictions. Both bureaucratic strivers and muddlers alike must signal to their superiors that they are on top of things. There are many issues on an official's plate. Protest makes some issues rise in prioritization. As the former petitioning office worker cited at several points in this chapter said to me, "Collective behavior . . . can have a big impact on the government's perception of the *urgency* of an issue" (Interview POS #2 March 2017, emphasis added). I have illustrated this process with a brief look at how worker resistance in Guangdong's portion of the Pearl River Delta has outstripped Jiangsu's portion of the Yangtze River Delta over the past decade – and how turnover rates among local officials responsible for maintaining stability have done the same. This bureaucratic churn, then, I have shown, has been accompanied by a greater eagerness in the PRD than YRD to demonstrate to higher levels of government that authorities are paying attention to labor issues, as measured by mentions of key workplace terms in the public security sections of local yearbooks. What does this mean in terms of actual policies? When confronting a popular challenge, each arm of local government swings into action in the way it knows best, whether coordinated or not, I argue. These scattered reactions together over time generate contrasting regional models of control. Where conflict is less intense, i.e., it takes a more contained form, a more orthodox approach to governance emerges; where conflict is more intense, i.e., it takes a boundary-spanning or transgressive form, a risk-taking approach instead emerges. In the next chapter, we will begin by examining in greater detail the YRD model as an example of orthodoxy.

4

Orthodox Control

We were seated around a banquet table at a restaurant in the old part of Yangzhou, a canal city northeast of Nanjing, a couple of professors, a labor inspector, and myself. My interview notebook lay largely untouched, as the revolving tray at the center of the table spun around, delivering dishes. The talk focused on the hot topics of the moment – protests in Hong Kong, China's economic slowdown, but not what I had come to discuss: the state's supervision of labor relations, particularly in this region, Jiangsu's portion of the Yangtze River Delta. Then, toward the end of the meal, the labor inspector suddenly launched into a passionate defense of the YRD's approach to governing workplaces as compared to the region's competitor further south, the Pearl River Delta. As he put it: "Thinking may be more open in the PRD by several years, may have felt more influence from the West, but there is better management in the YRD. In the north, politics tend to be more important ... Things are more balanced" (Group Interview 54). When I asked the inspector about the Jiangsu government's attitude toward labor civil society in particular, he continued, "In the YRD, the overall capacity to control is stronger than in the PRD – in terms of services provided, in terms of coordination, and in terms of *containment*" (Group Interview 54). The result, he said, is a win for everyone. Workers enjoy more attention, businesses earn more in the long run, and, most importantly, social stability is maintained. With a flourish, the inspector finished by declaring that Jiangsu is simply more civilized or, as he put it, a "culturally superior" place, and its form of governance follows suit. If I was looking for the best earthly approximation of the "harmonious society" desperately yearned for by the CCP leadership, I needed to look no further. The Yangtze River Delta had things figured out.

This chapter uses conversations like mine in Yangzhou, along with a close review of local government yearbooks similar to those relied upon in the previous chapter, to begin an exploration of how regional differences in the intensity and forms that worker resistance takes, in interaction with the system's bureaucratic incentives, yield distinct regional models of control. I show that the Yangzhou labor inspector quoted above may have gone overboard with his local boosterism, but he was right to portray the Yangtze River Delta as quite different from that of its southern rival. As I explained in the first chapter, the two regions are quite similar. They are both engines of the China's economic growth, deeply integrated into the global economy, reliant to similar degrees on the state sector, and (temporary) homes for large numbers of migrant workers. Nonetheless, there are important differences in their recipes for resistance. Jiangsu is more high-tech and, despite being a major destination for migrants nationally, still has a greater concentration of local workers. Resistance thus occurs at a moderate level and generally ranges from contained to boundary-spanning. Tactics include a high reliance on the legal system, along with routinized strikes and protests. Demands are couched in terms that show a high level of trust in authorities. And local labor NGOs generally stick to cultural programming or, at most, the provision of legal advice. As a result, the government is able to continue to pursue an orthodox approach to governing workplaces. Specifically, officials try to *preempt* conflict as much as possible. As the labor inspector's comments suggested, the government also takes pride in not rushing headlong into the latest governance fads, whether "Western" inspired or otherwise. Instead, it adopts a *cautious*, incremental approach to policymaking. Finally, as the inspector also hinted, the subtle coordination of social forces is the rule. Officials *nudge* employers and employees into line with incentives, along with quiet punishments, such as bringing reputational pressures to bear on recalcitrant employers and isolating NGOs deemed potentially dangerous. This is a specific model tailored to a specific form of pressure (or lack thereof) emanating from the grassroots. But before delving into these details, a little more background on the region is in order.

A POLITICAL AND ECONOMIC POWERHOUSE

The Yangtze River Delta is situated midway up China's coast. It plays an important role in China's economy and politics – and has for centuries. Since the Song Dynasty (960–1279), the YRD has been a center for trade and the merchant class. Cities like Suzhou and Wuxi, with their winding waterways and carefully cultivated gardens, have long represented a luxurious, sophisticated lifestyle. Nanjing was the first capital of the Ming Dynasty (1368–1644), the stronghold of the rebel Taiping Heavenly Kingdom (1850–64), and the center of government for the Republic of China under the Nationalists from 1927 until the Japanese army overran the city in 1937 (and again, briefly, after the war and before the founding of the People's Republic). During the Cultural Revolution, the city was rocked by factional conflict and brought under control relatively late (Dong and Walder 2011a, 2011b; MacFarquhar and Schoenhals 2006, 240–41). However, Nanjing was also the site of early and enthusiastic opposition to the Gang of Four and of support for the moderate Premier Zhou Enlai (MacFarquhar and Schoenhals 2006, 420–22). Following market reforms, Jiangsu, like its neighbor Zhejiang, experienced a boom of "capitalism from below," with private speciality suppliers, which were closed out of the credit available to the state sector, forming integrated industrial clusters and production chains marked by both competition and coordination (Nee and Opper 2012). The YRD opened to foreign investment during China's "second wave" of liberalization which started in 1984, five years after the establishment of the Special Economic Zones of the PRD (Naughton 2007, 409). The YRD has grown rapidly since and is seen as on the verge of overtaking the PRD (Lau 2016a).

A Note on Defining the Region

Throughout my book – including in the paragraph above – I refer to Jiangsu Province and the Yangtze River Delta interchangeably. However, the YRD technically only cuts through the province's south. The north and middle of the province, while also densely populated – the county Shuyang in the north is one of the largest in the country – are not as wealthy. Southern YRD GDP per capita is roughly 1.6 times that of the middle and 2.4 times that of the north (HKTDC 2014).[1] Moreover, the Yangtze River Delta is not fully contained by Jiangsu. Zhejiang Province and the directly administered city of Shanghai can also claim parts of the delta. I focus on Jiangsu's portion because these other places have very different political economies. While Zhejiang's economic growth has been driven to a unique degree by small and medium enterprises, Shanghai is the country's financial center. Finally, even within the part of the Yangtze River Delta controlled by Jiangsu, there is considerable variation. Labor markets, in particular, differ sharply from city to city. At the time of my research, for example, the Kunshan industrial zone was experiencing a labor shortage while the capital of Nanjing was experiencing a *job* shortage (Interviews 14–15, 21). Foreign sources of investment also vary between YRD municipalities. For example, Kunshan, popularly dubbed "Little Taipei," attracts considerable Taiwanese investment, while Wuxi had, at the time of my research, just signed an agreement to become the site of a China-South Korea Science and Technology Financial Service Cooperation Zone (Frank Chen 2014; China Daily 2015). These nuances, however, should not obscure what different parts of the region have in common (and what the region has in common with my other case study, the Pearl River Delta): they occupy a central place in China's politics and economy.

---

[1] On a brief bus trip to Shuyang, I was struck by how the large, newly tiled rural homes outside of Nanjing gave way to smaller, worn, whitewashed structures as I traveled north.

SECTORS AND WORKER DEMOGRAPHICS

Digging deep into any region's dynamics inevitably reveals nuances that escape even the most focused "most similar" case selection. This is certainly true of the Yangtze River Delta and Pearl River Delta. Despite their closely matched socioeconomic profiles, the two regions still differ significantly with regard to their dominant sectors and worker demographics. I provide more details on these distinctions below. Then, I explain their consequences for worker resistance and, after that, models of control.

A Leader in High-Tech Production

The YRD is a leader in high-tech, high value-added production. A 2008 report by Cambridge University's Institute for Manufacturing, in explaining why the YRD's growth has not come at the expense of the PRD, notes that whereas the "PRD is a production base of downstream, light consumer goods ... the YRD is a leading producer of raw materials and intermediate goods. For example, while the PRD produces 70 percent of China's toy exports and 90 percent of its watch exports, the YRD manufactures over 60 percent of the country's integrated circuit boards" (University of Cambridge Institute for Manufacturing 2008, 12). The YRD's Suzhou, Wuxi and Changzhou have "nine national-rank development zones, 16 provincial economic technical development zones and hundreds of suburban industrial districts among them" (J. Liu 2011, 66). Whereas productivity in the two deltas was roughly the same in the mid-1990s, by 2005, the YRD (understood more broadly to include Shanghai and portions of Zhejiang) was 20 percent more productive than the PRD (OECD 2010, 119). Guangdong, as I will explain in the next chapter, is trying hard to move up the value-added ladder, but Jiangsu, despite entering the reform era later, is a rung or two ahead. As a result, the YRD's firms tend to provide enhanced employment conditions. Based on a survey conducted in both deltas, Liu, Yong, and Shu (2011) find that YRD employees enjoy better wages, better work hours, better benefits, less frequent wage arrears, and lower deductions from their wages for work rule infractions (the sole area where the PRD scores better is work injury insurance). Moreover, a report by X. Wan (2005, 25) shows a sharp difference in the percentage of YRD workers who have experienced prohibitions on visiting the restroom during work, who have been subject to searches by factory guards, or who have suffered beatings, compared to the PRD. Although work in the YRD is still often grinding, it is unlikely to give rise to the same intense grievances found in the PRD. Moreover, as befits the demands of more high-tech industries, the workers employed in the YRD are more educated: they are 10 percent more likely to have a senior high school, technical secondary school, technical school, or higher degree (X. Wan 2005, 4). Capital in the region is thus cutting edge, comparatively less abusive, and more demanding in terms of talent. It represents the cream of Chinese industry.

More Local Workers

Both the YRD and PRD, as already established in the first chapter, draw large numbers of migrant workers. Jiangsu ranks fourth nationally in its total number of residents with their household registration somewhere other than the townships where they live (China Statistical Yearbook 2014). Nonetheless, migrants make up a much smaller percentage of Jiangsu's total workforce (18 percent) than they do of the Guangdong's workforce (34 percent) (China Statistical Yearbook 2014). In the words of an apparel factory manager I interviewed in Lianshui, Jiangsu:

A big difference between the YRD and PRD is that most of the workers in the YRD are local. They are simpler than in the PRD ... Workers are older. They go home in the evenings and have a family life. If you can see your family every day, things are more stable ... The factory ... is like a big family. Some employees' children have already begun working here. (Interview 19)

It should also be noted that the migrants who do work in Jiangsu tend to be from nearby – a few counties over or the adjoining province of Anhui. This contrasts with the nonlocal population of Guangdong, which hails from as far away as Guizhou and Sichuan in southwestern China; Henan, Hunan, and Hubei in central China; and scattered areas in Northeastern China. In recent years, Uighurs have even been sent to work in Guangdong from far off Xinjiang to encourage ethnic assimilation (E. Wong 2014). As such, migrants in the YRD fall somewhere between total outsiders and in-the-know locals. This, combined with the kinds of industries they work in, drives the sort of resistance they engage in: contained and boundary-spanning.

CONTAINED AND BOUNDARY-SPANNING TACTICS

Workers in the Yangtze River Delta tend toward contained tactics in their activism. For the year 2013, right after the close of the period featured in my statistical analysis, China Labour Bulletin's strike map showed 98 strikes, protests, and riots occurring in Jiangsu, as compared to the 606 in Guangdong. Given that these figures are likely only a small sample of the total number of incidents occurring that year, adjusting them by local population yields exceedingly small figures. Still, the spread between the regions remains more or less the same as it does for the aggregates: seven times as many conflicts in Guangdong per capita as in Jiangsu.[2] Nor is Jiangsu only quiescent compared to Guangdong. The province also lags behind neighboring Zhejiang and Shanghai – and even places like Hainan and

[2] Specifically, in 2013, China Labour Bulletin recorded 0.001 strikes per 10,000 people in Jiangsu versus 0.007 in Guangdong. Population figures are from the *China Statistical Yearbook 2014*.

Shaanxi – in unrest.[3] In contrast, although the PRD is also the leader when it comes to formally adjudicated employment disputes, the gap between the YRD and PRD is narrower for such cases: in 2013, Guangdong had 1.71 workers involved in labor litigation per 10,000 people, compared with 1.33 in Jiangsu, that is, only 28 percent more (dispute figures are from the *China Labour Statistical Yearbook* 2014; population, the *China Statistical Yearbook* 2014). The report by Wan cited above shows that YRD workers consistently rate their knowledge of labor laws higher than their PRD counterparts (X. Wan 2005, 31). Moreover, YRD workers surveyed by Wan were more likely to use complaint channels established at the workplace level than PRD workers, even though the latter said that they have more "opinions" about their working conditions (X. Wan 2005, 27–28). These are all indications of a by-the-rules orientation.

The preference of Jiangsu workers for contained resistance was also clear in my interviews. For instance, when I asked a construction worker on a train from the city of Zhenjiang (again, not to be confused with Zhejiang Province), what he usually did when he experienced workplace abuses, he said to me, "I first call the police station. If that doesn't work, I go to court ... we usually use formal channels" (Interview 3). One person looking for work at a Nanjing migrant job center responded to the same question by saying, "People go to the labor bureau" (Interview 21), while another at the center replied, "Most bosses are good; if not, you dial 110 [China's equivalent of dialing 911] ... you have them send a labor inspector" (Interview 22). These responses match what a researcher at a government think tank in Nanjing said of YRD workers: "They are aware when something is illegal. But here they won't strike as much. They might not know exactly who they should contact – for example, they might dial 110 when they should really get in touch with the labor department – but they'll ask the government for help" (Interview 37). These respondents do not represent everyone, but they capture a general tendency in the region. At least with regard to tactics, this is not a hotspot of resistance.

An impression of workplace calm was pervasive. For example, the head of a Nanjing state-owned enterprise's trade union said, "In general, Jiangsu is quite stable. There aren't as many disputes as elsewhere. Workers here are very reliable" (Interview 27). In the words of a provincial labor bureau official,

---

[3] Might these figures reflect biases in reporting, though? Some of my interviewees in the Yangtze River Delta wondered whether their region might rank higher in conflict if provincial authorities did not keep such strict control over information. As one Nanjing-based academic said, "I'm increasingly realizing that there are a lot of things that happen here in the YRD that you just don't hear about ... in general, things are covered up" (Interview 71). A labor lawyer in Guangdong concurred: "It's not like there aren't strikes in the YRD. I have connections with officials. They tell me about things. It's just that incidents are effectively concealed" (Interview 64). However, in contrast, even if officials in the PRD wanted to hide their conflicts, it is unlikely that they could successfully do so at this point. Unlike in Jiangsu, the turmoil in Guangdong is just too pervasive for anyone to pretend otherwise. It simply must be acknowledged.

"From a national perspective, we are pretty peaceful and quiet here" (Interview 113). A taxi driver and former factory employee in Kunshan concurred: "[There are] very few direct, open conflicts here, mostly just people saying bad things behind the boss's back" (Interview 29). In the words of a young worker I spoke to at a noodle shop in Kunshan, "If conditions aren't good somewhere, you either bear it or you leave" (Interview 17). A Nanjing-based NGO leader noted more of a willingness among workers to stand up for themselves than in the past but said, "Of course, it is still only a minority of workers who pursue rights protection" (Interview 50). There might be good incentives for all these people to downplay contention. But such statements were heard much less from those I interviewed in Guangdong, even among state representatives.

CONTAINED DEMANDS

Even when boundary-spanning tactics are deployed in the Yangtze River Delta, they are accompanied by contained demands: framing that emphasizes faith in the government's ability to fix problems. A conversation I had with protesting workers in Zhangjiagang, a county-level city under the administration of Suzhou, suggests that even in the midst of a protest, expressions of trust in YRD authorities runs remarkably high. The workers in question had recently blocked the road to their industrial park in an attempt to recover money owed them from before their factory went bankrupt. Standing by the guardhouse of her now empty plant in the rain, one of the workers explained, "We haven't been paid for four or five months ... Some of us have worked here for five or eight or nine years." Despite these dismal circumstances, when I asked her if officials had been helpful, she replied, "Yes, they've been a big help. They are hunting for the owner who ran away" (Interview 39). When I later approached one of the factory's remaining managers, he echoed this sentiment: "We're all ordinary people here. The government is responsible for this problem and we hope it will fix it" (Interview 39). As I will describe in the next chapter, Guangdong workers I interviewed expressed much more cynicism. And they had moved on to claims not just for backpay but higher pay and the reform of local unions.

CONTAINED AND BOUNDARY-SPANNING ORGANIZATIONS

Finally, worker organizations in the Yangtze River Delta are few and moderate. The list of labor NGOs nationwide provided to me by CLB and referred to in Chapter 2 listed only five organizations in Jiangsu as of the end of 2013, as compared to the thirty-five found in Guangdong. More importantly, YRD-based labor NGOs tend to focus on cultural programming for workers, education for migrant children, and legal advice. Usually, the emphasis is on the first two of these forms of service. In the words of a Suzhou-based activist, "For [our] organization, culture is the main focus but legal advice is given, too, albeit in an inconspicuous (*di diao*) way" (Interview 46). The director of an organization in Nanjing described her organization's work as "Providing information on the street. Showing movies and accompanying them with information on work safety" (Interview 50). She added, "We have organized plays, where people act out difficulties from migrant workers' lives; [it is a] way for migrants to have a voice and for them to interact with and build bridges to other social groups. We take migrant children to university campuses" (it should be noted that her group also provided legal services and had an elaborate map of hot spots for different issues around the city – although this work was not emphasized as much) (Interview 50). Nondispute work is not necessarily "easy," and it can be quite meaningful for the people it serves. For example, another Nanjing activist explained how her organization went to considerable effort to build connections between overworked migrant parents and their left-at-home children, some of whom exhibit serious psychological problems already at a young age (Interview 48). But these sorts of activities present much less of a challenge to authorities than involvement in court cases, let alone strikes and protests. Altogether, YRD authorities face much less grassroots pressure than their PRD counterparts.

PREEMPTIVE GOVERNANCE

What style of governance is the result? Orthodoxy. This means several things in the Yangtze River Delta. First of all, a low level and contained and boundary-spanning form of worker resistance allows authorities in the YRD the luxury of being able to micromanage things. According to a researcher I interviewed at a government think tank in Nanjing, "The government ... interferes much more in Jiangsu ... In Guangdong, it's 'big society, small government'; in Jiangsu it's 'big government, small society'" (Interview 37). A Nanjing-based law professor offered a similar analysis: "Government is more open in the Pearl River Delta, letting more be settled naturally between workers and government ... In the Yangtze River Delta, the government, in contrast, is constantly intervening" (Interview 9). According to an official in Jiangsu's provincial labor bureau: "You have to take the initiative. Lots of workers would not act on problems right away. Chinese people will put up with things for a while until they can't stand it anymore. Then, they will make things really big" (Interview 113). An NGO leader in Suzhou told me, "It's not that there aren't disputes here. It's just that the government tries to mediate everything quickly so nothing gets taken to court. There's a lot in people's hearts here but it never gets to rise to the surface. In Guangdong things explode more" (Interview 76).

This orthodoxy requires constant monitoring of the region's industrial zones. The trade union work section of Wuxi's yearbook, for example, reports the release of a "Wuxi Federation of Trade Unions Emergency Work Plan on Handling Sudden Incidents" and the expansion its network of early warning organizations to 11,435 across the city (Wuxi Yearbook 2011, 103). Yangzhou has established a "green channel" for reporting urgent information in order to "mediate labor relations contradictions and mass incidents in a timely manner" (Yangzhou Yearbook 2011, 98–99). Suzhou's union similarly trumpets a "labor relations early warning system and network to discover symptoms in a timely manner ... and report [them] to higher level Party committees and unions" (Suzhou Yearbook 2010, 158–59). Several YRD yearbooks document special efforts to keep track of "floating populations" (Huai'an Yearbook 2011, Wuxi Yearbook 2011). Such activities are also reported in PRD yearbooks, but an academic in Nanjing said that the YRD particularly stands out in its population registration work. When his research team visited Zhangjiagang, he said, "There were several people we met who were assigned to this, and they made regular visits to places and kept detailed records. They have organized a landlords' association to keep track of workers" (Interview 71). The academic observed, "In the PRD, by contrast, no one has any idea of how many workers there are at any given time" (Interview 71). More accurately, in Guangdong, workers are more likely to be housed in dormitories and therefore tracked by companies, not the state (Pun and Smith 2007). But the point remains: the YRD government keeps an exceptionally close tab on people.

Monitoring schemes like these are not limited to municipal unions or neighborhoods; they penetrate deep inside factories. The public security section of Wuxi's yearbook highlights police efforts to "enter enterprises and serve the enterprises, help enterprises resolve difficulties" and elsewhere says it makes special guarantees of service (*zhongdian fuwu baozhang*) to enterprises that are large-scale, have a lot of outside employees, produce high profits, and use new technology (Wuxi Yearbook 2011, 113, 115). Nanjing's yearbook writes of establishing police service units (*jingwu fuwu dui*) for especially big construction projects and setting up a communications system for enterprises that are experiencing difficulties (Nanjing Yearbook 2010, 399). The government think tank researcher cited above explained to me, "Some companies have an office specifically for [reporting conflicts] at the state's urging ... there are people with this as a permanent job. But maybe they are sent over from the union or the human resources department" (Interview 53). Asked about her company's response to labor disputes, a human resource manager in Wuxi said, "It depends on the situation. Usually, we will contact them [the government] and ask them how to handle things, will give them a heads-up if someone will be bringing a case to arbitration.... One person is specially designated by the factory to notify the government immediately about any incidents" (Interview 25). A manager of an apparel factory in Lianshui noted that his guards were trained by the local police and made a part of the district police force, though he hastened to add this was not intended to intimidate workers (Interview 19). Although similar arrangements may exist in the PRD, I never heard them discussed there.

CAUTIOUS GOVERNANCE

Another effect of the Yangtze River Delta's relatively quiescent workforce: the region's constant intervention is counterintuitively accompanied by caution in terms of the labor laws it enacts and the programming of its trade unions. The region is not a center for policy experimentation – and it seems to like things that way. As the provincial labor official I interviewed said, "Our work style is to 'first, look; second, move slow; and third, only later put something through' (*yi kan, er man, san cai tongguo*). Governance, we believe, is like crossing a street" (Interview 113). "Looking" here can be understood as "looking both ways": down toward labor (and a given policy's potential for sparking unrest) and up toward Beijing. The YRD tends to pass legislation that complements or fills in gaps in national regulations, with the aim of incrementally crafting a more "complete" array of rules (Interview 113). An example of typical law-making in the region is the 2013 Jiangsu Province Labor Contract Regulation, which includes restrictions on labor dispatch and the use of student interns,[4] as well as new rules on open-ended contracts, work hours, and work-related illnesses.[5] These kinds of measures can make a real difference in the lives of workers.[6] They also carry few political risks. Workers can, of course, use the laws to bring new kinds of lawsuits, but they are not empowered to collectively challenge their employers the way they are under Guangdong's legislation governing strikes and representation in workplace negotiations (more on this in the next chapter). With only middling numbers of strikes, protests, and riots, the incentives for Jiangsu officials are clear: Why risk introducing conflict where there is none at present? Why needlessly rock the boat?

Caution is not just evident in the YRD's legislative activity but also in its trade union work. The most common topics featured in the union sections of Jiangsu yearbooks are charitable activities ("sending warmth"), jobs skills competitions, selecting "model workers" for praise, providing legal aid, and signing collective contracts, especially contracts with Fortune 500 companies.[7] A union leader at a state-owned enterprise in Nanjing described her organization's work: "Because [the enterprise] does not have a lot of grievances, the union doesn't do much rights protection work. Instead, it focuses on creating entertainment and health facilities for workers. It has a cultural center with a

---

[4] For instance, it requires that any work carried out by students be related to their majors and forbids schools from arranging work via intermediary organizations (Article 42).

[5] For example, it requires that companies notify workers about their legal qualification for open-ended contracts a month in advance of their second fixed contracts expiring (Article 38).

[6] In particular, subcontracting to human resources agencies and recruiting of young people from vocational schools to avoid legal obligations and cut costs have become serious issues over the past decade (Brown and deCant 2013; C. Zhou 2007).

[7] Collective contracts, as noted in Chapter 3, often simply restate the parties' existing legal obligations. With regard to Fortune 500 companies, a campaign has been launched to expand their use in major foreign firms.

gym. Workers with family difficulties, such as ones with a family member in the hospital, are helped financially by the union" (Interview 27).[8] In its yearbook, Yangzhou claims that 95 percent of "normal" manufacturing enterprises with preexisting unions signed collective contracts before the close of 2010 (Yangzhou Yearbook 2011, 98). Wuxi reports that 34,468 enterprises with unions, or 95.4 percent, had conducted "collective consultation" by the end of 2010 (Wuxi Yearbook 2011, 103). Changzhou notes that 40,000 enterprises, or 80 percent, had reached agreements by the end of 2012 (Changzhou Yearbook 2013, 79). As a local academic observed, "Reforms, such as the recent push for collective bargaining agreements, are implemented as orders from above; officials don't want to make mistakes, just want to 'do the job right'" (Interview 9). Jiangsu unions try to be responsive to workers' concerns – after the financial crisis, yearbooks noted union efforts relating to layoffs, for instance – but they are not eager to push their work into uncharted territory.

Two exceptions that prove the rule in terms of cautious YRD union programming are the region's use of Staff and Workers Representative Congresses and its limited trials with sectoral collective bargaining agreements. China had introduced SWRCs by the 1960s but backed them most actively in the 1980s as a vaguely Yugoslavian-style forum for worker input in factory decision-making and as a way to avoid the dreaded "Polish disease," that is, independent trade unionism (Estlund 2013, 3–8; Pringle and Clarke 2011, chap. 2; X. Zhu and Chan 2005). Traditionally, SWRCs have been limited to the state sector (Estlund 2013; see also Interview 52). In the late 1990s, these bodies were sometimes effective in challenging corruption during SOE restructuring (X. Zhu and Chan 2005). There are glimmers of activity in SWRCs today, but they remain weak (Estlund 2013, 8–11). In Jiangsu, yearbooks nonetheless make frequent mention of them (see, e.g., Changzhou Yearbook 2013, 78; Nanjing Yearbook 2010, 375; Nantong Yearbook 2006, 150; Suzhou Yearbook 2010, 158; Wuxi Yearbook 2011, 103; Yangzhou Yearbook 2010, 98). In contrast, SWRCs did not appear at all in the PRD yearbooks I examined. Until these bodies begin to engage in real oversight, the prevalence of SWRCs in Jiangsu should not be read as a sign of innovation but rather traditionalism.

Sectoral unions and collective bargaining agreements show more promise. As E. Friedman (2014a, 483) explains, in the Chinese context, sectoral unions "are organizations, typically established at the municipal level, that aim to organize all of the employers in a specific industry within their jurisdiction to either engage in collective negotiation or provide legal and other types of assistance to workers." Most famous in Zhejiang, where they were used to raise (but also place a ceiling on) wages in the Wenling wool sector, these unions have been pushed by the ACFTU nationally as a means of resolving

---

[8] Unionists at SOEs across China highlight similar efforts, of course – the state sector is not a leader in ACFTU innovation – but the YRD stands out relative to the PRD in its regional embrace of such programming.

disputes (E. Friedman 2014b; Mingwei Liu 2010; Pringle 2011; X. Wen 2015). Sectoral bargaining is clearly more common in Jiangsu than Guangdong (Mingwei Liu, Li, and Kim 2011). Its attraction for policymakers, lies not in its ability to empower workers but rather in its ability to forge a consensus between employers and the state; in fact, employers' associations have sometimes provided the initial impetus for such bargaining, not the ACFTU (X. Wen 2015). Compared to SWRCs and sectoral unions, Guangdong's experiments with union elections and substantive bargaining described in the next chapter, although flawed, come across as quite daring. In Jiangsu, there is no *need* to be daring. Why be daring if you do not have to?

NUDGING GOVERNANCE: CAPITAL

As a final point in the discussion of the styles of governance, moderate worker activism yields a nudging, passive-aggressive approach to managing capital and labor (unless things veer into Pearl River Delta–style confrontations). I focus on capital first. Yangtze River Delta employers face pressures and incentives for good behavior – formal and informal – from the local government. When companies are caught committing serious abuses, the state moves quickly to increase its leverage over companies. For example, in August 2014, an explosion occurred at an auto parts–polishing shop run by the Taiwanese-invested Kunshan Zhongrong, killing at least seventy-five people (X. Lin 2014). Afterward, a manager said, "There has been more pressure on Taiwanese firms. The government is using the accident as an opportunity to put pressure on the Taiwanese, forcing them to turn over more information on their operations" (Interview 24). One formal shape that such pressures can take is the state's cutting off of funding. The union leader of a state-owned enterprise in Nanjing noted, "Some industries . . . have more problems. For example, the construction sector still has a lot wage arrears. But the government is doing something about this. If you as a construction firm don't pay your workers' wages, the government will cut off your investment [projects]" (Interview 27). The Jiangsu labor bureau official I interviewed said, "You can make companies who have a history of having wage arrears set aside a certain amount of money as insurance" (Interview 113). Such policies are not uncommon in China. In Shenzhen, for example, certain kinds of firms (such as, again, construction companies), are required to place wages in a special account to ensure payment (NewsGD.com 2006). What is more distinctive is Jiangsu's "harmonious enterprises" program, which is administered by a tripartite commission and certifies as "harmonious" those companies that apply for and pass a rigorous evaluation of their business practices. In the words of the Jiangsu labor bureau official:

We grade each enterprise, focusing on several details: 1) whether they are employing people in a standard manner, including signing contracts, providing social security, etc.; 2) whether payments are made correctly, i.e., whether there are any wage arrears; 3) whether social insurance is paid fully and on time; 4) whether they have signed collective agreements and set up internal mediation systems and communications channels—they should have a special department inside the enterprise to resolve things inside the factory—and finally, 5) whether they are practicing corporate social responsibility in a number of very detailed ways. An enterprise has to score above 85 points on all these aspects combined to be considered a 'harmonious enterprise'. (NewsGD.com 2006)

Companies can use their "harmonious" status to attract customers and to avoid frequent state inspections, but the designation can be revoked if a company has "experienced a lot of petitioning and a lot of labor disputes" (NewsGD.com 2006). Other provinces have begun to study the program. Chongqing, for example, has sent officials to Jiangsu to learn about it (Interview 107). In the PRD, the city of Nanhai reports that 4,814 enterprises were designated "model harmonious enterprises" in 2010, in an apparent direct borrowing from the YRD (Nanhai Yearbook 2011, 166). In Guangzhou, 1,528 enterprises were declared "harmonious" in 2015 (Tencent 2015). And there are many other examples. The program is a rare instance of Jiangsu leading the way on a labor policy – but it is a policy that very much fits with the YRD's cautious approach. There is little risk that the certification of an enterprise as "harmonious" will itself lead to conflict, unlike the establishment, for instance, of new bargaining channels. The program works by quietly coaxing companies to behave.

Not all nudging of firms is so institutionalized. As the labor inspector in Yangzhou cited at the beginning of this chapter said to me, "You can't rely on the law alone. You have to pay attention to local distinctions, have to rely on traditions, have to use personal connections to work things out" (Interview 54). Sometimes reputational pressures are brought to bear on employers in the YRD. The same inspector told me, "If people know you have wage arrears, developing [your enterprise] will be very hard, and you might even go bankrupt" (Interview 54). In some circumstances, the government junks questions of legal responsibility altogether and itself steps in to make things right by employees. According to the Nanjing think tank researcher, "The government might even lend money to make sure things are paid" (Interview 37). The Yangzhou official concurred: "The government will pay companies to keep jobs. This isn't the case in the PRD . . . The YRD will intervene. This is better for the long-term. Enterprises here feel a lot of pressure" (Interview 54; a similar statement was made in Interview 51). Contrary to his assertion, there are actually many reported instances of authorities paying off workers in the PRD, too, especially in the early days of the 2008 financial crisis.[9] But there was much more discussion of the practice in my YRD interviews. And it fits well with other Jiangsu policies. Paying off labor is a politically safer way of handling disputes, at least in the short term, than allowing them to run their course via protests or

---

[9] For example, when the Smart Union toy factory in Dongguan went bankrupt, the local government compensated employees using 24 million RMB of public money (Eimer 2008).

litigation. This is not "nudging" in the sense used to describe policies intended to unconsciously shape citizen behavior in the United States and elsewhere (Thaler and Sunstein 2008), but rather one of a constantly evolving set of tools, some written up in regulations but many ad hoc or relationship-based, that are intended to solve problems with a minimum of fuss.

NUDGING GOVERNANCE: LABOR NGOS

The nudging of labor takes a different form. Labor NGOs in the Yangtze River Delta are co-opted or isolated. Increasingly, local authorities are buying the services of these organizations. One group in Nanjing shares its offices with the Ministry of Civil Affairs (Interview 50); a Suzhou organization has used space provided by the municipal government to seven or eight other groups in the past (Interviews 46); the Zhangjiagang Ministry of Civil affairs provides space to NGOs, with "cubicles for each group" (Interview 71). In the words of the Nanjing organization's leader, "Work for [my] organization is slowly getting better. People didn't fully understand organizations like this at first. Now, the government is supportive" (Interview 50). According to another activist in Nanjing, "If there's a gap in services, the government puts lots of money there and all the groups flock to that area. For example, there's been a lot of money recently for helping old people and children" (Interview 48). Although this interviewee was critical of the herd mentality of fellow civil society organizations, she also took away a positive lesson from this development: "The government is opening up more to NGOs, changing. In the past, it wouldn't help an organization like mine" (Interview 48). Importantly, state funding comes with strings attached. Politically sensitive work is discouraged. A Suzhou-based activist/intellectual noted: "The government supports work that helps migrant workers' children. It's different with rights protection" (Interview 42). According to a Nanjing academic, engagement "gives the appearance of supporting civil society, but it also keeps people under tight control" (Interview 71). For the most part, organizations do not stray too far from what is deemed acceptable.

When NGOs cannot be co-opted or the situation is deemed serious enough, YRD authorities shift to isolating civil society groups. A Beijing-based organization specializing in labor litigation that established a branch in Jiangsu said that carrying out programming in the YRD was difficult due to local political sensitives (Interview 20). Others in the labor NGO world told me that this was an understatement, and that the Beijing organization had had a next to impossible time operating in the YRD, with its staff more or less confined to their offices. When large conflicts crop up, the Jiangsu government moves quickly to seal off activists from workers. This tendency was on full display in the aftermath of the 2014 explosion at the Taiwanese-owned auto parts polishing shop mentioned earlier. As authorities used DNA tests to identify the dead, relatives of missing workers protested outside of government offices (X. Lin 2014). Notably absent were NGOs. An academic explained:

Jiangsu moved quickly and controlled the situation. There were probably a lot of families who wanted to protect their rights and NGOs like maybe [the Beijing group with a Jiangsu branch] wanted to involve themselves. But the government in Kunshan had the resources to promptly pay the families a relatively reasonable compensation so that things didn't escalate; this combined with their tight control of the situation kept things from getting more serious. (Interview 53)

A Suzhou-based labor activist echoed this description of the incident. He said he went to the site of the explosion in Kunshan and stood in the crowd. However, he could not get past security: the factory was being guarded too closely. "The victims were separated from any social groups and protected in the hospital," he added (Interview 46). Such a quiet, surgical approach no longer seems to be possible in Guangdong. There, incidents escalate further, and nudging – whether in the form of carefully doled out incentives or quiet pressure and exclusion – is not enough. To the YRD's preemption, caution, and nudging, the PRD offers a contrasting regional model of control: reaction, experimentation, and crackdowns: a different model for a different level and different form of contention.

FEEDBACK FROM POLICIES

The Yangtze River Delta's polices undoubtedly reach back to affect the nature of worker resistance. The Jiangsu government's low-key strategy of co-optation and isolation likely encourages moderate initiatives by nongovernmental organizations, for instance. One interviewee observed of an NGO in Suzhou that had been the object of both state pressure and co-optation: "[the organization] used to run a lively library. Now it is quiet. They still do music, but it's mostly just him [the organization's leader] playing. Workers have cooled ... The organization goes out less, seems afraid of contacting workers. The group is focusing more on migrants' children now" (Interview 24). Less heavy-handed repression is doubtless partially responsible for the high level of trust workers show in authorities. And to the extent that less overt disciplining of companies is more effective, it likely encourages compliance of the sort that in turn reduces the need for harsher measures. Better compliance means, again, less angry labor. The YRD model, in other words, is to some degree self-reinforcing. However, as will be pointed out in the next chapter, the PRD once employed similar governance strategies to those of the YRD. But the PRD's fundamental characteristics – and the innovations of its activists – set the region careening off on a different course. Jiangsu's interlocking relationships perpetuate themselves as well as they do because nothing has changed at a structural level to encourage a wave of unrest that would throw things off-balance. An alteration in the composition of local capital (and therefore working conditions) or in the backgrounds of the region's workers would likely encourage more anger and cynicism and a greater willingness to reach outside safe institutions for redressing grievances. Although activism has a strong element of contingency and it is difficult to predict how it will develop, with time and experience, workers and their allied NGOs would likely become bolder and better at protesting (and NGOs might, like their PRD counterparts, turn down state offers of office space and money). Preemption of the sort currently practiced by authorities in the YRD would eventually become impossible and nudging and co-optation would be inadequate. The system's bureaucratic incentives would then work differently. Risk-averse officials would see more career benefit in trying out new things rather than staying with the tried and true. And, in the end, the region's once smoothly functioning machine would be found inadequate and in need of repairs, meaning that the government would have to start taking risks.

IS THE GOVERNMENT RESPONDING DIRECTLY TO STRUCTURAL FACTORS?

One can also imagine ways in which the characteristics of sectors and worker demographics described above directly affect governance. For instance, local officials might be more sympathetic to local people and therefore craft gentler policies, making resistance of a confrontational sort unnecessary. Or they might be anxious to keep their high-tech industries and high-skilled workers and therefore approach conflicts with a gentler touch. Resistance itself would therefore, not be as important as a driver of policy. Yet, there are strong reasons to believe that this is not the case. When Jiangsu workers *have* adopted a more militant stance, as when over 2,000 of United Win Technology Ltd Co. workers in Suzhou protested against hexane gas exposure, riot police have been deployed, just as in the PRD (Qian 2010). Labor NGOs that have gone too far have not just been isolated. They have been shut down. This happened to a university-connected labor law clinic recently. It is hard to argue that riot police not being deployed more in the YRD is not primarily a function of the region's relative scarcity of high-profile incidents. Or that NGOs being co-opted is not mainly a result of their being weak, underdeveloped, and willing to be co-opted. Resistance is the intervening variable through which all others must pass – and is, therefore, the essential one.

POLITICAL CULTURE

So, is it possible that Jiangsu simply has a very different political culture? The labor inspector quoted at the beginning of this chapter certainly believes that governance in the YRD is more "civilized" at a fundamental level. Others I interviewed echoed this sentiment. For example, an activist based in Suzhou who once worked in the PRD as a migrant said to me, "The PRD has a backward culture. It was nothing before reform and opening. The YRD has a better cultural background, traditions to fall back upon, traditions of following what the government says. Rights protection is better here" (Interview 42). Yet, if a certain approach to politics is deeply ingrained in the region, then that would seem to affect officials more than workers. After all, although more workers are locals in the YRD than in the PRD, a large percentage of YRD workers are still migrants. And many are employed in foreign-invested enterprises. In contrast, most officials – at least up to a certain level in the system – are from Jiangsu and embedded in Jiangsu bureaucracies. Thus, to the extent culture is important, it affects the policy side of the equation more than the protest side. It is, then, another of many contributors to the way governance plays out, but it does not seriously confound the protest-policy relationship.

SUMMARY

Particular industries and worker demographics in the Yangtze River Delta yield not only lower resistance but more moderate forms of resistance. More high-tech industries in need of more educated workers paired with more locals and fewer migrants mean activism that involves contained or boundary-spanning tactics, demands, and organizations. This, in turn, results in an orthodox approach to governance characterized by preemption, caution, and nudging. Specifically, the government rules by carefully monitoring industrial zones for signs of impending disturbances, avoiding daring reforms to labor laws or the role of local branches of the ACFTU that might upset the equilibrium, and using quiet incentives and punishments – certification programs, offers of support, reputational blackmail, isolation – to keep capital and labor in line. Feedback loops certainly exist, making certain relationships, such as that between state management of enterprises and their compliance or state control of NGOs and their choice of activist styles, self-reinforcing. But a structural change that spurred more intense worker resistance would likely cause these patterns to break down. It could furthermore be argued that the YRD government is crafting its policies in direct response to the sectoral and demographic drivers of unrest (or the lack thereof) – again, high tech industries and locals – as opposed to the (low) level of unrest itself. Alternately, it could be posited that everything comes down to the region's unique political culture. However, the reactions of authorities to local resistance that does go beyond the region's norms undercut purely structural interpretations, while the still heavily migrant composition of the YRD's workforce undercuts analyses focused exclusively on regional culture. The YRD's model of control is primarily a product of the region's form of resistance (interacting with the system's bureaucratic incentives). With more pressure from below, the YRD would likely become like the PRD, which I describe in the next chapter.

5

Risk-Taking Control

The previous chapter on the Yangtze River Delta began with a short anecdote concerning a dinner party. The Pearl River Delta, in contrast, requires at least two stories to start things off. The first takes place in a very different setting: the backstreets of Zhongshan, a manufacturing center across the mouth of the Pearl River from Shenzhen and abutting the gambling center of Macau. I made two brief trips to Zhongshan in the spring of 2015. The reason for my trips: employees of a Japanese-owned handbag factory in an outlying district of the city had become frustrated at their low wages and lack of social security contributions and, moreover, were concerned that cutbacks in their work hours might portend layoffs. As they had before when they came up against otherwise unresolvable grievances, the workers responded by going on strike. Unlike in their previous mobilizations, however, the workers were met with a violent crackdown. On my initial visit to the handbag factory, a worker chatting in a convenience store across the street explained to me what happened: "People were beaten ... They were beaten by people in military-style uniforms. I don't know if they were police or mafia. [It happened] when we were all gathered outside, [and] the police and labor bureau people just laughed at us. How can you not do anything for people and then just laugh at them? It was so cruel!" (Interview 60). Nor apparently was it just workers who had been attacked. I read online that NGO activists who had gone to the strikers' aid were brutalized by plainclothes policemen. One subsequently had to be treated for a lumbar disc protrusion. On my follow-up visit to the factory, workers were streaming out of negotiations with factory management. The discussions had already dragged on a month. But the intimidation continued. The workers pointed out a thuggish individual loitering outside the plant's gates: "That man with the phone there was responsible for beating people up; he takes revenge on people" (Group Interview 61). The effect of all this violence was, unsurprisingly, a paralyzing atmosphere of fear. In the words of one worker, "There's just no more feeling of safety" (Interview 60). Creating precisely such an atmosphere was obviously the intention of the authorities handling the dispute. They were coming down hard on challengers.

My second Pearl River Delta anecdote is closer to the one that began the previous chapter. Like my recollection of the Yangzhou banquet, it concerns an official. This time, though, the official in question was a retired leader of the municipal trade union federation of Guangdong's capital, Guangzhou. The scene was not a banquet but a low-key walk around the older part of the city, near the official's old offices. As we passed worn but still grand colonial buildings, the official criticized the ACFTU's internal organization, the legal structures in which it operates, its international interactions, and its general outlook. On internal organization: "Even when enterprise-level union leaders are elected, their union positions are only part-time responsibilities ... The company doesn't want them to speak up for the workers and the union leaders have to think about their own futures ... We need systemic adjustments. In other countries, a workplace union leader can find work later in his or her sectoral union. However, in China there are no opportunities for professional advancement" (Interview 62). Moreover, the official said, "The union has too many responsibilities. In one small union there are 15 departments, the same as the corresponding government agency. Not all are related to workers. This forces the union to separate itself from the masses" (Interview 62). On legal structures, he commented about a recently passed provincial law on collective consultation: "It does not protect labor, does not regularize collective actions as it was intended to" (Interview 62). On international interactions: "The Chinese union doesn't play its role sometimes ... Early on, Obama adopted protections against tires from China. He did this at the urging of the steel workers. This is a powerful union! They were looking out for their jobs. Why doesn't the ACFTU do the same?" He further commented, "The union joins big international events but does its own thing. It is not joining the big labor family" (Interview 62). As an example, he related how on a trip to Africa, the ACFTU delegation had spouted the same vague slogans at every stop and were unable to engage meaningfully in discussions about important issues of globalization their African counterparts raised (Interview 62). Most bitingly, the official commented, "The union [among workers] should be like fish in the water. However, it is really more like oil and water" (Interview 62). Not all of the conversation was devoted to criticisms, though. At points, he also reflected on his own career: an early and controversial push to make a textile company union he headed more a part of setting wages, a law he later supported that prevented managers from being union leaders, and daring outreach to American unions that drew censure back home. This was an individual used to operating in an environment where original thinking was encouraged.

Like the previous chapter, this one uses extensive interviews, a close review of local government yearbooks, and news reports to explain the different approaches to governing workplaces found in different parts of China.

I show that the Pearl River Delta's approach – its distinct model of control as exemplified by the brutality unleashed on the Zhongshan workers and the thoughtful perspective of the retired Guangzhou union leader described above – is quite different from that of the Yangtze River Delta. As noted, Jiangsu is more high-tech and, despite being a major destination for migrant workers nationally, still has a greater concentration of local workers. The converse of this is that light industry and migrants feature to a greater degree in Guangdong. Worker resistance thus occurs at a high level and generally ranges from boundary-spanning to outright transgressive. Tactics include not only relying on legal channels and routinized strikes and protests, but also well-coordinated, high-profile showdowns. Demands extend beyond the basics afforded by law and are no longer couched in deferential terms that show trust in authorities. Finally, in terms of organizations, local labor NGOs, at a minimum, provide legal advice and have increasingly (at least until the last couple of years) engaged in openly organizing and negotiating ends to strikes. As a result, an orthodox approach to governance like the YRD's is no longer tenable. Instead, local authorities take risks. Specifically, they adopt a model of control that is characterized by reaction, experimentation, and crackdowns. After fleshing out these dynamics, I tackle some analytical complications, as in the previous chapter. Are workers spurred on by the creativity of local officials? Or angered by the violence of police? And what of the PRD's famed culture of reformism and, relatedly, foreign influences? First, though, I once more begin by providing some general background on the region.

THE WORKSHOP OF THE WORLD

Like the Yangtze River Delta, Guangdong's Pearl River Delta has a long history as an economic and political center. With the Nanling Mountains hindering the region's land access to northern China, the PRD had already oriented itself toward the ocean in Imperial times (Vogel 1971, 13). In the Qing Dynasty, all foreign commerce was initially restricted by law to the provincial capital of Guangzhou (Canton), but following the first Opium War in 1842, the city was made one of several "treaty ports" where foreigners enjoyed extraterritoriality. Cantonese, meanwhile, made up half of all the Chinese who emigrated abroad (Vogel 1971, 20). Many early reformers and revolutionaries were from Guangdong, including Sun Yatsen, Liang Qichao, and Kang Youwei. For two brief moments, from 1925 to 1927 and again for several months in 1949, Guangzhou was the capital of the Nationalist government. Worker organizing in early-twentieth-century Guangzhou was extensive. In 1927, the Nationalists suppressed a Communist-organized uprising there – the "Canton Commune" – at the cost of thousands of lives. Cultural Revolution violence was intense in the PRD and, as in the YRD, it persisted for years (Vogel 1971, chap. 8; Yan 2015). The country's successive political storms rocked Guangdong profoundly.

For much of Mao Zedong's rule, Guangdong lapsed into underdevelopment, but with Deng Xiaoping's Reform and Opening, the PRD became *the* center for the country's market experiments, with labor protections loosened and investment flowing in from Hong Kong and further abroad (Howell 1993, chap. 6; Vogel 1989). J. Friedman (2005, 28) writes, "For a decade or two, the region was China's Wild West, a case of 'primitive accumulation.'" When economic policy briefly took a statist turn following the 1989 Tiananmen Square Massacre, Deng traveled to the PRD city of Shenzhen on his famous "Southern Tour," reviving reforms. A statue of Deng is now located in the city's Lianhuashan Park. Shenzhen itself is almost wholly a product of the post-state socialist era. Into the early 1980s, what is now the city was only a collection of farms and fishing villages; today, it is the residence of more than 15 million people. As Shenzhen grew, other brand new metropolises, like neighboring Dongguan, sprouted up and followed suit, renting out agricultural land for manufacturing and housing (Saich and Hu 2012). Visitors traveling through the PRD today are treated to a seemingly endless sea of tiled factories, hastily assembled worker housing, and dusty roads, with ragged farms, tucked into the small slices of remaining land. Liberal economists laud Guangdong's growth model (The Economist 2017).

Again, a note about terminology is in order. As with the "YRD" and "Jiangsu," I use the words "Guangdong" and "the PRD" interchangeably here. Guangdong Province also contains poorer, inland regions. And the PRD itself is economically divided, "both between the east and the west and between the inner and outer circles," with the east and inner areas (demarcated by the Beijing-Kowloon Railway line) more developed (B. Yang and Jin 2011, 81–82). However, the PRD is, for all that, remarkably cohesive – indeed, the "most economically agglomerated region in China" – and it dominates Guangdong to an even greater degree than the YRD does Jiangsu. In 2013, a full 79.1 percent of Guangdong's GDP and 95.4 percent of its exports were from the PRD (HKTDC 2015). When observers refer to China as the "workshop of the world," they usually have both the PRD and Guangdong in mind.

SECTORS AND WORKER DEMOGRAPHICS

As in the Yangtze River Delta, the sectors and worker demographics of the Pearl River Delta generate unique local patterns of unrest. Investment in the PRD has been concentrated in light industries that are known for workplace abuses and that simultaneously gather workers together in great numbers. The workers themselves are, meanwhile, overwhelmingly migrants and from further away than their YRD migrant counterparts. The result: boundary-spanning and transgressive resistance through all dimensions: tactics, demands, and organizations. Authorities in the PRD face a different recipe of resistance and consequently feel much greater pressure.

A Leader in Light Industry

In contrast to the high-tech Yangtze River Delta, the Pearl River Delta's strength has traditionally been in light manufacturing, including toys, electronics, clothing, lighting, jewelry, and furniture. B. Yang and Jin (2011, 84) write of the region: "Most of the industries ... are made up of small-scale enterprises concentrating on the processing phase that is dependent on imported resources. PRD enterprises are labor-intensive ... and are defined by low-level technology and machinery." Xianming Chen (2007, 193) notes that the region's factories "rely on suppressed low wages and razor-thin profit margins but ... lack local integration and innovation." The PRD has long been synonymous with abuses: forced labor, corporal punishment of workers, and factory fires (A. Chan 2001). Guangdong has continually striven to upgrade its industries. Automobile production has picked up over the past decade, as has Internet commerce (HKTDC 2015). By connecting its companies with research and development conducted in Hong Kong and at local universities, the PRD has tried to leapfrog in "strategic emerging industries" like LED manufacturing (Butollo 2015). Still, as noted in the previous chapter, even as it leads the YRD in raw GDP terms, the PRD lags behind its northern competitor in value-added terms. Production is crude and workers have ample grievances.

More Migrant Workers

The previous chapter noted that migrants dominate the Pearl River Delta to a greater degree than the Yangtze River Delta. But numbers alone cannot convey the degree to which Guangdong has become a microcosm of China's diversity. In much of the PRD, outside of the older neighborhoods of Guangzhou, the local language of Cantonese is rarely spoken and Cantonese restaurants can be hard to find. The region's factory zones are dotted with "urban villages" (*chengzhong-cun*), which are home to groupings of people from particular places – a Sichuan village here, a Hunan village there. Underground native place associations protect their members, with violence if necessary (C. K.-C. Chan 2010, chap. 3). According to a manager at a Dongguan shoe factory that experienced a massive strike in 2014, "Guangdong has a high number of migrants. They have nothing to lose by creating havoc, asking for more ... Migrants group together" (Interview 36). The phrase "nothing to lose" is key. Less embedded in the city as a whole, migrants are immune to some of the pressures brought to bear on locals. And in their isolated micro-communities, they find the footing to resist.

BOUNDARY-SPANNING AND TRANSGRESSIVE WORKER RESISTANCE

Worker resistance in the Pearl River Delta occurs at a high level. As noted, the PRD leads the country in strikes, protests, and riots, as well as formally adjudicated disputes (though, again, the gap between it and the YRD in the latter dimension is smaller). Not enough information is available for an accurate accounting of changes in the size and duration of workplace clashes over time. However, anecdotal evidence suggests that the PRD's conflicts are occurring on a larger scale and lasting longer than they did in the past. In an interview, one Shenzhen-based labor NGO staffer commented to me, "It used to be just small conflicts, but they have expanded to include big factories" (Interview 63). An example of the scaling up he described is the 2014 Dongguan shoe factory strike which involved upward of 40,000 protesters, making it likely the largest work stoppage in the history of the People's Republic. According to another activist in the PRD: "Strikes used to just last a couple days at most; now they will last a week or two" (Interview 78). Some have dragged on for a month. I received no such reports in the YRD. In their study of strikes in France from the 1830s through the 1960s, Shorter and Tilly (1971) found that "small but long" strikes had given way to "short but large" strikes, a change they attributed to the growth of national union federations and the politicization of French workers. In contrast, Guangdong labor activism is expanding through *all* dimensions – and without, of course, the support of unions, national or otherwise. This means much better coordination and a shift from routinized, boundary-spanning contention into something more transgressive.

BOUNDARY-SPANNING AND TRANSGRESSIVE DEMANDS

Pearl River Delta workers are also increasingly sidestepping narrow legal claims. They are the leading edge of the national trend toward "offensive demands" documented in Chapter 2 (see also Elfstrom and Kuruvilla 2014). Scholarship from the late 1990s and early 2000s portrays the migrants flocking to Guangdong as cautiously rights-oriented in what they were calling for (see Lee 2007). But during my fieldwork, interviewee after interviewee attested to migrants' claims having changed. For example, in the spring of 2015, a junior cadre with the Shenzhen Federation of Trade Unions said to me, "Increasingly, workers' demands are not limited to the law" (Interview 69). Specifically, according to a Guangdong labor lawyer, "Workers are demanding 1) higher wages (the cost of living is rising); 2) more respect; and 3) organizations" (Interview 64). The last of these demands – for workers' own organizations or for more representative branches of the state union federation – features in seven PRD conflicts in the *China Strikes* dataset, including not only factories that were a part of the 2010 Honda auto parts plant-inspired strike wave, but also Uniden Electronics (already in 2005), the Yantian Port (in 2007), TDI Power workers (2011), Ohm Electronics (2012), and the 2014 Dongguan shoe factory strike. No such claims can be found in the dataset from the YRD. In the words of one of the PRD labor NGO leaders quoted above, "Workers know ... that litigation is not enough ... Workers are acting collectively to get more than the law by itself provides" (Interview 78). Increasingly, rules and regulations and their enforcement organs are becoming irrelevant.

Of course, nothing is set in stone. With the economy beginning to slow, people could return again to making defensive claims and utilizing arbitration panels and courts more in the future. I observed some evidence of growing backward-looking activism already in 2015, during my fieldwork. For example, people I interviewed outside of an electronics factory in Shenzhen who had recently been on strike said,

The strike was over overtime. We used to put in seven days a week at the factory and earned over 5,000 RMB, because of the double pay on weekends. But now the factory is giving everyone two days off per week, so, without overtime pay, we are just making 3,000 RMB. We could stand 4,000 RMB, but 3,000 is just too little. Many of the people at this factory are parents with kids. We are not afraid of working hard (*bu pa xinku*). (Interview 106)

At another Shenzhen electronics manufacturer where employees had blocked the entrance to their plant, the manager of a neighboring cafeteria said, "The protesters were cleaning workers, I believe. They were really deserving of pity: they hadn't been paid for three or four months. And when they wanted more work, the boss kept saying to just come back another day. Some threatened to jump from a building" (Interview 105). An employee at the handbag factory in Zhongshan that was mentioned at the beginning of this chapter, where workers had been on strike for almost a month, complained to me, "The factory kept reducing the hours of the older workers, cutting their overtime, sometimes bringing them down to just 22 hours a week or so. These people used to earn about 3,500 RMB a month. Now, they are just bringing in 1,500 or 2,000-something RMB" (Interview 60). However, as the industrial actions in each of these instances demonstrate, even if their claims change to more defensive ones, PRD workers are unlikely to adopt less aggressive tactics. Guangdong workers' organizing skills, honed via repeated conflicts, will probably simply be put to the service of new demands.

In my interviews with Pearl River Delta employees, I furthermore picked up little of the trust for the state I had felt from their counterparts in Jiangsu. For example, in Shenzhen and Dongguan, I held a series of group interviews with plaintiffs in industrial illness and injury lawsuits. During one of these interviews, a worker complained, "If local governments really practiced good oversight, there wouldn't be illnesses like mine. But the officials just come around to the factory near the end of the year, basically just to collect money from the company. You can ask any worker! Every factory is like this" (Group Interview 96). Another injured worker said of his experience with bringing a case to the local offices of the labor bureau, "The Labor Station stood with the company, not workers like me, despite their rhetoric. One wonders: are their parents actually devils? They just sent us elsewhere" (Group Interview 97). Said another: "Only if someone dies does the government do anything, start to pay attention" (Group Interview 97). And yet another: "They [officials] are just delaying, delaying. The main problem is the government is not doing its duty." In the words of a Shenzhen activist,

Workers' consciousness is changing. They used to trust in the government and they would put a lot of energy into legal cases. Now, that trust has been lost. I met a worker once who was crying – not because he hadn't succeeded in getting what he wanted but because he was so disappointed in the government, in how it hadn't matched up to his idea of it. (Interview 79)

The bitterness workers in the PRD felt – and feel – toward authorities should be deeply concerning for the government.

Moreover, from workers' own descriptions of their interactions with officials, it seems that their cynicism is already translating into rougher encounters with officialdom. One of the injured workers I interviewed described his argument with a labor bureau representative: "I cursed out the local government. I said: 'If you always have to sue to get anything, what use are you? There's no implementation of laws!' Of course, I didn't curse at the higher levels. If your attitude is good, I won't quarrel with you. But with that local official, the more we argued, the angrier we got" (Group Interview 98). Another from another plant said, "We blocked the entrance to our factory. Four government departments visited the factory. Not *one* told the factory they should compensate us ill workers. So, we blocked the local government office's entryway. *Then*, the Labor Bureau called the factory and put some pressure on them, so they paid a bit" (Group Interview 96). Again, these quotations contrast starkly with the expressions of gratefulness to authorities made by the workers' counterparts in the YRD. Labor in Guangdong is no longer waiting patiently for benevolent authorities to step in and right wrongs. It is framing its aims in starker, more transgressive terms.

BOUNDARY-SPANNING AND TRANSGRESSIVE ORGANIZATIONS

Cynicism also means reaching beyond government bureaucracies or shop floor networks for help. For example, a manager with a Shanghai-based company that had experienced a strike in Shenzhen showed me an internal PowerPoint analysis of the incident that read, "Employees did not trust [the company], the union or the government ... Workers engaged with external bodies, ex-employees and the media" (Interview 11). This corporate analysis is echoed by academic studies of numerous strikes in which PRD workers have reached out to 'external bodies', sympathetic journalists, in particular (e.g., Becker 2014; Leung 2015). Trying to rope other actors into a group's framing of an issue is a classic means of growing a struggle (McAdam, McCarthy, and Zald 1996; Tarrow 2011). In the context of Chinese environmental activism, Mertha (2008, 23) finds that for "a victory to be decisive," it is necessary, among other things, to expand "the sphere of political conflict through the mobilization of new groups into the policy process." Guangdong workers appear to be learning this lesson. And they are applying it in many ways.

Pearl River Delta labor NGOs are particularly numerous and ambitious. They started early – the very earliest was formed in 1996 – and have exploded since. On the list of nationwide organizations provided to me by the CLB, there were thirty-five from the PRD or 40.6 percent of the total. Like their YRD counterparts, NGOs in the PRD also offer cultural and educational services to workers. But PRD groups have always focused more on providing advice and training for winning legal disputes – programming that, as discussed in the previous chapter, lies at the extreme of what YRD organizations feel comfortable carrying out. Moreover, from their inception in the late 1990s, Guangdong NGOs have quietly been involved in strikes and protests, as well as petition efforts around labor legislation. Most academic studies of these organizations have focused on their more individually oriented, institutional activities (e.g., Franceschini 2014; Gleiss 2014; Halegua 2008; Hsu 2012; Lee and Shen 2011), but the groups' hidden, more collective action-oriented side has begun to be receive attention that is long overdue (Becker 2014, chap. 8; Feng Chen and Yang 2017; Fu 2016, 2018; Pringle 2017). Fu (2018), for example, documents organizations providing advice to workers on verbal threats, sit-ins, and staging a "suicide performance" – programming that is certain to make the state uncomfortable. Feng Chen and Yang (2017) portray the groups as taking over tasks traditionally associated with trade unions. This move should be deeply concerning for authorities.

Nor are groups entirely shy about this shift. In recent years, NGOs have become more open about this politically riskier aspect of their work. Some have put themselves forward as representatives of workers in informal collective bargaining during high-profile disputes (Fu 2018, 153–56). Others have stayed in the background, helping draw up lists of demands. For example, during the 2014 Dongguan shoe factory strike, an NGO used a series of accounts on the QQ social media platform to compile complaints from the factory's workers and then post them online in the form of an open letter, urging the formation of a committee that could present those complaints to management (Group Discussion 83). Another group assisted protesting workers at the Lide shoe factory in electing representatives to negotiate with management over the handling of social security arrears (Han 2016). The same organization helped with bargaining following strikes by workers at the Lianshen Metal and Plastics Moulding Factory, the Hengbao Jewelry Factory and in Guangzhou University Town, and elsewhere (Han 2016). When a draft Guangdong law on NGOs included language barring funding from overseas, several organizations came together to meet with the Ministry of Civil Affairs and pressed for a change; the language was ultimately dropped (national legislation would later include similar restrictions, though). This sort of activism is unheard of in Jiangsu.

Increasingly, PRD labor NGO activists, like workers themselves, are expressing reservations about simply addressing problems within the framework of the law. In an interview with me, the leader of one organization aligned himself with workers' wishes in this regard:

Only if workers take action will there be change. It is no longer a question of a law resolving things. The laws are too full of loopholes. Workers are making demands without regard to whether they are "reasonable" or legal. For example, many protests are over changes to companies' names [i.e., corporate reorganizations]. Workers want their contracts bought out in these cases. But actually, this is not a legal issue; companies *can* change their names if they want. So, the solution to workers' demands must come from outside the law.

If you only rely on laws, you can't protect your most basic rights. These can only be protected through collective action and collective bargaining. The younger generation of workers understands this. They see the shortcomings of the previous generation's purely legal activism. These young people regard bringing a case to court too much trouble. Given the current labor shortage, they can always find jobs elsewhere. (Interview 79)

In contrast, an activist I interviewed in Jiangsu's city of Suzhou thought such activism was hopeless: "Down south, organizations are all focusing on collective bargaining. But what if a factory moves, like Beverly Silver describes?[1] Capital is always fluid, moving. Bargaining can only do something short-term" (Interview 76). Despite the activist's left-leaning rhetoric and reference to Silver's research (which has been translated into Chinese), his criticism may have been a cover for organizational caution: he later revealingly added, "We don't pick fights with the government" (Interview 76). Guangdong organizations do not intentionally "pick fights" with authorities either – but they operate up to and sometimes over the line of what is politically acceptable. Jiangsu groups do not. Between more frequent, larger, and long-lasting strikes featuring more ambitious labor demands, less worker trust in state institutions, and increasingly sophisticated labor NGOs, the PRD government faces a much more boundary-spanning and transgressive challenge from below. This results in a distinct model of control.

REACTIVE GOVERNANCE

The first characteristic of the Pearl River Delta model of control is *reactive* governance. Officials do not set out to nip every conflict in the bud before it occurs. And not every conflict that *has* occurred is even seen as requiring an immediate response. When I asked a leading official in the Shenzhen Federation of Trade Unions (SZFTU) if labor unrest had come to be treated as routine in the PRD, he replied in the affirmative: "It used to be that a strike was a big deal for the government. The moment something occurred, they would send a lot of

---

[1] Here, the activist was referring to Johns Hopkins University sociologist Beverly Silver and her book *Forces of Labor: Workers' Movements and Globalization Since 1870* (Silver 2003).

police. Now strikes are … [treated as] normal" (Interview 101). In fact, the state is sometimes remarkably slow to intervene in industrial conflicts. For example, a manager with a Taiwanese company that experienced that massive shoe strike in Dongguan in 2014 said:

When the strike started, the company wanted to get [guidance] directly from the provincial government. But the provincial government was not at all visible. Their big delay caused a lot of problems … The company learned a lesson from the strike. Now they will communicate more with the central government. The company needs a consistent message and a consistent decision-maker. (Interview 36)

A researcher in Beijing who visited Dongguan following the strike backed up the manager's account: "At first, the Dongguan authorities didn't think it [the protest] was a big deal" (Interview 23). Even an NGO leader involved in the case, who eventually suffered considerable police blowback for his involvement, concurred: "It is strange how tolerant the police were at first" (Interview 78). The PRD is no less concerned than the YRD with social stability, of course. However, as the Shenzhen union leader cited above also commented to me, "The government can't influence/direct everything here" (Interview 101). Rather than pretend otherwise, authorities in the PRD save their resources for what they deem to be serious long-term problems – and for reining in conflicts that have begun to truly spiral out of control.

EXPERIMENTAL GOVERNANCE

The Pearl River Delta's relatively hands-off approach to disputes should not be understood as disengagement on labor issues. On the contrary, where the YRD exercises policy caution, the PRD is a center for labor law experimentation. In 2008, when China's national Labor Contract Law went into effect, the city of Shenzhen enacted a yet more ambitious piece of legislation. Its Regulations on the Growth and Development of Harmonious Labor Relations in the Shenzhen Special Economic Zone mandated a day off per week for all employees, limited the fines and deductions employers could levy from employees for various infractions, and set a new base rate for overtime pay. Such tweaks would not be out of place in YRD legislation, but other items went much further than anything contemplated in Jiangsu. Most significantly, Article 52 (Article 47 in the draft regulation) specified that in the event of a work stoppage, unions should represent workers in "negotiations" (*tanpan*, not the more common term "consultations" or *xieshang*). This contrasted sharply with Article 27 of the 2001 national Trade Union Law, which ordered unions to "assist the enterprise or institution in properly dealing with the matter so as to help restore the normal order of production and other work as soon as possible." At the time of its passage, some observers interpreted the Shenzhen law as "one step away from the right to strike" (e.g., China Labour Bulletin 2008). Another provision in the law (Article 58) allowed for fee shifting in employment disputes, that is, it required employers to cover employees' legal costs if the employers lost cases. In 2014, Guangdong finalized the Provincial Regulations on Collective Contract of Enterprises. These contained new rules on the selection of worker-representatives for bargaining, outlawed retaliation against such representatives, and punished intentional delaying of negotiations by enterprises. A potentially more far-reaching piece of legislation, the Guangdong Regulations on the Democratic Management of Enterprises, which would have theoretically mandated the involvement of workers in core company business decisions, died under sustained lobbying by Hong Kong employer groups in 2010 (see, for example, Garver 2010). Although frequently watered-down or blocked – a source of frequent frustration for individuals like the former Guangzhou union official quoted at the beginning of this chapter – legislative initiatives in the PRD clearly outstrip their YRD counterparts in daring.

Legislative dynamism in the Pearl River Delta has been paired with a more engaged role for the state-controlled union federation. PRD yearbooks attest to this. They describe local branches of the federation performing the same welfare functions and meeting the same centrally mandated targets as their YRD counterparts. But they also note experiments with enterprise-level union direct elections. For example, Foshan's yearbook reports that 157 basic-level unions held such elections in 2011, with an aim to "raising union chairs' sense of responsibility and sense of mission, advancing union organizations' mass character, democratization and legality" (Foshan Yearbook 2012, 98–99). In the yearbook sections allotted to them, PRD unions also delve into more specifics with regard to the sectors and social groups that are the targets of their union organizing and collective bargaining efforts than do their Yangtze River Delta counterparts. For example, the Shantou and Zhongshan unions both highlight organizing directed at workers in labor dispatch companies (Shantou Yearbook 2013, 218; Zhongshan Yearbook 2013, 132). Dongguan notes experiments in collective consultation initiated in the Humen textile industry and the Wanjiang tea industry (Dongguan Yearbook 2012, 137). The yearbook of Guangzhou notes its municipal union's success in raising the earnings of sanitation workers 10 percent above the minimum wage and the ways in which the union has looked after this group's illnesses and family financial difficulties (Guangzhou Yearbook 2013, 109). Many of these programs are likely window-dressing. Guangzhou, for instance, has been the site of a series of large strikes by garbage collectors and street cleaners, so it is not surprising that the city wishes to demonstrate progress (however small) toward resolving their grievances. But YRD unions, in contrast, rarely feel it necessary to even window-dress in this manner.

Particular cities are at the forefront of Pearl River Delta union efforts. In 2009, I attended a presentation in Guangzhou on efforts to bring construction workers and other especially vulnerable groups under the municipal union's umbrella. Then, in 2010, the Guangdong provincial union organized a pioneering election for a new enterprise union chair at the Nanhai Honda plant in

Guangzhou's neighboring city, Foshan, which was at the center of the auto factory strike wave that year. As early as 2007, SZFTU had responded to a strike in the Yantian port by engaging in serious collective bargaining on behalf of the strikers (Pringle 2011, chap. 3; Pringle and Meng 2018). Now, the union is said to be sending cadres to "live with workers, eat with them in their cafeterias, and work alongside them for a month" (Interview 41). In contrast to the staid career officials who often end up in union positions elsewhere, the SZFTU is drawing in idealistic young people as staffers (Interview 68). Starting with relatively "easy" areas of the city with big, profitable, and stable firms, the union is organizing elections in thousands of enterprises and trying to reinvigorate district-level union organizations (Interview 69). The campaign is quite comprehensive, covering issues like the fees that sustain local unions. A Beijing-based researcher observed, "Normally enterprise-level unions get 60 percent of union fees and the other 40 percent goes to the higher level unions," but Shenzhen "has raised the enterprise-level unions' cut to 80 percent!" (Interview 102). According to a leader in the Shenzhen union, "The workers have been taught how to express their demands. They often say, 'I want a higher wage.' OK, but which part of your wage do you want to raise? Your hourly rate or a year-end bonus? And what are you willing to give up for this raise? We are making the whole process more professional" (Interview 101). These efforts, the same leader said, have drawn some corporate pushback: "We organized an election recently and the capital side closely observed things. The company put pressure on people who were going to take part in the union and fired the most important person in the process or, rather, pushed him to resign of his own accord" (Interview 101). If, as this anecdote suggests, the bosses' anger is strong, the union's programs have some teeth: more teeth, in fact, than anything further north.

The depth of the labor legislation and union reforms enacted in the Pearl River Delta should not be overstated, of course. Speaking at a conference in Beijing, the former leader of the Guangzhou Federation of Trade Unions quoted earlier described the Regulations as an ugly, "late born baby," highlighting a loophole in the law regarding retaliation against workers, as well as the way the law expanded the role of the police in industrial relations (Interview 6). As C. K.-C. Chan and Hui (2013, 13) state in their article, after the historic elections at the Nanhai Honda plant, "By manipulating candidateship and isolating the active workers' representatives, who had close contact with civil society organizations during the strike, the GDFTU [Guangdong Federation of Trade Unions] and company management succeeded in getting most of the newly elected enterprise trade union officials drawn from the managerial or supervisory levels." Guangzhou's previous union head, who reached out eagerly to international labor activists and was a vocal critic of union bureaucratism, was replaced upon his retirement by someone who, by most accounts ... is a bureaucrat. When I interviewed him, the retired leader told me, "The union offices are over there. I don't go back much, though. Things have tightened and become more bureaucratic. We'll see if things are different in a couple years." When activists organized at the Jasic Technology Company in 2018, district union officers encouraged them to form an enterprise-level union, but the officers subsequently withdrew their support and sided with management (two officers who had been helpful to the workers were later detained by the police, see China Labour Bulletin 2018d). A 2013 undercover investigation by a group of university students found few workers knew their enterprise even had a union, including at factories that had been singled out as models by Shenzhen's union federation (Rosenman 2013). Tellingly, a young union staffer said to me:

> Our best unions can really bargain over wages and benefits. They are quite good at this now. But workers don't pay any attention to the elections. Often, they just vote for whichever person they know. In fact, the unions that do the best job are the least likely to have the base know about their work (*zuode yuehaode gonghui, jiceng yue buzhidao*). We hold democratic elections so that representatives from every production line can be part of negotations. But the workers still do not care. (Interview 70)

I asked the same staffer if workers simply disliked the union. He responded: "No. Eighty percent of workers, I think, have *no* sense of what the union does. It's not that they have bad feelings toward the union; they just don't know anything about it. To dislike something, you have to have some understanding" (Interview 70). Indeed, in many ways, as E. Friedman (2014b) argues, if Guangdong represents the leading edge of trade union reform in China, this is a sad commentary on the reform effort more generally. Yet, it bears pointing out that, imperfect as they are, the initiatives undertaken in Shenzhen and Guangzhou would be inconceivable in the YRD. Workers can use union reformers as an opening to press for change, in a manner reminiscent of the way that, for example, disabled people have used reformers from the Chinese Disabled Persons Federation to press for better protection of their rights or business people have used state-backed chambers of commerce to pursue their economic interests (Xi Chen and Xu 2011; K. S. Tsai 2006). For Jiangsu officials, any reform in the realm of labor relations carries the danger that it will introduce unrest where comparatively little exists at present. In Guangdong, the conflict has reached a point where officials have little to lose – and perhaps something to gain – through experimentation.

CRACKDOWN GOVERNANCE: MOSTLY LABOR

If the orthodox approach of Yangtze River Delta authorities is to constantly intervene and coordinate, nudging with quiet punishments and rewards for companies, while co-opting or nipping civil society in the bud, then the hands-off Pearl River Delta authorities, when they *do* intervene, take a more direct approach. They are actively encouraging the worst sweatshops to leave Guangdong – or at least move further inland in the province, away from the

PRD proper. More dramatically, after initially reaching out to labor NGOs, the government is coming down hard on civil society, harassing, kicking out, and arresting activists, while acting increasingly coercively toward ordinary striking workers. The state is not omnipresent; it saves its coercive arm for what it perceives as the most serious threats. Then, it takes a hard line.

Letting Go of Backward Enterprises

In contrast to the Yangtze River Delta's nudging of companies to obey the law, the Pearl River Delta is taking more public action against recalcitrant employers. As noted, Guangdong is eager to move up the value-added ladder and join Jiangsu in high-tech manufacturing. But it also clearly realizes that workplace abuses spur protest. Thus, authorities have started to go after the worst of the worst. Already in 2005, the provincial labor bureau publically condemned twenty "sweatshops," prominently posting a list of the abusive employers at job centers (China Labour Bulletin 2005a). Article 38 of the 2008 Regulations on the Growth and Development of Harmonious Labor Relations in the Shenzhen Special Economic Zone states that when an enterprise seriously violates laws regarding the timely payment of wages or safe working conditions, relevant government departments should ensure that the problems are reflected in the company's credit ratings, deny the company awards, cut the company off from government contracts, and ensure that for five years, the company's owners not be allowed to register new enterprises. According to Article 46, business groups should also monitor their members' compliance with labor laws and publically report the most egregious violations. It should be pointed out that efforts like these stalled in the early days of the global financial crisis. At that time, the provincial government put out "ten pieces of advice," including the recommendation "don't publish reports that will affect company image at will" and the suggestion that executives suspected of "normal crimes" not be arrested. Local governments like Foshan's went further, stating that companies in violation of the national Labor Contract Law would "not be fined, and [would] not have their operating licenses revoked" (E. Friedman 2012, 467–68; see also Y. Wang 2015, chap. 3). But after the crisis, the public pressure picked up again. Wang Yang, the provincial Party Secretary at the time, famously called for "emptying the cage and letting the right birds in," that is, allow polluting and labor-intensive enterprises to move out of the PRD – or even encourage them to do so – in favor of bringing in more value-added firms. In some conversations, it was suggested to me that authorities had allowed particular protests to occur in a bid to speed the exit of certain firms (e.g., Group Discussion 83). It does not appear that "social upgrading" necessarily accompanied this "industrial upgrading" drive (Butollo 2014). However, Wang Yang's rhetoric stood in sharp contrast to the gentler, behind the scenes coaxing and prodding of YRD authorities: he understood that simply nudging capital would not bring the PRD's industrial zones under better control.

Harassing Labor Activists

If the Pearl River Delta authorities' handling of backward enterprises can be blunt, the state's approach to labor is blunter still. Full-time labor activists and ordinary striking workers alike are facing pressure across Guangdong. This was not always the case. At one time, authorities in the PRD tried to co-opt labor NGOs in a manner similar to the way it was done in the YRD. In 2007, for example, Shenzhen union leaders attended a conference hosted by a prominent local organization, despite the fact that the conference included edgy human rights activists. They also sent cadres to help with the organization's legal trainings for migrants. Fu (2018, chap. 3) covers these interactions in fascinating detail. In 2012, Guangzhou authorities set up an umbrella federation under the ageis of the municipal union. Organizations were invited to join the federation and several did. Offers were made of financial support for the groups' services and there was an assumption that those who participated would receive a measure of state protection. Howell (2015) describes this as a high point in Chinese "welfarist incorporation." But the initiative fizzled. A PRD activist said to me, "That was maybe a final, image-building gesture by [the former head of the Guangzhou Federation of Trade Unions] before he left, something he wouldn't have to maintain. It [the umbrella group] had one meeting but never got off the ground, was never formally set up" (Interview 12). A Hong Kong–based organization concurred: "The effort never really went anywhere. It was never clear what the group should do" (Interview 58). At any rate, the state's attitude seems to have changed dramatically in recent years.[2] Outreach initiatives like this have more or less halted. The fist has been ungloved.

Labor NGOs in Guangdong are now objects of intense harassment, not mere isolation as they are in Jiangsu. The pressure comes and goes, and it affects different groups differently. One factor determining who is targeted may be funding sources. The leader of a group in Shenzhen said he had only been visited by state security two or three times in the past year, explaining to me, "This is less than in years past. They have come less [often] because I have not been receiving foreign funding for the last period. They come when you get funding" (Interview 80). Another group had a similar experience: "Our organization has always felt some government pressure. But the government knows that we haven't had much funding recently, so they haven't come after us

---

[2] There are still many purely service-oriented groups that receive state support (Interview 75). A Shenzhen activist said he was sometimes urged by authorities to move his organization in this direction: "Sometimes, they will point out other organizations that have registered with the Ministry of Civil Affairs. There are two or three that did so in Dongguan, I believe, under Wang Yang. But they just carry out very basic social work. For example, they help guide traffic with a whistle. Or they post people inside hospitals to guide you to the section you need from the waiting room" (Interview 79). Such groups are more properly classified as "government-organized non-governmental organizations" (GONGOs).

much" (Interview 56). A second factor may be China's political calendar. An activist said, "Whenever the 'two meetings'[3] occur in Beijing or other big events are going on, they'll tell us not to distribute pamphlets, etc. Often, they'll stop by before big events and ask what sorts of events we have planned. They'll offer to help organize them!" (Interview 63). But for some organizations, the interference has become unremitting. In the words of a long-time NGO leader based outside of Guangzhou, "Different years have different pressures. But basically, things have stayed at the same level of high pressure. It has always been there. The government has always interfered (*ganyu*) and tried to control things" (Interview 104). The general trend over time seems to be toward more harassment for everyone. Each increase in control – 2010, 2012, 2016 – sets a new floor for the future. The pressure is ratcheted up.

The harassment meted out to activists can take a number of forms. One basic form is surveillance. An activist formerly based in the PRD and in contact with sympathetic low-level bureaucrats said, "I talked to the daughter of one such official and sent her stuff over QQ [a social media platform]. I never imagined that they were monitoring something like QQ so closely back then. She lost her job as a result" (Interview 73). Another form of harassment is pressure on family members. A Shenzhen activist said that police had visited his parents in his hometown in the interior. He said, "Security told them that I was working with anti-China forces. My family are simple rural people and this really frightened them" (Interview 78). The activist's children are now also prevented from attending school in Guangdong (Interview 78). Organizers' moves are constantly followed. The same activist said of occasional trips he made back to his old office: "The moment I arrived with my van, the police came out and said that I couldn't drive in there. I asked, 'What law says I can't drive in here?' They said there would be consequences, but they haven't done anything" (Interview 79). In a sign of cross-regional collaboration, one PRD-based activist said that his family home in another province now had a security camera pointed at it and his wife there frequently felt followed (Interview 12). This all can take a psychological toll. That is obviously the point – authorities want to make labor organizing emotionally unbearable for organizers.

More dramatically, organizations' offices are frequently forced to move. The aforementioned Shenzhen organizer whose van was stopped had his organization sent packing more than a dozen times in 2014; he now keeps the group's materials in big plastic containers for easy transport (Interview 78). Some have adapted by decentralizing. Another activist said, "I was just forced to move my home again. But it's not a big deal. They can't find my office, so they make me move my home. In fact, I don't really have much of an office anymore.

---

[3] These are the annual meetings of the National People's Congress and Chinese People's Political Consultative Conference.

My employees are spread out" (Interview 77).[4] Other labor organizers have become itinerant "troublemakers," chased around the country from province to province. The activist whose QQ communications had cost an official's daughter her job said, "I have been kicked out of Dongguan and Shenzhen in Guangdong. In Hunan, Huaihua City and Hongjiang City both made me leave. Fenghuang City in Hunan was beautiful, but they checked in on me because of some Gene Sharp[5] books that were mailed to me ... and they forced me away from there, too" (Interview 73). Even if the organizers can personally adapt to this lifestyle, the constant moving makes it difficult for workers to find them (Interview 97). Addresses and phone numbers must be updated. The communities activists carefully cultivate become strained and must continually be rebuilt.

In more extreme circumstances, organizers are detained. In December 2015, police took seven NGO leaders into custody in one night, while interrogating a dozen others; three of the activists were subsequently formally arrested on charges of "gathering a crowd to disturb social order" and another was charged with "embezzlement." They were denied access to their lawyers on national security grounds for several months. Two were eventually given suspended sentences and the third a twenty-one-month sentence because he initially would not confess. The same pattern was repeated in 2018 when police detained scores of Marxist students protesting in support of the striking Jasic workers in Shenzhen, first raiding an apartment the activists shared, then shoving some student leaders into vans in the broad daylight right off their elite campuses far from the PRD and forcing some to appear in confession videos shown to deter classmates (Yuan Yang 2019). In early 2019, another group of NGO leaders was detained, mostly around Shenzhen, and a sub-group was charged with disturbing order again (they were released roughly a year later) (Elmer 2019a). Then, young Guangzhou journalists connected with a website called iLabor.net were swept up by authorities, too. Their apparent crime: telling the stories of workers who had contracted pneumoconiosis (CPJ 2019). At the end of the year, an activist and researcher advocating for sanitation workers in Guangzhou was taken into custody for two weeks before being let go (Elmer 2019b).

Again, in the PRD, the approach is reactive. As noted above, when the massive shoe strike occurred in Dongguan in 2014, police were, at first, slow to respond. However, after initially being able to meet with the strikers, the NGO activist most involved in the dispute had one of his meals with workers interrupted by police. The next day, security took him to dinner and tried to force him to stay at a hotel of their choice. A week later, police detained one of his employees for posting a message on social media about *another*, unrelated

---

[4] Koesel (2013) has shown how Chinese underground "house churches" have used similar tactics.
[5] Gene Sharp was a theorist of non-violent resistance whose books have been translated into many languages and are used by actiivsts around the world.

strike that turned out to be a rumor. The employee remained in custody for a month, and the group's QQ account was shut down (Interview 78). Now, the organization's leader says he is afraid of being arrested himself: "They are looking for me to make a mistake. No one can avoid making any mistakes whatsoever" (Interview 79). He described to me having a couple of drinks with a group of workers and driving home only to find police already at his door, ready to administer a breathalyzer test (which he passed) (Interview 79). When the activist went to the aid of another group of striking shoe plant employees a year later, he said, "State security was already there, waiting ... I was told that the government had had a meeting about me and had given me a new name, 'cancer cell'" (Interview 79). Organizers are understood as serious threats – and handled accordingly.

Violence toward labor NGO leaders is rare but not unheard of. As noted, activists supporting the Zhongshan strike described at the beginning of the chapter were attacked. An NGO leader was also attacked by toughs after helping shoe factory workers who were involved in a long-standing dispute. Meeting with me in his office, the activist said, "I'd never been beaten before! It happened right here ... they came up to the office and beat me. I was in the midst of a meeting with some university professors when the attackers came in" (Interview 104). Violence by company thugs has occurred in the past. In 2007, for example, a Shenzhen-based NGO director was knifed outside his organization's offices. But then, the Deputy Chairs of the Guangdong Federation of Trade Unions and the SZFTU both visited the activist upon his release from the hospital, and police arrested the assailants – and the factory owner who had hired them – after two months (China Labor News Translations 2009b). No such efforts have been made following more recent attacks. In fact, in both of the recent incidents mentioned above, the violence was a prelude to the arrests of not the attackers but the activists themselves! Organizers are under a sustained, comprehensive assault.

Cracking Down on Strikers

Labor NGO leaders are not the only ones coming in for retribution. When Guangdong's usually hands-off authorities *do* decide to take action regarding a strike, the striking workers themselves are treated more poorly than in the recent past. Policing in the Pearl River Delta has always been rough. Until 2003, workers from other parts of the country could be detained if they did not have temporary residence permits. An interviewee based in the YRD who used to be a migrant laborer in Guangdong and now edits collections of labor poetry recalled, "Back then, people thought of the police like the mafia. Police would ask for your registration. And even if you were registered, they could tear up your card" (Interview 42). The situation is once again tightening, with workers who participate in collective action at greater risk of detention than at any point in the recent past. A labor lawyer in Shenzhen explained:

The pressure started in 2010. It was then that the police started hassling workers. Before, there was no pressure on workers. Why? This was when unrest peaked. The government's response was 1) not supporting the workers and 2) using the police more. In 2014, over a 100 workers were detained by police and 1,000 were fired by their employers with the support of the courts. (Interview 64)

An activist concurred that things were worsening, "Whenever there is a strike, police are sent. It is said that they are sent to 'maintain stability' (*wei wen*), but they are really there to suppress (*zhenya*). If things go too far, they will detain workers" (Interview 80). In a conversation with me, a former leader of the Guangzhou Federation of Trade Unions echoed this analysis:

Workers are being detained more. In the past, this also occurred, but then they just took some worker leaders down to the police station and urged them to tone things down. As long as things stayed contained within the factory grounds, the police would just warn them. Now, it is different. They will bring charges against workers, though usually they just hold them for a few days. (Interview 62)

The most prominent worker to be arrested in recent years is Wu Guijun, who was charged with "gathering a crowd and disturbing the order of public transportation" for taking part in a protest at a furniture-making facility in Shenzhen in 2013. Other detainees have included a group of hospital security guards who faced the same charges following a rooftop protest the same year. Repression is comprehensive, reaching professional and shop floor organizers alike.

Police are also increasingly moving to force strikers back to work, not just guarding the perimeter of demonstrations (or beating and detaining workers). In the words of one activist, "The police are intervening and suppressing workers' protests much more than in the past. Definitely much more. They go inside the factory and make sure the workers on the line are working! Isn't this forced labor?" (Interview 77). Said another activist, "Before 2014, you rarely heard of police forcing workers back to work. It used to be that if you didn't block an entrance or a road, they would leave you alone and not make you resume production. But in the past year, I know of over 30 instances in which this has happened. It is a new situation" (Interview 79). The most prominent instance of this kind of strikebreaking was the 2014 Dongguan shoe strike, which has been discussed at several points in this chapter. In an interview with me, a manager at the shoe company defended the actions of his employer and authorities but ended up essentially confirming the active role of police: "I wouldn't say that the police were pushing people back to work. Workers were going into the factory and clocking in in the morning and then clocking out at the end of the day but not working at all. Police saw this pattern and addressed it. If you want to go in, you work ..." (Interview 36). A Beijing-based academic who has been consulted on PRD union reforms explained:

The police definitely don't *want* to intervene themselves. But the local governments are making the police force workers back to work. Why? Because workers are raising demands that go beyond the law and involve political questions that are difficult to resolve. And even if there are representatives to negotiate for the workers, those representatives don't necessarily have the workers' trust. So, disputes go unsolved and strikes last longer and longer. The government then feels a lot of pressure to get people back to work. (Interview 102)

In other words, under increasing pressure, the government is coming down hard especially in high-profile showdowns. This is occurring even as the state pulls back from micromanaging industrial zones and as it creatively tweaks its labor laws and trade union roles. Risk-taking of a repressive and responsive sort is occurring. Rising boundary-spanning and transgressive resistance precludes traditional approaches to governance. Thus, officials must prove that they are willing to go out on a limb to restore a modicum of order.

FEEDBACK EFFECTS

As in the Yangtze River Delta, there may be feedback effects at work in the PRD. Governance patterns cannot help but affect contention. The passage of legislation such as Shenzhen's Harmonious Labor Relations Regulations likely encourages some workers. Police violence, meanwhile, may harden disputes. But in the course of my fieldwork, interviewee after interviewee emphasized that protest shapes policy more than policy shapes protest. A prominent labor lawyer in Shenzhen, for example, stated, "The government changes because of what workers are doing. The government is not the main force" (Interview 64). Meanwhile, a civil society leader said, "NGOs are taking on some of the tasks that the government *should* be doing, such as stepping in and mediating conflicts. Now, the government is taking up some of this work, too, but this is just because of pressure from the NGOs" (Interview 56). Nor was it just labor-side interviewees who said these sorts of things. Officials made similar points. For example, according to a young staffer in the SZFTU, "Worker pressure plus pressure from NGOs leads to union reform" (Interview 68). A former head of the Guangzhou Federation of Trade Unions echoed this: "Union reform doesn't come from companies and it doesn't come from the union itself pushing it. Reform is pushed forward by the labor movement ... There is no momentum from the top" (Interview 62). From the number of NGOs in the PRD to the region's dramatic rise in strikes from the mid-2000s onward, activism has developed so fast that it seems that the government has had to scramble to keep up (unlike the government in the YRD, which has been able to adapt in step with a more moderate surge of pressure from below – and by observing what is happening in PRD). In the final analysis, the causal arrow running from unrest to governance is the dominant one. But the changes wrought by workers are mixed.

POLITICAL CULTURE

Finally, there is, again, the issue of political culture. I have already noted the Yangtze River Delta's claims to a more "civilized" style of governance.

The PRD, in turn, may have a down-to-earth, pragmatic political culture that encourages greater reformism. From the immediate post-revolutionary period onward, Guangdong has chafed at northern influence and wanted to do things its own way (Vogel 1971). Some of its innovativeness may be the result of policy trials pushed on the region by the central government or models of governance consciously imported from elsewhere. For example, in Chapter 6, an interviewee in Jiangsu characterized Guangdong as "small government, big society" (Interview 37). Whether the interviewee knew it or not, "small government, big society" is the slogan attached to a specific program of offloading certain government functions to the private sector and civil society that started in Hainan Province (Brodsgaard 2006). However, pragmatism and reformism seem to run deeper than any particular policy in the PRD. The former leader of the Guangzhou Federation of Trade Unions cited at the beginning of this chapter noted to me, "Here, government offices tend to be fairly small. Up north, they build them much bigger. They care more about face there" (Interview 62). A PRD-based corporate social responsibility officer added, "The YRD has a stronger sense of hierarchy. Levels are clearer in the north, even though there is more conflict in the south" (Interview 62). Some interviewees also noted the influence of Hong Kong civil society on Guangdong labor activists (e.g., Interview 2; Interview 8; Interview 46; Interview 50). But Hong Kong's influence on ordinary workers is likely weak. These activists come from even farther away than migrants in Jiangsu, after all. Their greatest cultural influences spring from Hunan, Henan, Sichuan, and elsewhere – as well as the villages-in-cities where they now make their homes. If they come in contact with the Hong Kong advocacy world, it is second-hand, via NGOs. As in the YRD, culture would seem to have the greatest impact (if it has any impact at all) among officials – many of whom are locals – and on the margins of state decision-making. In other words, it does not affect both sides of the protest-policy equation equally and does not fundamentally confound our analysis.

SUMMARY

If the YRD constitutes a relatively stable region in the greater sphere of Chinese labor politics, the PRD is a region in tumult – if often creative tumult. The careful coordination of social forces practiced by authorities in the YRD, with companies nudged to obey the law, workers engaged through pragmatic bargaining, and NGOs co-opted or isolated, appears to be impossible in the PRD. Standard operating procedures must be junked and the government must think more on its feet. Strikes, protests, and riots are frequent and, it seems, large and long-lasting. Workers are also raising new, more ambitious demands and show little trust in the state. Their organizations are sophisticated and aggressive. In the face of this challenge, and in keeping with their bureaucratic incentives, authorities have sped up changes to their labor laws and trade unions, that is, made serious efforts to be responsive. They will likely need to change these even more in the future. The Guangdong government has also fitfully moved to push out the lowest value-added and most abusive companies. This thrust, too, may need to increase, as long as employment opportunities do not fall too much. Finally, police are treating both labor NGOs and ordinary strikers in a more overtly repressive manner than in Jiangsu. Yet more severe crackdowns should be anticipated. In the PRD, change is the rule, and no change on the government's part ever seems to be enough. Guangdong shows what might be in store for other parts of China, if current dynamics deepen: not just more police spending or pro-worker judicial decisions, but a qualitatively different approach to governance. In the next chapter, we will dig beneath these different models of control to try to identify average trends in Chinese governance, exploring how the state is becoming stronger through its encounters with labor, albeit in a paradoxical manner that may generate new challenges in the future.

6

Increased Repressive and Responsive Capacity

The Yangtze River Delta and Pearl River Delta dynamics that were described in the previous chapters show the different models of control that have developed in different parts of the country facing different forms of worker resistance but the same bureaucratic incentives to maintain stability. However, focusing only on such models risks missing the forest for the trees. Beneath the country's various local approaches to managing industrial relations, we can also identify broad, average trends. Specifically, where unrest is more intense, the government is enhancing both its repressive and responsive *capacity*. Capacity does not map neatly onto the specific tactics discussed in previous chapters. For instance, is preemption more responsive or repressive? Does it require more capacity than reaction? Does not nudging mix both repressive and responsive elements? But as local governments clash repeatedly with labor and develop their distinct models of control, they accumulate repressive and responsive resources – everything from riot shields to informants, to arbitrators, to skilled trade union leaders – and a greater facility for using them. Gradually, the Chinese state as a whole is strengthened in a dual manner. In this chapter, I first describe the variety of forms that repressive and responsive capacity can take in the Chinese context, some of which have appeared in previous chapters and some of which have not. Using spending on the paramilitary People's Armed Police and formally adjudicated employment dispute data, I then show how capacity has risen in tandem with strikes, protests, and riots, all else being equal. Finally, I draw on interviews to address a lingering issue that I cannot control for in my statistical analysis, namely the overlap between labor and land use conflicts in some areas. The stage is then set for my penultimate chapter concerning the role of elites in Chinese labor politics and final chapter reflecting on what all this means for China: Is this all just further evidence of the state's adaptability? Is becoming empowered along these two clashing dimensions sustainable?

DIFFERENT FORMS OF REPRESSIVE CAPACITY

Repressive capacity can take many forms in China. Some forms are of a traditional, brute force sort. At the beginning of the book, I described how riot police contained the second Stella shoe factory strike in 2015. Scores of clashes have occurred between such forces and workers. To take just the year 2012 as an example: a mobilization by Pangang Steel and Vanadium workers in Chengdu in January drew over one thousand police, who reportedly beat organizers (Mudie 2012); protests at the Pingdingshan Cotton Company in Henan in May were met by what a journalist described as "more than 1,000 uniformed, riot and plainclothes police ... with a special black-clad unit, armed with clubs, riot shields and a don't-mess-with-us attitude" (Schiller 2010); and, as shown in images posted on a dissident website, over a hundred police formed a human chain around a handful of workers during a confrontation at the Saidaxin electronics plant in Shenzhen in December (and the site reported that several workers had been assaulted and detained) (Zhongguo Molihua Geming 2012). Sometimes these crackdowns have taken a yet more blatantly coercive shape. During the height of the mobilization of state-owned enterprise workers in the late 1990s and early 2000s, for instance, the government reportedly deployed a tank division to suppress labor protests in the northeastern oil town of Daqing (Han 2002). Similarly, following riots by migrants in 2011 in the blue jeans production hub of Zengcheng, police fired tear gas, patrolled with armored vehicles, and imposed a curfew on the city (BBC 2011). This is the type of clampdown that readers familiar with the Tiananmen Square Massacre might expect. But interventions on this scale are actually relatively rare in China, at least outside of the country's semi-colonial fringe of Tibet and Xinjiang (Y. Li 2019a, 2019b). More common is an overwhelming show of police power aimed at preventing escalation to violence.

Other forms of repressive capacity are subtler. In fact, higher forms of capacity are arguably harder to observe. Control can, first of all, be quite high-tech. Table 6.1 gives some examples of recent purchases by the public security bureau of Guangzhou, the capital of Guangdong Province and a major manufacturing center, as documented by government procurement websites: riot shields and riot control barriers, but also a new video surveillance system for one district of the city and mobile security cameras for another (these are confusingly sometimes categorized as "anti-terrorism" expenses in public documents).[1] The Chinese government's use of video surveillance, in particular, has skyrocketed. A full accounting of expenses from the same procurement websites would show that most big police purchases over the past years have been for these systems. Analysts expect the country's share of the global surveillance market to dwarf that of any other country and even any whole region of the world by the year 2019 (Statista 2018). Some of this spending is, of course,

---

[1] Here, I am inspired by the work on Xinjiang conducted by Zenz and Leibold (2020) and others.

TABLE 6.1 *Examples of public security spending from Guangzhou*

Item	Cost (budgeted)	Year
Surveillance system for the Huangpu District	2.4 million RMB	2018
Mobile surveillance cameras for the Panyu District	2.47 million RMB	2017
Riot control barriers for Guangzhou City (rental)	477,000 RMB	2017
Anti-riot vehicle for the Haizhu District	1.01 million RMB	2016
Pavilion for anti-riot police in the Tianhe District	410,000 RMB	2015
Anti-riot shields for the Panyu District	112,100 RMB	2015

Sources: Guangdong Government Procurement System (www.gdgpo.com/) and Guangzhou Public Resources Trading Center – Government Procurement (www.gzggzy.cn/). Accessed on February 1, 2018.

carried out by private companies and individuals wishing to protect their property, but one analyst interviewed by *The Wall Street Journal* estimates that government purchasing accounts for 90 percent of surveillance expenditures in China (Areddy 2014). These cameras are being installed across industrial zones. Already in 2008, in an essay describing China as a model "police state 2.0," the journalist and activist Naomi Klein predicted that the export processing hub of Shenzhen would soon be "the most watched city in the world" (Klein 2008). Several years ago, I witnessed this surveillance apparatus first-hand when a friend's satchel was stolen and Shenzhen police tracked the motorcyclist who had stolen it from intersection to intersection on big screens at their station. Today, their tracking would be aided by powerful facial recognition software tied to a national database. This combination of resources was used to identify and arrest nineteen "drug addicts" trying to enter a festival in Qingdao in 2017 (C. Xie 2017). In Xinjiang, where the government has embarked on an extraordinary effort to monitor citizens belonging to the Uyghur minority, biometric data are added to the mix, along with things like QR codes stamped on kitchen knives and applications that must be downloaded on phones (Human Rights Watch 2018). It is no exaggeration to say that a "Panopticon" is being rolled out in China that possesses a power to observe individuals that would startle even Foucault (1977, 195–228). Labor activists have good reason to fear the system is being turned on them.

Some forms of repressive capacity are more old-fashioned and human-scaled. For instance, labor organizers are frequently asked to "tea" with security personnel, who try to persuade them to reveal information about other activists and their donors. Police develop close ties with the organizers over time, offering various perks and showing concern during hard times (Franceschini 2017). Grassroots workers' center leaders complain of their groups being infiltrated by new employees, volunteers, and workers "needing help" who are secretly on the payroll of the Ministry of Public Security

(Fu 2018, 55, 57). A Chinese academic described to me how authorities in Tianjin demobilized striking workers at a particular factory: "Cadres were sent to every family, telling them to make sure that their children stopped making trouble" (Interview 74). Finally, a vast web of informants is maintained. Even in remote Kailu County, Inner Mongolia, there is reportedly one informant for every twenty-five residents (Q. He 2012). Although not as flashy as surveillance technology, deploying these traditional forms of control also requires considerable skill and financial resources. Police must know who to talk to about what. Pressure must be applied just so. Informants must be paid. Yet, the effect can be powerful.

Finally, repressive capacity is sometimes outsourced. For example, during my fieldwork, I observed that the property management office of my apartment building in Shenzhen contained a full array of riot control equipment, including helmets, shields, and body armor. This equipment seemed to have been stocked by the managers themselves. It was unclear if the target of the preparations was potential protests by angry tenants or by construction workers who were then busy expanding the complex. I suspect the latter. But the company clearly wanted to be ready for something. Thugs are regularly hired by local authorities to attack protesters (Ong 2018). Xi Chen (2017) argues that this practice is the result of competing pressures on officials: to reduce unrest but not cross any legal lines themselves (or at least not openly). Regardless of the cause, criminals have frequently physically harmed labor organizers. In 2007, the activist Huang Qingnan was nearly knifed to death in such an incident (China Labor News Translations 2009b). Less dramatically, landlords, acting on government orders, force organizers to move their homes (Harney 2015). And employers and authorities collaborate to blacklist persistent "troublemakers" from job opportunities (Fu 2018, 92–101; Leung 2015, 88–91). In all these instances, third parties dole out the punishments, and whether or not the government issued the orders, it benefits from a private reserve of coercive power. To summarize: the Chinese state's repressive capacity is diverse.

DIFFERENT FORMS OF RESPONSIVE CAPACITY

Identifying responsive capacity is less straightforward than identifying repressive capacity. My basic intuition is that the ability to respond positively to the grievances of people outside the state's "selectorate" of elite insiders shows flexibility and skill (on selectorates, see de Mesquita et al. 2003). Responsive capacity so defined also appears in many forms in the context of Chinese labor issues. Some would not be out of place in liberal democracies. In particular, as unrest has grown, the country has passed scores of new labor laws. Several of these were noted in the previous chapter. In 1994, for instance, China introduced its first Labor Law, which stipulated a range of workplace protections but was weakly enforced (Cooney 2007; Gallagher 2017). A Trade Union Law was adopted in 1992, only three years after the Tiananmen Square protests had

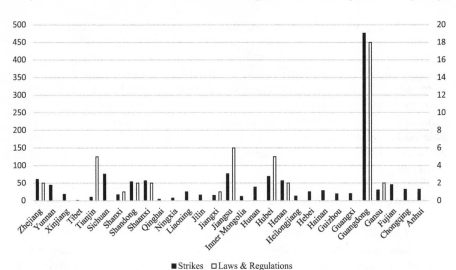

FIGURE 6.1 Important labor regulations versus labor unrest.
Beijing and Shanghai excluded. Strikes are tracked on the left *y* axis; labor laws and regulations, on the right.
Sources: China Strikes (2017) and PKULaw.cn (2017).

given birth to short-lived autonomous worker federations, and the legislation was amended in 2001. In 2007, after a wide-ranging debate, which included an unprecedented outpouring of public comments online and considerable opposition from the business community, including foreign chambers of commerce (K. Chang 2009, chap. 5; Gallagher and Dong 2011; Global Labor Strategies 2007), the National People's Congress passed a new Labor Contract Law that reinforced with stiffer penalties a number of existing rules and added new provisions, especially about hiring and firing (Cooney et al. 2007). This law is credited with increasing the number of workers with formal contracts, although its effectiveness in other areas is debatable (Becker and Elfstrom 2010; Freeman and Li 2013; Gallagher et al. 2014). With wage arrears continuing to pile up, especially in the construction sector, the government criminalized "malicious" non-payment of wages in 2011 (Halegua 2017, 90). Other legislation has touched indirectly on workplace issues, such as the 2011 Social Insurance Law that made it somewhat easier for migrants to transfer their insurance contributions back to their hometowns (Frazier and Li 2017). At a regional level, authorities have gone further, as noted in my case study of the Pearl River Delta in the previous chapter. Importantly, subnational legislative activity in the arena of labor law has closely tracked local incidents of worker unrest. Figure 6.1 shows the provincial count of significant legislation dealing in some way with trade unions, as documented by Peking University's legal database, alongside the provincial count of strikes, protests, and riots from China Strikes (minus Beijing and Shanghai, which, as the country's political and financial capitals, have a disproportionate number of laws in general). Peaks for both strikes and laws include Guangdong, Hubei, Jiangsu, Sichuan, and Tianjin, followed by Zhejiang, Shaanxi, and Shandong. The two counts are almost perfectly correlated (0.91). Contention is being matched by an expanded legal framework.

Other forms of responsive capacity reflect the resilience of institutions from China's state socialist past. In particular, the state has enacted several reforms via the All-China Federation of Trade Unions (ACFTU). In 2003, the year that the migrant worker Sun Zhigang was killed in police detention and "custody and repatriation" rules were abolished, the ACFTU finally recognized migrants as a part of the working class (rather than as peasants and therefore not their responsibility) and committed to representing them (Xinhua 2003). In some places and industries, most famously the wool sector of Wenling in Zhejiang, branches of the union have engaged in extensive sectoral bargaining with employer federations. This bargaining has been criticized as thin and, to the extent it has, in fact, delivered any benefits, as helping employers more than employees, but it has nonetheless served to place real negotiations on the agenda for the union, to some degree (E. Friedman 2014a; Mingwei Liu 2010; Wen 2015; Wen and Lin 2014). Union drives and bargaining in foreign firms such as Wal-Mart in 2006 have involved novel elements including clandestine meetings with workers, although the campaigns have usually wound down once the first contract is signed (the contract agreed upon at the first Wal-Mart store to unionize was imposed on all other stores as they unionized, even though workers in some instances wanted much more; activists from early campaigns were meanwhile sidelined by the union) (Blecher 2008; China Labor News Translations 2009c; Unger, Beaumont, and Chan 2011). Following high-profile showdowns, like the one at the 2010 Honda auto parts plant or the Yantian crane operators strikes in Guangdong, the union has increasingly supported direct elections for the heads of its enterprise-level branches, something long guaranteed by law but rarely carried out in practice. But again, elected leaders have subsequently often been undermined and pushed aside as troublesome (Lyddon et al. 2015; Pringle and Meng 2018; C. K.-C. Chan and Hui 2013). More modestly, union branches have provided legal aid to individual workers (Pringle 2011, chap. 5). Some of the more notable ACFTU reforms made at a regional level were explored in the previous chapter on the PRD. At its best, the organization has been pushed to act as something of a fourth player in what F. Chen (2010) calls China's "quadripartite" industrial relations system: neither fully on the side of workers or employers, but closely tied to the Party – if sometimes charting its own course within the Party's general framework. The union is a barometer, not a driver, of worker empowerment. But it is a barometer that is revealing: when the ACFTU engages in reforms, it shows that the government is feeling real pressure from below. And if the union represents a still thin form of responsive capacity, it becomes stronger when conflict is more intense, as the previous chapter, again, showed.

Finally, responsive capacity can take a very symbolic and personal form. Chinese leaders frequently try to send sympathetic signals to labor like eating dumplings with miners underground over the Spring Festival holiday (Xinhua 2005) or hosting delegations of migrant workers, as the current President Xi Jinping did at the headquarters of the ACFTU on May Day in 2013 (Xinhua 2013). In 2011, Chongqing's populist Party Secretary Bo Xilai went further and ordered a SWAT team to help a group of construction workers recoup wages (Fauna 2011). Premier Wen Jiabao was approached in 2003 by a woman named Xiong Deming, whose migrant worker husband was owed over 2,000 RMB in wage arrears from a construction project, and the Premier saw to it that the man was paid in full, generating headlines (Becker 2014, 67–68). The Premier also visited migrants stranded at a Guangzhou train station in 2008. Xinhua reports that Wen addressed the crowd with a megaphone, saying, "You all want to go home and I completely understand how you feel. We are now fixing the power grid. Once the power supply resumes, trains will be running" (Xinhua 2008). These kinds of interventions by politicians are not unique to China, of course. As in other countries, they are intended to give the state an accessible, human face. But in a state like the PRC, where officials are frequently far removed from ordinary citizens – rarely holding press conferences or unstructured "town halls" of the sort seen in democracies – gestures like these mean more. They are an important part of the state's responsive arsenal. And that arsenal is broader than a naive observer might imagine.

DOCUMENTING HOW RESISTANCE IS DEEPENING REPRESSIVE AND RESPONSIVE CAPACITY

To show how worker resistance is increasing both repressive and responsive capacity over time, statistical analysis is needed. In Chapter 2, I introduced two quantitative measures of resistance: my *China Strikes* dataset of strikes, protests, and riots (boundary-spanning or transgressive resistance) and official numbers of formally adjudicated employment disputes (contained resistance). We now require measures of repressive and responsive capacity to match them. These measures must similarly be available for an extended period and, to maximize the number of observations available and thereby give us greater leverage on trends, it should similarly be possible to break them down into subnational units (King, Keohane, and Verba 1994, chap. 6). For the sake of convenience and to keep elite politics constant, a useful time period to study is that covered by *China Strikes*: the decade in which Hu Jintao and Wen Jiabao were in office. The best level of analysis would arguably be the prefectural level. However, official data is simply not consistently available for cities. As a second-best option, I therefore use provinces as my unit for the investigation.

With China's "soft centralization" of the late 1990s more decision-making power became concentrated at the provincial level, making this a reasonable place to also focus (Mertha 2005). Two measures that are available for all or most of the Hu-Wen era and can be gathered on a province-by-province basis are spending on the paramilitary People's Armed Police (representing repressive capacity) and the outcomes of formally adjudicated employment disputes, specifically the total number of disputes decided in a pro-worker or split manner (responsive capacity). Below, I begin by providing details on each measure in turn. After that, I explain what other important variables must be controlled for and introduce appropriate statistical models, before summarizing the results obtained when those models are estimated. Much of my analysis here echoes a piece I published in *China Quarterly* (see Elfstrom 2019b). Throughout, I will keep the discussion as straightforward as possible. Readers interested in equations and tables of coefficients can consult the footnotes and the Appendices.

MEASURING REPRESSIVE CAPACITY

Spending on the paramilitary People's Armed Police (PAP) is a useful measure of repressive capacity. Whereas "public security" expenditures more generally include a broad swath of the budget reported in the *China Statistical Yearbook* – covering public security agencies, procuratorial agencies, and courts (through 2006) and more vaguely "expenditure for public security" (2007 onward) – the PAP has more focused responsibilities. It is charged with "handling rebellion, riots, large-scale criminal violence, terror attacks and other social safety incidents" (Wines 2009). The organization in its current form had already been established by the 1980s, but it received new power following the Tiananmen Square Massacre, when the reputation of the People's Liberation Army (PLA) was tarnished by its role in the bloodshed (T. M. Cheung 1996). For a period, the PAP's precise place in the Party-state hierarchy was unclear. T. M. Cheung (1996), for example, posited that the PAP was, in fact, mostly controlled by the PLA, while Blasko (2012, 7) cited a 2006 white paper as placing the PAP largely under the leadership of the Ministry of Public Security. Recently, however, things have become clearer: the force has been moved directly under the Communist Party's Central Committee and Central Military Commission, detaching the force entirely from the State Council and any government (as opposed to Party) control (Xinhua 2017). Regardless, the PAP has always been decidedly "political" (Greitens 2017, 11). Its troops are not routinely called out to tamp down protests, but their buildup in particular regions is a strong show of state concern – and a forward-looking investment in increased *capacity* for coercion (regarding the changing rules for PAP deployment, see Tanner 2014). Thus, following the 2010 Honda strike outside of Guangzhou, Lam (2010) reports that then-President Hu Jintao cited former leader Deng Xiaoping's warnings about the Polish Solidarity movement and sent massive PAP reinforcements to the province, where the troops were put on

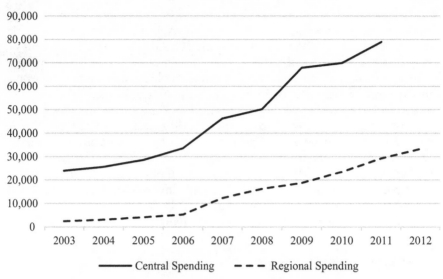

FIGURE 6.2 People's Armed Police spending (100 million RMB).
Source: CEIC 2017. "ISI Emerging Markets and CEIC." *CEIC Data Manager.*

"standby" status, ready to "swing into action to crush prolonged labor militancy" if necessary. Unfortunately, data on paramilitary spending by individual provinces is only available (via the *Financial Statistics of Cities and Counties* or *Quanguo dishixian caizheng tongji ziliao*) through the year 2009 (shortening our analysis somewhat). Figure 6.2 tracks spending on the PAP, both by the central government and by all of China's provinces combined (data for which are available for a longer time frame than just for individual provinces), from 2003 to 2012. The trends at both levels point steadily upward, although central spending has grown faster.

MEASURING RESPONSIVE CAPACITY

The most neatly parallel way of measuring responsive capacity would probably be spending on courts or arbitration panels or the labor inspectorate. Unfortunately, much of this data is either not consistently available at the provincial level or, as noted, rolled up in the general public security budget (and not the PAP budget). An alternate way of capturing responsive capacity is to use the outcomes of employment disputes taken to mediation, arbitration, and court. The rising total number of such disputes and their breakdown by province were noted in Chapter 2 in the context of changes in contained resistance. However, the decisions rendered in them are also revealing. The *China Labour Statistical Yearbooks* helpfully divide cases into pro-worker, pro-business, and split outcomes. Pro-worker decisions mean rulings that are

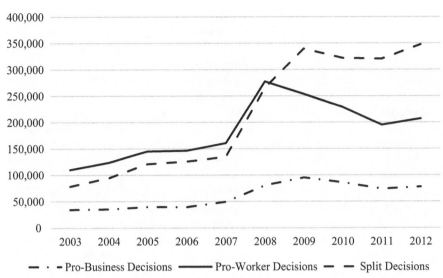

FIGURE 6.3 Outcomes of formally adjudicated employment disputes.
Source: *China Labour Statistical Yearbooks* 2004–13.

fully in workers' favor. Pro-business decisions mean rulings that are fully in employers' favor. Split decisions, which come closer to realizing the Communist Party's preference for harmonious "win-win" (*shuangying*) solutions, mean rulings that hand partial victories to employers and employees alike. In practice, splitting frequently entails compromising on workers' rights, for example, awarding employees only a portion of the compensation they are legally owed for an occupational injury or only part of a mandated severance package while not compromising on companies' prerogatives. Still, even such decisions are an improvement over rejecting labor's demands outright. And they require a certain *capacity* to overcome the objections of local elites. Aggregate numbers decided in each manner per province per year are listed in the yearbook for the full time span of my *China Strikes* dataset. Figure 6.3 shows that dispute decisions of all types are rising – not surprising since, after all, the total number of disputes to be decided is rising – but pro-worker and split decisions have far outstripped pro-business decisions. This suggests a greater ability to override powerful interests and respond to working-class grievances – not perfectly, of course, but better than before. Responsive capacity, like repressive capacity, is trending ever upward.

NECESSARY CONTROLS

A number of factors, including some noted in Chapter 2 in its discussion of recipes for resistance, could conceivably both spur or dampen worker resistance and, at the same time, affect our measures of state repressive and responsive capacity. Historically, Chinese workers, like their foreign counterparts, have responded to increased job opportunities with greater militancy, as they did during the surge in protests demanding higher wages around the 2010 Honda strike, when the economy was on the upswing (on this pattern abroad, see Ashenfelter and Johnson 1969; Franzosi 1989; Tracy 1987). But they have also become more active during downturns, like during the 2008 financial crisis, albeit with different demands. Growth simultaneously generally means more tax revenue and therefore a greater ability on the part of authorities to satisfy workers. One can further imagine that wealthy areas might be less concerned about siding with labor, as such places can always attract other investment. Conversely, bigger government coffers might mean more money to spend on repression. To control for all these possibilities, I include in my analysis the natural log of provincial GDP per capita, drawn from the *China Statistical Yearbooks*, on the assumption that any flaws in this data are not systematic (I also log government revenue per capita in place of GDP, using the same yearbooks, although revenue should only affect state reactions to worker resistance, not the resistance itself).

The presence or absence of particular groups of workers might also confound my analysis. In Chapter 2, I described the rich literature that exists on the protests of SOE workers in the late 1990s and early 2000s, and I documented a link between migrant worker density and unrest today. It seems likely that authorities will also react differently to protests from these groups. As discussed, one group (SOE employees, who are generally locals) is more embedded in local political institutions than the other (migrants). There might also be less reporting on conflicts involving the state sector, biasing my measurement of unrest. For these reasons, I control for the percentage of a province's residents with their household registration somewhere other than where they live or work and the percentage employed in SOEs. Both these figures, like GDP data, are obtained from the *China Statistical Yearbooks*. As noted, light industry and worker skills overlap considerably with migrant worker density; this makes the inclusion of industries and skills in our analysis unnecessary.

Certain institutions could also affect both resistance and responsive capacity at once. As explained, Chinese labor nongovernmental organizations (NGOs) have expanded their above-ground activities in recent years from legal training for workers to more risky engagement in collective action, that is, have moved from boundary-spanning to transgressive mobilization. Their mere presence in a region could conceivably both spur more strikes and protests and make the state respond less sympathetically to the same incidents. I thus include a control for the number of NGOs in a given province and given year, using a list of groups and their founding dates provided to me by CLB (also used in Chapter 2). Meanwhile, the strength of the ACFTU in a place might both factor into workers' decision about whether to strike (as demonstrated in the Vietnamese context by Anner and Liu 2015) and affect how strike demands are handled if they are brought to arbitration or court. I thus control for the number of enterprises with "wage only" collective contracts in a given province-year, documented by the *China Trade Unions Yearbook*.

Finally, there are a few potential confounders that are less easily categorized. Because there may be variation across regions and across time with regard to the abuses suffered by workers – the raw exploitation highlighted in early scholarship on Chinese labor issues – and this variation might, in turn, affect variation in both the strength of the cases that are formally adjudicated (and therefore the workers' win rate) and the number of strikes, protests, and riots that occur, I include a control for the percentage of cases featuring the single type of claim with the most intra-provincial variation, namely remuneration (wage arrears, etc.), drawing on the *China Labour Statistical Yearbooks* (Appendix 5 shows the variation that exists for different claims). I also control for the percentage of a province's population living in an urban area to account for any remaining particularities of such metropolitan areas: more sophisticated judiciaries, more crime, etc. Here, again, I rely on the *China Statistical Yearbooks*.

APPROPRIATE MODELS

With these controls in hand, basic time cross-sectional series models can reveal the correlations between resistance, repressive capacity, and responsive capacity. Such models take advantage of China's immense geographic variation in worker-state interactions already noted, while accounting for the changes that occur in those interactions. As I have pointed out, the measures introduced thus far – *China Strikes* data, total numbers of formally adjudicated employment disputes, People's Armed Police spending, and dispute outcomes – all evince upward trends. Although revealing in their own right, when combined together, these trends can lead us to imagine causal relationships where there are, in fact, none. Therefore, in our models, we must use the first difference of each measure, that is, the change in its values year to year, rather than its absolute value at any given point in time. This yields what is called "stationarity."

RESULTS OBTAINED

If we estimate models with these specifications,[2] we find a strong relationship between boundary-spanning or transgressive resistance and repressive capacity.

---

[2] Specifically, I estimate models that take the form $\Delta Y_{it} = \alpha_0 + \beta_0 \Delta x_{it} + \beta_1 X_{it} + \varepsilon_{it}$, where i is the province and t is the year, ΔY_t is the year-to-year change (first difference) in either provincial PAP spending or the number of disputes in a given province that have a particular outcome; α_0 is the intercept; β_0 is the coefficient of the year-to-year change in my main independent variable, strikes; β_1 is the coefficient of a vector containing all my controls; and ε_{it} is the error term. The results are the same if I also use the first difference of each of the controls $(\beta_1 \Delta X_{it})$. With a panel fixed effects

Specifically, an increase of one strike, protest, or riot in my China Strikes dataset is correlated with an increase of 4.8 million RMB in funding going to the PAP (at a 99.9 percent confidence level).[3] Of course, my dataset only represents a small sample of all the contention occurring in China's workplaces, and a single strike among the full "population" of incidents in the country would likely have much less impact. Even so, resistance stands out from the other variables. Only one other is significant: an increase of a single labor NGO in a province is correlated with an increase of 10.7 million RMB in spending (at the same level of significance), reminding us that greater worker organization, too – not just instances of contention – is unsettling for authorities. Interestingly, GDP per capita does not appear to drive policing investments, all else being equal (and neither does government revenue per capita, if the log of it is substituted for log GDP). These relationships are perhaps best presented visually. Figure 6.4 thus plots the standardized coefficient of strikes, protests, and riots and of each of my controls, along with their 95 percent confidence intervals. Variables with their coefficients to the right of the zero line in the figure have a positive correlation; those to the left, a negative correlation. Confidence intervals that cross the zero line are insignificant (i.e., they are not significantly different from zero). For a complete table of results, see Appendix 6. But the general trajectory is clear: more intense resistance means considerably more investment in the organization most directly responsible for repression.

The relationship between boundary-spanning or transgressive resistance and *responsive capacity* is similar. There is a significant, positive correlation between strikes, protests, and riots and both pro-worker and split decisions, but not pro-business decisions. Moreover, despite the aggregate, national trend toward split decisions, the coefficient for pro-worker decisions is also highest. Specifically, an increase of one incident in my China Strikes dataset is associated with an increase of 130 disputes decided in a pro-worker manner and 66.2 decided in a split manner (at a 99 percent confidence level). There are also interesting ancillary results. In particular, higher GDP per capita is associated with more split decisions but has no significant correlation with pro-worker decisions. Perhaps wealthy provinces can afford to try to please everyone. Or such places might have more white-collar workers, yielding more complicated disputes. But log *revenue* per capita works in the opposite manner: more pro-worker and pro-business decisions but only a significant relationship with split decisions at the 10 percent level

___

model, with year and province fixed effects and strikes lagged or with strikes lagged plus a lagged dependent variable, instead of differencing, the results are similar, but it is split decisions alone that are positively and significantly correlated with more strikes. A simple panel fixed effects model with no lagged or differenced variables does not yield significant results in the expected direction. Employing the natural log of PAP spending gives results that are in the expected direction but not significant.

[3] More precisely, here and in the rest of my discussion, given that the first difference of the main independent and dependent variables is used, this sort of relationship should be interpreted as an increase *in the increase* of the independent variable being correlated with an increase *in the increase* of the dependent variable.

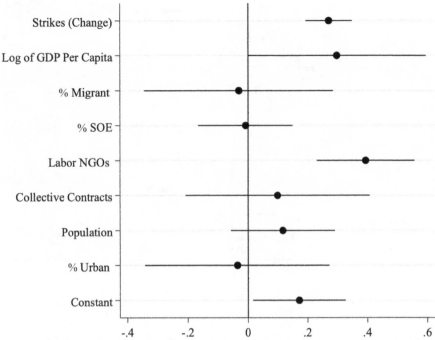

FIGURE 6.4 Strikes, protests, and riots and People's Armed Police spending.
Sources: *Financial Statistics of Cities and Counties* (*Quanguo dishixian caizheng tongji ziliao*) collections from 2003 to 2009 for PAP spending, *China Strikes* (2017) for strikes, *China Trade Unions Yearbooks* from 2004 to 2013 for collective bargaining agreements, a list of NGOs and founding dates provided to the author by China Labour Bulletin, and *China Statistical Yearbooks* from 2004 to 2013 for everything else.

of significance. Again, worker organization also matters. But strangely, NGOs show the same association with split decisions as GDP (perhaps because such groups often only have the clout to mediate compromises, as explained by Halegua 2008). Figure 6.5 plots the standardized coefficient of strikes, protests, and riots and of each of my controls, along with their 95 percent confidence intervals in a similar manner to Figure 6.4. This time, though, the results of three models are displayed simultaneously, one for each type of dispute outcome. Bars representing pro-worker, split, and pro-business decisions are stacked on top of each other. Readers who wish to review a complete table of results can consult Appendix 7. However, again, the broad direction of change is obvious: as with increased repressive capacity, intense resistance is yielding an increased capacity on the part of the state to be responsive to working-class concerns.

What form, then, do the results of contained resistance take? If we substitute the total number of formally adjudicated employment disputes for strikes, protests, and riots, we find that more disputes are, of course, significantly correlated with more of all of the possible dispute outcomes – but the coefficients for pro-worker and split decisions (0.3 and 0.37, respectively) are much

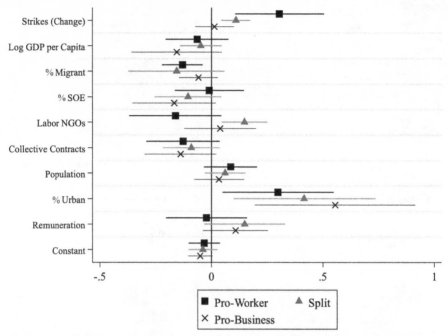

FIGURE 6.5 Strikes, protests, and riots and formally adjudicated dispute decisions.
Sources: *China Strikes* (2017) for strikes, *China Labour Statistical Yearbooks* from 2004 to 2013 for dispute outcomes and the percent of disputes focused on remuneration, China Trade Unions Yearbooks from 2004 to 2013 for collective bargaining agreements, a list of NGOs and founding dates provided to the author by China Labour Bulletin, and *China Statistical Yearbooks* from 2004 to 2013 for everything else.

higher than for pro-business decisions (0.08). However, there is no significant relationship between disputes and PAP spending, although the correlation is in the same direction. See Appendix 8. This should not be surprising. Workers taking cases to the legal system instead of the streets lessen direct pressure on the public security apparatus. But this should not be understood to mean that as long as labor stays within the boundaries set by authorities, there are no negative repercussions for activism. As I showed in my case studies of the Yangtze River Delta and Pearl River Delta in Chapters 4 and 5, contained activism just draws a qualitatively different form of repression. Raw beatings and detentions give way to subtler forms of control, specifically an approach that can be characterized as preemption, caution, and nudging.

FEEDBACK EFFECTS

The results above could be the result of reverse causality, meaning that PAP spending or more pro-worker or split decisions actually encourage greater unrest rather than the other way around, or that there is a two-way relationship between state and worker actions, generating an endless loop of cause and effect. It might seem that greater investment in paramilitary forces would, if anything, deter protests. Certainly, few of the incidents in my dataset appear to be directly driven by grievances related to policing (forty incidents, or under 3 percent). However, some theories of state coercion suggest that it gradually pushes activism in a more radical direction (Lichbach 1987). At any rate, one can certainly imagine that employees might be buoyed by positive outcomes in formally adjudicated disputes, interpreting them as evidence of state support.[4] The best way of dealing with this issue, along with related ones, is to use what is called an Arellano–Bond Estimator and include on the right-hand side of my model a lagged dependent variable, namely PAP spending or dispute decisions made a certain way the year before, and to instrument on the past levels of my main independent variables, namely strikes, protests, and riots or the total number of formally adjudicated employment disputes, lagged two years back (see Arellano and Bond 1991). This ensures that my independent variable really is exogenous to the model, that is, not determined by my dependent variable in some way – because instrumented change in strikes or lawsuits in year t-2 cannot be said to have been influenced by the change in police spending or disputed outcomes in year t – and also takes care of the possibility that using the first difference of the dependent variable (police spending or dispute outcomes) might have inadvertently introduced auto-correlation. If readers find this all confusing, they should just note the results: when I estimate this more complex model, I get almost exactly the same results for PAP spending as I did with the simpler one (at a 95 percent level of confidence). However, when I use the new model with the different formally adjudicated dispute outcomes, things change. Specifically, strikes, protests, and riots are no longer significantly correlated with pro-worker decisions or split decisions, but are now both significantly and negatively correlated with pro-business decisions (at a 99 percent level of confidence). In other words, there seems to be strong reverse causality at work with regard to any dispute outcome that gives something to workers. But worker mobilization is nonetheless driving down straight-out employer wins, as expected – and now in a more significant manner. Unrest is pushing courts away from capital. See Appendix 9. Although, as already noted in the preceding case study chapters, aspects of the protest–policy relationship are clearly circular, resistance is still found to increase both repressive and responsive capacity.

ACCOUNTING FOR POTENTIAL BIASES IN DATA

In Chapter 2, I argued that *China Strikes* represents the most complete collection of strikes, protests, and riots for the period that it covers. Some of the

---

[4] By pairing protest event data with data on posts to local government message boards, Zheng and Meng (2020) provide evidence that greater access to institutionalized channels for raising complaints increases protest in China.

controls used above were intended to account for remaining problems, such as the possibility that there is less reporting of SOE worker activism than migrant worker activism because of political sensitivities around the former. However, it is still conceivable that there are regional disparities in the dataset's coverage. For instance, some parts of China, especially Guangdong, the subject of Chapter 5, have comparatively open local media, large communities of foreign reporters, and high rates of internet use (Guangdong is, of course, also right across the border from Hong Kong and its human rights groups and labor NGOs, which publicize conflicts). Other areas are more cut off but might nonetheless feature workplace unrest. There is no perfect solution to this problem. However, if I re-run my regressions with provincial fixed effects, which control for any time invariant characteristics of regions, or drop Guangdong, in particular, entirely from my analysis, I get the same results (see Appendix 10 for fixed effects). The country's hotspots deserve extra attention because of their unique models of control, as explored in the previous chapter. But the average dynamics documented in here are not artifacts of those hotspots having skewed the data.

A CONTROL NOT INCLUDED: RURAL UNREST

A final issue presents itself for my analysis, especially when it comes to the relationship between unrest and repressive capacity: might the correlations I find actually reflect state reactions to challenges from groups other than workers? China is, of course, the site of many forms of contention: protests over air pollution by middle-class urbanites, public awareness campaigns by feminists around issues like sexual harassment, nationalist demonstrations against perceived insults from countries like Japan or the United States, and national self-determination struggles in Tibet and Xinjiang. For the most part, these various mobilizations, while important in their own right, are either too few in number to undermine my analysis (e.g., feminist campaigns and nationalist demonstrations) or are geographically separated from labor unrest and therefore work against my finding any significant correlations between worker activism and state policy (e.g., the struggles in Tibet and Xinjiang). However, one form of contention is both common and can overlap geographically with workplace conflict. This is rural unrest.

Chinese farmers protest a lot. Driven first by excessive taxation (Bernstein and Lü 2003) and more recently by land expropriation (Heurlin 2016), they have frequently confronted authorities in protracted, violent conflicts. For instance, in 2005, in the village of Shengyou in Hebei Province, peasants dug foxholes and trenches to protect their fields from an army of hired thugs, who attacked them with shotguns, pipes, and clubs, killing six, at the order of local authorities anxious to build a power plant (Pan 2005). In 2014, outside Kunming in Yunnan Province, farmers captured and burnt to death thugs sent to clear them from their land (BBC 2014). Although by no means always so dramatic, these sorts of incidents rival industrial incidents in number

(C.-J. J. Chen 2009; Tong and Lei 2014). After the sorts of showdowns that are the subject of this book, they are arguably the government's *other* key concern.

Importantly, farm activism can also occur in roughly the same parts of the country as workplace activism. As cities expand outward and farmland is expropriated for industry, hotspots of labor unrest have become centers for rural insurgency, too (Svartzman 2013). Thus, Guangdong Province, the leader in industrial contention, was the site of two of the bigger farmer mobilizations of the last two decades: the 2005 Dongzhou Village protest and the 2011 Wukan Village protest, both of which centered on expropriations (although these did not occur at the center of the province's industry). In my interviews for the case studies that are the focus of subsequent chapters, I found evidence of these dynamics in places like Zhenjiang in Jiangsu Province (Interview 1). The turmoil in China's countryside could complicate my analysis of the drivers of PAP spending, in particular (employment dispute outcomes are restricted to workers by definition).

Nonetheless, interviews I conducted suggested that rural unrest is not a serious confounding variable. People were generally of the opinion that the state responds very differently to disputes by farmers versus those by workers. In particular, they argued that policing the countryside is cheaper. For example, one Nanjing academic said, "In rural areas, the government is more direct in how it resolves disputes. It's easier there to reduce the size of conflicts ... It's hard to say about costs ... but more is probably spent in cities on disputes than in the countryside" (Interview 43). An instructor at the Central Party School who leads training for officials on handling mass incidents meanwhile commented, "In the cities, there's a saying that if you make big trouble, you get a big resolution; small trouble, a small resolution ... people push for more money ... It's different in the countryside. The issue is not just money. For example, in Wukan, it came down to organizing new [village] elections" (Interview 115). Finally, an activist I spoke with who had been involved in both worker and farmer organizing explained, "The difference is that in the countryside, at the beginning, the police won't use as much violence. Relationships in the countryside are 'personal relationships' (*shurende guanxi*), and police will at first try to use these relationships to deal with issues" (Interview 73). The activist added: "There is definitely more 'stability mainten-ance' spending in urban areas! Wherever there are more young people, there is more 'stability maintenance' spending" (Interview 73). Whatever the precise cause, there seemed to be a consensus that police investment operates in a different manner for labor than it does for farmers. Rural unrest is unlikely to be a major issue in my analysis.

SUMMARY

The different regional models of control developed by local authorities to counter worker resistance provide important insights into qualitative shifts in China's governance. However, if we squint, we can observe a broad, national process of capacity-building at work, too. Specifically, resistance is simultaneously building the state's repressive and responsive capacities. Where strikes, protests, and riots – boundary-spanning and transgressive resistance – increase, we see a concomitant deepening of investment in the People's Armed Police and a greater ability to overcome the objections of employers and deliver wins or at least split decisions to workers in employment disputes (contained resistance – more pursuit of grievances through approved channels – seems to have a somewhat different effect: it is not correlated with PAP spending, though other forms of repressive capacity may conceivably be strengthened as workers litigate more). This dynamic is self-reinforcing. More worker wins in mediation, arbitration, and court mean more strikes, protests, and riots. But police investments do not seem to either spark more resistance or deter it. Rural conflict might seem to constitute a confounding variable, but interviews suggest that it operates very differently. In the next, penultimate chapter, I address an important question that has hovered in the background of this and previous chapters without being confronted directly: might not elite politics – the policies of Chinese leaders at different levels – complicate the picture of bottom-up change that has, up to this point, been painted?

7

Bottom-Up versus Top-Down Change

Throughout this book, I have argued that worker resistance is powerfully altering governance in the People's Republic, albeit in a contradictory manner. This is a forthrightly bottom-up perspective on the Chinese system. I have acknowledged complications to this schema at various points. For example, in the case studies in Chapters 4 and 5, I noted how state policies could double back to reshape the nature of labor mobilization regionally, for example, the Yangtze River Delta's co-optation of labor NGOs might mean less boundary-spanning or transgressive organizations for the state to contend with down the line, making harsher measures less necessary. Moreover, in the statistical work in the previous chapter, I explicitly tested for reverse causality and found evidence that pro-worker and split decisions in formally adjudicated employment disputes are both a product of *and* a cause of strikes, protests, and riots (although I found that resistance drives down pro-business decisions even when this feedback is accounted for). Nonetheless, the issue of the precise role played by elite politics in labor politics deserves more focused attention for at least two reasons. First, at a regional level, officials, while all disciplined by the same cadre promotion system, clearly approach stability maintenance in ways that are informed by their own, idiosyncratic perspectives, with implications for both sub-national policies and local levels of unrest. Second, nationally, changes between administrations have obviously coincided with different degrees of political openness, including in the arena of industrial relations. The current government of Xi Jinping has been extraordinarily harsh on dissent. Again, this dynamic could affect both ends of the protest-policy relationship, encouraging/discouraging workers while ramping up/dialing down repression and responsiveness. Do these dynamics fundamentally undercut the arguments advanced thus far? Put differently, could top-down pressures dominate bottom-up ones in the final analysis?

In this chapter, I address these issues in several ways. First, I examine the power of local officials through a brief study of the directly administered city of Chongqing and its charismatic leaders, Wang Yang and Bo Xilai, to argue that, although some officials may be more motivated to engage in far-reaching reforms, where, exactly, they focus their reformism is principally determined by conflict on the ground. More workplace contention means more interventions in industrial relations policy, while less of the same means that leaders direct their interventions elsewhere. Thus, although both Wang and Bo had reputations for shaking up politics, neither innovated much in the realm of labor issues per se while in charge of Chongqing, because the city is simply not a hotspot of worker unrest. In contrast, Wang initiated several of the reforms in Guangdong noted in Chapter 5 when he was reassigned there, as the province's industrial conflict put labor on his front burner. Some of these interventions are thought to have provided "political opportunities" for mobilization, in turn. But Wang's contrasting actions suggest that protest, not policy, is the key independent variable to consider. Second, I describe in some detail the chilling crackdown on worker rights activists that has been underway nationally since Xi came to power at the end of 2012. This crackdown, I acknowledge, shows that it matters profoundly who exactly is in charge in Beijing. But I argue that China's current coercive turn should not blind us to the significant waves of repression that occurred under previous administrations, too – or the modest signs of responsiveness under Xi. Finally, more broadly, I argue that while the balance between the state's reliance on its repressive versus responsive capacity shifts over time, yielding a lurching quality to political development, the proliferation of regional models of control and the general buildup of these two forms of capacity move steadily ahead. The change documented here has a momentum – albeit one, not that does not clearly point forward – that, while sometimes obscured by short-term political fluctuations, is ultimately immune to them. From a long-term perspective, the government is gradually becoming more adept at both confronting and conciliating workers with each wave of contention.

THE INFLUENCE OF REGIONAL LEADERS

Regional leaders have the potential to constitute something of a "confounding variable" in the study of labor politics. As noted in Chapter 3, they all have to meet the same conditions to move up the CCP hierarchical ladder. However, a strong case can be made that their idiosyncratic approaches and outlooks are quite important to the kinds of policies they enact (see, e.g., P. T. Y. Cheung 1998). Especially disruptive local politicians could conceivably influence both labor unrest *and* state responses to it. For example, a powerful reform-minded official's expressions of sympathy for a strike at a certain factory might be interpreted as an indication that strikes more generally will receive government support, spurring an upsurge in work stoppages. Or the placement of a known hardliner in charge of some place might intimidate potential strikers there enough to prevent them from taking action. At the same time, leaders personally direct government responses to unrest, formulating new labor laws or urging trade union reforms. In other words, they could be the beginning and the end of the contentious process we have traced thus far. What at first might appear to be an impact of protest on policy could simply turn out to be the result of the machinations of certain individuals or top-down, not bottom-up change.

Leadership Types

If influential regional leaders are *the* key factor in Chinese labor politics, we would expect politicians, especially those with strong ideological reasons for intervening in industrial relations, to be associated with relatively consistent sets of policies with regard to labor wherever they reside and, perhaps, to consistently spur or dampen labor unrest in those places, too. In other words, local circumstances should not much affect the actions and impact of these people. If, instead, dynamics on the ground are decisive, then the same individuals should behave differently in different places and, consequently, leave different legacies in different places. Leaders might, of course, be more or less reformist by nature (see again P. T. Y. Cheung 1998). But if labor unrest is key, then whether they choose to focus their reformism on labor per se in a given place, as opposed to other issues, should be easily explained by the level of unrest in that place. There is no reliable way of rating the ideological leanings or reformism of all mayors or provincial party secretaries in China and then subjecting these to rigorous statistical study. I therefore choose to focus my analysis on one particular place and its leaders as a sort of plausibility probe for the idea that individual officials can be important. My choice: the booming southwestern city of Chongqing and its successive Party Secretaries, Wang Yang and Bo Xilai. Chongqing is a dynamic city, ripe for policy experimentation. And these two politicians were both reformers, albeit of very different stripes. Thus, if anyone in any place in the country were to have a clear approach to and impact on labor relations it would be these people in this city.

Chongqing on the Cutting Edge

In terms of the best areas of China to examine for evidence of the power of leadership, those places that are at the center of change would seem to be ripest for elite legacy-building and therefore reforms. The directly administered municipality (i.e., province-level municipality) of Chongqing is just such a place. The city is up and coming (Rithmire 2012). Through the Mao era and early reform period, it remained a backward interior outpost devoted to weapons manufacturing and other state industries. But in 1997, as a part of the administrative reorganization necessitated by the Three Gorges Dam construction downstream (and the millions of people the dam displaced), Chongqing and its vast surrounding rural areas were broken off from Sichuan Province and elevated to the same status as Beijing, Shanghai, and Tianjin. China's leadership further made Chongqing a hub in their "Develop the West" and then "One Belt, One Road" initiatives (HKTDC 2016; Lai 2002). Major Taiwanese and foreign electronics firms have now established operations in Chongqing, including Hewlett-Packard, Foxconn, Inventec, and Acer (HKTDC 2016), as have auto companies like Hyundai, Iveco, General Motors, Ford, and China's own Chang'an Automobile (S.-L. Wong 2016). The city has long been a source of migrant labor for other provinces, but it is becoming an important destination for migrants in its own right. For example, in a cafeteria near Chongqing's massive Foxconn facility, I spoke with workers from neighboring Hubei Province who had chosen to move further inland to Chongqing to work, rather than make the more traditional migrant journey to the coast (Interview 110). As economic growth in the rest of China slowed to 6.9 percent in 2015, the year I visited Chongqing, the city's growth powered ahead at 11 percent (S.-L. Wong 2016) – the highest in the country for the second year in a row. A Chongqing arbitrator I interviewed said to me, "There is a relatively high rate of disputes here, the most of the interior [cities]. If coastal areas represent the 'Himalayas' of disputes, then Chongqing and Sichuan are 'Mount Tai'" (Group Discussion 107). But being "Mount Tai" means falling behind not only Guangdong, but also Beijing, Shanghai, Fujian, Hubei, Zhejiang, and Jiangsu, as well as even Hainan, Shaanxi, and Ningxia, in strikes, protests, and riots per capita. In sum, the city is the kind of place where risk-taking officials are sent. If elites are crucial to Chinese labor politics, then Chongqing should be a site of considerable labor policy innovation (and, maybe, dramatic clampdowns on labor activism, too). But if levels of industrial contention are instead decisive, then Chongqing is not necessarily where you would expect important policies to be enacted. Thus, the city constitutes a "most-likely" case for political elites mattering more than unrest: if a top-down approach to labor politics were to be convincing anywhere, it would be in Chongqing; such an approach is not convincing in Chongqing, we should doubt the approach elsewhere.

Chongqing's Powerful Local Leaders

Two of the country's most influential politicians of the past two decades have led Chongqing: Wang Yang (from 2005 to 2007) and Bo Xilai (2007 to 2012). For a period, these men were understood to represent distinct ideological poles within the CCP: Wang, liberalism; Bo, populism – or, as they themselves put it in their widely followed "cake debate," "dividing the cake" (Bo) versus "making an even bigger cake" (Wang) (Cartier and Tomba 2012, 50–55).[1] Contemporary Chinese liberalism combines two characteristics not normally

[1] Wang Yang's role in China's repressive policies in Xinjiang has tarnished his liberal reputation recently (on this role, see Gan 2019).

associated with each other elsewhere in the world: first, a deep faith in markets and suspicion of an overbearing state, and second, a powerful concern for the welfare of "vulnerable groups" (J. Pan and Xu 2017; Tian and Wu 2007; C. Wang 2003, chap. 5). Thus, during his stint in Chongqing, the liberal Wang might be expected to have supported reforms that allowed workers to resolve their own problems, such as through collective bargaining with their employers or streamlined judicial procedures. Populist Bo, meanwhile, might be expected to have gone even further in supporting labor: the fiery Party Secretary was in close contact with many of the country's New Left and Neo-Maoist intellectuals, who have frequently expressed concern about the fate of the Chinese working class since Deng Xiaoping's rollback of the planned economy (Fewsmith 2012; Freeman III and Wen 2011). And in his own speeches, Bo decried "the polarization of rich and poor" as a symptom of "the backward culture of slave owners, feudal lords and capitalists" (Yuezhi Zhao 2012, 7). When he was ultimately brought down in a scandal involving allegations of corruption and murder, Bo's supporters saw this as a "coup" directed by the wealthy (Yuezhi Zhao 2012). Bo was also known for a brutal streak. In particular, he was accused of running roughshod over civil liberties during a crackdown he led on organized crime (W. He 2011). One can easily imagine that Bo would have clamped down hard on labor civil society groups ("bourgeois liberalization"), even as he supported workers in other ways. Yet, a close analysis reveals that neither Wang *nor* Bo chose to initiate significant overhauls of Chongqing's workplaces, whether in the form of repression or responsiveness. For all their flare, neither politician devoted themselves in a sustained way to industrial relations or had much of an impact in this arena.

Wang Yang in Chongqing

True to his reputation, Wang Yang was a liberal reformer when he was in charge of Chongqing. He drew national attention by negotiating a peaceful settlement to a high-profile standoff between developers and a "nail house" homeowner who had held out against demolition for three years (Fong 2007).[2] Such property conflicts are common in China, especially in places with breakneck growth like Chongqing (Heurlin 2016, chap. 2). In addition, Wang made waves by issuing a circular on media reform that pushed state news outlets "to prioritize reports according to the importance of news events rather than to the ranking of the officials concerned," which had the result of shifting local reporting to grassroots social issues, including the lives of migrant workers (Heurlin 2016, chap. 2). In a prominent speech, he called for "liberating thought" (*jiefang sixiang*) – a phrase associated with Deng Xiaoping and the

---

[2] Homeowners in China who resist eviction in this manner are compared in popular discussion to stubborn nails that stick out from boards.

reformer Hu Yaobang – and vigorously supported a strong private sector (Chongqing Daily 2007). In terms of more thoroughgoing changes, Wang worked to break down the distinctions between Chongqing residents with rural and urban household registration, a policy carried on by Bo Xilai after him (Jin 2007). In 2007, Wang declared that, by 2012, there would only be one form of household registration in the city, namely a "Chongqing resident registration" (*Chongqing jumin hukou*), and that this change would help migrant workers with "employment, training, settlement, their children's education, and other difficulties" (Jin 2007). (He subsequently engaged in similar, if perhaps less far-ranging initiatives on the urban-rural divide while in charge of Guangdong). Many of these policies doubtless directly or indirectly affected the city's work-place relations. But none in a big way.

Wang Yang did not choose to concentrate on labor policy per se in Chongqing. No important workplace regulations were passed during his tenure. Nor did he launch any major rounds of repression against labor activists. A prominent local labor lawyer said to me, "Wang Yang was only here a short time. His main thing was opposing bureaucratism" (Interview 141). A Chongqing-based academic agreed that little changed in terms of industrial relations under Wang, commenting, "It was more or less the same under Wang Yang and Bo Xilai. Wang Yang focused his work on migrants and pulling together the city and countryside. But Wang Yang was only in power a short bit" (Interview 138). Wang's speeches to municipal trade unions were anodyne and focused on things like, again, bridging the rural-urban divide (G. Li 2006). The final municipal trade union congress he presided over called for the construction of a harmonious city and basic legal rights protection work (G. Li 2007). If not labor laws or union programming, then the registration of labor civil society groups might seem to be a likely area for a breakthrough under someone with Wang's outlook. However, a local NGO leader com-mented to me, "Chongqing was the same under Wang Yang and Bo Xilai. There was no change" (Interview 111). The activist added, "It was only last year that Chongqing allowed NGOs to register directly with the government without a sponsoring department. In Chengdu, you could register directly a long time ago" (Interview 111). In other words, while in charge of Chongqing, Wang was a reformer, just not a workplace reformer; he was a liberal, just not a liberal concerned with labor issues or even labor civil society, in particular. He did not have any great impact on industrial relations because this area was simply not a priority for him.

Wang Yang in Guangdong

In contrast to his relatively modest contributions to workplace governance in Chongqing, when Wang Yang was subsequently made Party Secretary of Guangdong, from 2007 to 2012 (when Bo Xilai took over the reins in Chongqing), he oversaw significant changes to PRD industrial relations.

Many of these changes are described in the section of Chapter 5 concerning experimental legislation in the region. During Wang's reign in the south, for instance, the Shenzhen Special Economic Zone Harmonious Labor Relations Regulations were passed and the Guangdong's abortive Regulations on the Democratic Management of Enterprises were discussed. Moreover, Wang seemed to be unfazed by – and even perhaps to find value in – worker organizing. A Beijing-based academic explained to me that while in charge of the PRD, "Wang Yang would observe how things developed first and only afterward decide how to react. If there were leaders among the workers, Wang Yang saw this as a good thing, as there was thus a way to negotiate a solution to the conflict" (Interview 74). Thus, under his watch, the police did not intervene in the 2010 Nanhai Honda strike and, after initial missteps by the relevant municipal-level trade union, he allowed the Guangdong Federation of Trade Unions to take charge and organize direct elections for enterprise-level union leaders (Chan and Hui 2013; Meng and Lu 2013). This kicked off a wave of union elections across the PRD that continues today. Wang also adopted a different approach to Guangdong NGOs than his successor, Hu Chunhua, encouraging organizations to take over certain government services and, unlike in Chongqing, lowering their barriers to registration (Simon 2011b, 2011a).[3] A number of Guangdong labor NGOs even received state funding, although a crackdown, the most intensive up to that point, was launched against the groups during the last year of Wang's term (Franceschini 2012). Wang Yang's ideology clearly did not change between his tenure in Chongqing and his tenure in Guangdong, but his policy focus did. Guangdong was deemed ripe for labor reform (and later, repression); Chongqing was not.

Bo Xilai in Chongqing

Unlike Wang Yang's stint in Chongqing, Bo Xilai's rule in Chongqing was widely viewed as pro-worker in a general sense. A labor lawyer who served as counsel to one of the alleged mafia leaders targeted in Bo's crime crackdown said to me appreciatively, "Bo Xilai was better for labor relations. You can't say because he broke the law we must therefore deny everything he did. Yes, he broke the law and no one is above the law. But he did a lot that was good for labor" (Interview 141). One thing Bo did that was "good for labor" was negotiate an end to a Chongqing taxi strike on live television in 2008, offering the drivers a range of concessions. Cabbies I interviewed in city were unsurprisingly uniformly nostalgic for the Bo years. One typical response to my questions about the former Party Secretary: "Things were better then. Things were better in all respects" (Interview 123). Or, in the words of another driver: "Everyone

---

[3] In fact, the rule changes regarding NGO registration in Chengdu noted in Interview 111 and cited above followed on the heels of Wang Yang's reforms in Guangdong.

says things were better under Bo. If he had become the top leader and not been taken out by Xi Jinping, things would be much better [now]" (Interview 126). Yet another remarked, "There are no good leaders. They are all corrupt. If there's a good leader, the others will knock him down" (Interview 131). When I pressed this driver for an example of such a "good leader," he responded quickly, "Need one say? Bo Xilai" (Interview 131). However, did this mean that workers were encouraged to challenge their bosses during Bo's time in power? A driver who helped organize the 2008 strike denied this in 2011, while the party secretary was still in charge, saying to me, "The decision to strike didn't have anything to do with Bo Xilai and people's opinion of him. The drivers would have struck no matter what, no matter who was secretary. This was about the masses' interests" (CQ TX #12). Indeed, the number of Chongqing incidents in my *China Strikes* dataset were not any higher during Bo's than they were under his predecessors; he had no galvanizing effect.

Like Wang Yang before him, Bo mostly pushed initiatives that indirectly impacted the city's workplaces. Bo tried to permanently integrate large numbers of migrant workers by fairly compensating them for giving up their rural land (again, an extension of Wang's efforts) and, in a revival of the Mao-era "mass line," forced officials to spend time among the masses (S. Wang 2011). He engaged in a massive round of public housing construction and bolstered state industries alongside the private sector, providing more stable jobs (Zhiyuan Cui 2011). Bo also made several dramatic, one-off interventions on behalf of workers. His high-profile role in resolving the 2008 taxi strike was unusual and contrasted with the reactions of leaders in some other cities experiencing taxi strikes around the same time. Guiyang, the capital of Guizhou Province, saw a more lukewarm response (GY TX #21, 25 Interviews). In Xining in remote Qinghai Province, for example, authorities arrested eleven cabbies they claimed had "organized a plot, agitated people to cause trouble, instigated people to petition, and ... maliciously caused a ruckus" (China Labour Bulletin 2009a).[4] There were other examples. Bo provided free meals to 1.3 million left-behind children of migrants (John Chan 2012). And in May 2011, as I noted in the previous chapter, he dispatched a city SWAT team to recover protesting construction workers' wage arrears and confront the thugs hired to intimidate the protesters (see again Fauna 2011). These gestures cemented Bo's populist reputation. But they were mostly just that: gestures. Did he substantially change labor governance in Chongqing? In a word, no.

In terms of the staples of industrial relations policy – rules on the working conditions or the resolution of conflicts or trade union reforms – just as with Wang Yang, little changed in Chongqing under Bo Xilai's leadership. One of the most important labor laws passed in the city in recent years has been the

---

[4] It should be noted, though, that during his organized crime crackdown, Bo later arrested an individual who had played a prominent role in the strike. See Interview 128.

Chongqing City Employee Rights Guarantee Regulations, which a local labor bureau leader described to me as a "relatively big deal, a substantive law ... [that] put restrictions on labor dispatch companies before the national Labor Contract Law was passed" (Interview 112). Another significant piece of legislation was the (procedural, not substantive) Chongqing City Labor Guarantee Inspection Regulations, which "clarified the division of responsibilities with regard to handling cases [and] set standards for levying fines" (Interview 112). These two laws were enacted in 2003 and 2014, respectively, before and after both Bo and Wang's tenures (and neither law diverged dramatically from countrywide trends). Meanwhile, in the cab sector, where change would perhaps be the most probable, not much that was concrete actually came out of the 2008 negotiations. A taxi activist who played a central role in the strike said, "Bo Xilai raised a number of good ideas – such as [establishing] a cab drivers' union and lowering cab fees – but these were not implemented" (Interview 140). Drivers, too, said little had changed for them, despite their appreciation for Bo's intervention (e.g., Interviews 119, 124). Interestingly, this lack of action extended to repression. Chongqing labor NGO leaders may not have been able to register easily during either Wang or Bo's tenure, but when I visited the city at the height of Bo's power, they seemed relatively unmolested, contrary to liberal critiques of his rule, whereas the groups were afraid to even meet with me two and a half years after his fall. To sum up, despite these leaders' distinctiveness, neither repression nor responsiveness was particularly marked for labor or labor activists under either politician, and workers did not act differently than they otherwise would have under the two administrations.

Average Chongqing

As I have argued, Chongqing and its leaders arguably constitute a "most likely" case for the influence of elite politics on Chinese labor politics (similarly, on "crucial cases," see Gerring 2008). If particular personalities and their ideologies are key to where policy change occurs, then if any city or any politicians could be said to be especially likely to engage in wholesale reforms of labor institutions or large-scale crackdowns, they would have to be Chongqing, Wang Yang, and Bo Xilai. Yet, aside from some one-off interventions and policies that were indirectly beneficial to workers, little occurred with regard to industrial relations innovation in the municipality from 2005 to 2012 – unlike in Guangdong. See Table 7.1. Summarizing labor programming in Chongqing across its different administrations – Bo's, Wang's, and others' – one local academic said, "There have been no real distinctive local policies enacted that I can think of, no real breakthroughs, especially compared to Guangdong. For example, Guangdong recently passed the – what's it called? – 'collective consultation regulations' or whatever. Chongqing might try out some new things, but they are usually not theoretically innovative like that" (Interview 108). Said another academic, "Chongqing doesn't have the

TABLE 7.1 *Leaders compared*

Leader	Wang Yang	Bo Xilai	Wang Yang
Place	Chongqing	Chongqing	Guangdong
Years	2005–7	2007–12	2007–12
Worker resistance	MODERATE	MODERATE	HIGH
Policies	Efforts to bridge rural-urban divide	Efforts to bridge rural-urban divide	Passing pioneering local labor laws
	Supporting basic trade union legal work	Symbolic interventions on behalf of workers	Trade union reforms
			Allowing strikes to be resolved in new ways
			Engaging labor NGOs
			Cracking down on labor NGOs

courage to pass a right to strike, but maybe Shenzhen will have the courage" (Interview 139). Yet another: "There's nothing very unusual about local legislation here. Beijing, Shanghai, and Guangdong are representative [of where labor policy is right now] – not Chongqing" (Interview 138). In other words, in terms of workplace governance, despite the presence of such powerful personalities at its helm, Chongqing most closely resembles Jiangsu. It is a dynamic spot, just not in labor policymaking.

Political Elites as Barometers, Not Drivers of Regional Labor Politics

All this suggests not so much that leaders are entirely unimportant as that they are barometers and conduits more than drivers of regional labor politics. Local Chinese officials may increasingly act as "policy entrepreneurs" (Mertha 2008). As Fewsmith (2013) found in his study of local political reform initiatives, certain experiments are only possible because of the intervention of a particular person at a particular time (and those initiatives often fizzle when the person moves on to another position). But different popular pressures in different places create different opportunities for entrepreneurship and experimentation. Where worker resistance is intense and labor NGOs are well developed, labor issues rise to the top of a Party Secretary's agenda – both as a challenge in need of addressing and as a chance to make his or her mark. Guangdong's PRD is such a place. Where workplaces are less contentious, other issues dominate and labor policy develops more or less as elsewhere, regardless of the ideological orientations of the leaders. Chongqing is such a place. Thus, while in Chongqing, Wang Yang focused on issues like housing rights and media freedom; in Guangdong, he turned his attention to labor reforms and civil society. Dramatic interventions aside, neither did the populist Bo Xilai do much to change workplace fundamentals while in Chongqing. Instead, like Wang, he focused on more general issues of integrating the city's rural and urban areas, as well as building social housing and fighting official corruption and crime. Leaders may determine the precise balance between responsiveness and repression. Thus, under both Wang Yang and his successor as Party Secretary of Guangdong, Hu Chunhua, trade unions experimented with direct elections and labor NGOs were harassed, but the emphasis was different: there were more reforms under Wang and more crackdowns under Hu. If their impact on policy priorities is marginal, leaders do not seem to especially spur or dampen labor unrest, either. Protest in Chongqing did not spike under Wang Yang or even Bo Xilai. And Guangdong was already a cauldron of contention before Wang was assigned to govern it (although certain decisions, like his approach to the 2010 Honda strike, may have shaped the demands of workers in subsequent strikes, at least for the remainder of that year and that strike wave; on the "political opportunities" created by the strike, see Meng and Lu 2013). Knowing something about the ideology of a leader in a given place can help us understand some of the specific ins and outs of the evolution of governance in that place, but influential leaders do not fundamentally confound the protest-policy relationship. What is happening on the ground is the true driver of change. The bureaucratic process – with its benchmarks, opportunities for promotion, threats of punishment, and all its imperfections – then carries grassroots pressure up through the system, gradually transforming governance.

THE INFLUENCE OF NEW ADMINISTRATIONS NATIONALLY

If regional leaders are mainly barometers or conduits of grassroots pressures, what of changing national administrations in China? Baum (1994) described the country as continually passing through successive periods of political loosening (*fang*) and tightening (*shou*). These shifts are felt at all levels of society. Politicians and bureaucrats scramble to align themselves with whatever the dominant trend is, accommodating or even encouraging critics in loose periods and harshly clamping down on dissent in tight periods. Meanwhile, activists respond to what social movement scholars have dubbed changes in the "political opportunity structure" by engaging in more daring activities or dialing back their efforts and lying low, depending on the prevailing winds from Beijing (Tarrow 2011). Even in good times, organizers feel pressure to frame their demands so that they are in step with central government rhetoric (again, see O'Brien and Li's [2006] discussion of "rightful resistance"). I recall, for example, during a period of relative relaxation, how an activist hurriedly added references to a "harmonious society" – the Hu Jintao and Wen Jiabao government's catchphrase – into his slide presentation before he spoke at a meeting that included representatives from the Ministry of Human Resources and Social Security and the official trade union. These adjustments are all the more pronounced when the atmosphere tightens. Activity by organizers can come to a virtual halt when things get repressive enough. At the same time, of course, at the other end of the protest-policy equation, the policies themselves evolve. Risky reforms are shelved. Legislative activity more generally may even slow. If regional leaders are not decisive, the change observed thus far in this book could conceivably instead reflect alterations at the very top of the Chinese system. Specifically, my findings may be the product of the special circumstances of the current Xi Jinping administration. I address this possibility next.

The Tight Xi Era

The policies of Xi Jinping administration have thus far been tight. In fact, they are the tightest they have been in decades. Some scholars see Xi's politics as a sharp repudiation of the reform era's cautious moves toward greater openness in various spheres. *Economy* (2018, 5), for instance, writes that today's leadership "has embraced a process of institutional change that seeks to reverse many of the political, social, and economic changes that emerged from thirty years of liberalizing reform." Other scholars, such as Minzner (2018), see Xi's policies as simply the acceleration of a retreat away from openness that has been underway for some time. In a recent paper, Yao Li and I provide evidence that, on average, under Hu and Wen, protests occurring in provinces that spent more on public security were *less* likely to be met with violence or arrests, whereas in the early years of Xi's rule, at least, higher spending translated into a *greater* likelihood of such overt repression. We also provide evidence that this inflection point came in the late Hu-Wen era, not with Xi (Li and Elfstrom 2020). Fu and Distelhorst (2018) argue that while repression has become more centralized and devastating under Xi, channels for public participation, like petitioning or freedom of information requests, have continued to expand. Regardless, Xi's rule has been tough for those activists and ordinary citizens who have come into the government's line of fire. For instance, shortly after Xi came to power, in 2013, when individuals connected with the New Citizens' Movement pressed for officials to disclose their personal assets, seemingly in line with the new leader's anti-corruption drive, the movement was crushed and its leader, Xu Zhiyong, was arrested. In March 2015, police arrested feminists organizing against sexual harassment ("the Feminist Five"), and in July of that same year, the government launched a wide-ranging crackdown against rights lawyers ("the 709 crackdown"). Most dramatically, Uyghurs and other Muslims in Xinjiang have been subjected to a dramatic escalation in the government's attempts to control their culture and religion, including the establishment of concentration camps that aim to "re-educate" an estimated one million or more citizens in the region (Zenz 2019; Zenz and Leibold 2020). When the virus COVID-19 began to spread at the end of 2019 and beginning of 2020, police detained whistleblower doctors. This is a period of extreme control – sometimes with disastrous consequences.

Xi Jinping's tightening has unsurprisingly touched Chinese labor politics. Readers who wish to are invited to go back through previous chapters to actively note that the most egregious instances of repression directed at worker-activists I have described as occurring in the Pearl River Delta happened after Xi took office. These are worth recapping. In December 2015, several activists in the vicinity of Guangzhou were detained, and two of them were put on trial. Then, in 2018, as a campaign by Marxist student groups in support of striking workers in Shenzhen gained momentum, authorities responded by arresting workers and disappearing leading student activists, forcing some of them into vans right off their elite campuses in cities like Beijing and Nanjing, only to later feature the students in confession videos shown to their classmates. An NGO staffer who participated in the strike in a minor capacity was captured, as well. In January 2019, five labor NGO leaders mostly from Shenzhen were arrested on the same day. Over subsequent months, police detained contributors to a website called iLabour that supported the efforts of workers seeking compensation for work-related pneumoconiosis, and an activist and researcher advocating for sanitation workers in Guangzhou was briefly taken into custody. In total, 2018–19 resulted in over a hundred detentions (China Labor Crackdown Concern Group 2019).

The January 2019 crackdown on labor NGO leaders deserves a more detailed explanation, as it shows the lengths to which the current government will go to contain labor activism. One of the leaders, Zhang Zhiru, once a factory worker himself, had formed one of the most influential organizations in the Pearl River Delta but had not engaged in high-profile work on collective bargaining – the focus of the 2015 roundup – in some time (for a good profile of Zhang, see Roberts 2020). On January 20, 2019, he was taken into custody by police while working in his modest office. Simultaneously, authorities arrested the organizer Wu Guijun, who had previously been arrested at the beginning of Xi's term for his organizing of furniture workers (and had been featured in a short *New York Times* online video). The same day, police captured two former staff members of Zhang's NGO, Jian Hui and Song Jiahui, as well as He Yuancheng, a former legal assistant at a labor law firm, who had edited a webpage about collective bargaining. The arrests crossed provinces: Jian was taken into custody in Hunan. Eventually, all the activists were charged with "gathering a crowd to disrupt social order," but they did not have prompt access to lawyers (for overviews of the cases, see CHRD 2019; RFA 2019). It seemed that in most cases, the charges were prompted by industrial actions that had occurred almost half a decade earlier. Appeals by Hong Kong NGOs, international trade unions, and the ILO fell on deaf ears. Then, in May 2020, the activists were abruptly allowed to return home. This all stood in contrast to the treatment given these individuals earlier. Zhang had been lauded by the nationalistic state newspaper *Global Times*. He had been pressured at points by authorities but had never faced criminal charges (though Wu had). The law firm that had been He's base was once a fixture of gatherings of officials and academics.

There is no denying that China's present administration has changed the options for worker-activists, and this must be included in our analysis of what is happening on the ground. The Xi Jinping factor is real. Yet, we should not overstate the alterations that have occurred, either. The policies of Xi Jinping may be chilling for labor NGO leaders, who are shifting away from transgressive programming, but workers are still both taking to the streets and lodging cases via approved channels in extraordinary numbers – and with a new sophistication. China Labour Bulletin's strike map shows a continued upward trajectory in protests. After leveling off, formally adjudicated employment disputes seem to have picked back up. There are new rumblings of discontent from state-owned enterprise employees. For example, in 2015, angry at wage arrears and plans for layoffs, miners employed by the Longmay Group in Shuangyashan, Heilongjiang Province, in the northeast, protested by the thousands, inspiring similar actions by SOE employees in Jilin, Hebei, Jiangxi and elsewhere in Heilongjiang (Lau 2016b). Most impressively, in 2018, there were nationally coordinated strikes by both crane operators and truckers. In the face of intimidation, labor is still flexing its muscles. What is different is that formal civil society groups are much less at the forefront than before. Whether or not this ends up being beneficial to authorities trying to resolve disputes remains to be seen.

Government responsiveness to labor's concerns has not ended entirely, either, although it has been downgraded somewhat. The "Constructing Harmonious Labor Relations" document jointly released by CCP Central Committee and the State Council in 2015 (and mentioned at other points in this book) endorsed many of Guangdong's innovations (People's Daily 2015). A union cadre in Shenzhen confidently told me in 2017, "We have now expanded the area of our experiment. I am working in a new district. Everyone is talking about union reform ... Other places also *want* to reform, but they don't know how. There's pressure from above" (Interview UOS 1, March 2017). Moreover, big state initiatives inevitably still include concessions to labor. For example, the government's plans for restructuring the coal and steel sectors include US$23 billion in funding to help laid-off workers find new employment (Lim, Miller, and Stanway 2016). When the Heilongjiang miners protested recently, the province's governor, who had falsely claimed that no one was even a penny in arrears, was forced to apologize in Beijing – and the restructuring program was temporarily halted (J. Huang 2016). New national rules on the taxi sector and ride-hailing apps seem to be a direct response to cabbie protests (Zuo 2016). In other words, authorities still possess a willingness and capacity to attempt to mollify workers when they wish.

Nor is today's repression altogether new. The arrests of activists in 2015 went further than anything in the preceding decade. And the 2019 arrests pushed the number higher still. But these rounds of repression built on smaller clampdowns that occurred in 2010 and 2012, before or just as Xi Jinping took power. And those clampdowns, in turn, were seen as major escalations at the time. For example, Franceschini (2012) described the government's pressure campaign in 2012 as "a landmark change compared with past practices of coercion." Few remember now, but authorities also went to extraordinary lengths to crush SOE worker mobilizations in the early 2000s. In Liaoyang, one of the cities at the center of the unrest, public security personnel and a unit of the People's Armed Police attacked protesting workers and detained the worker-activists Pang Qingxiang, Wang Zhaoming, Xiao Yunliang, and Yao Fuxin in March 2002. Two of these individuals, Yao Fuxin and Xiao Yunliang, ended up being sentenced to seven and four years in prison, respectively (for a summary, see Human Rights Watch 2002). As I noted in Chapter 6, a People's Liberation Army tank division was even reportedly deployed in Daqing to suppress workers the same year (Han 2002). Riots in 2011 by migrants in Zengcheng, Guangdong, were suppressed through the imposition of a curfew and a massive PAP presence. Human rights lawyers with an interest in labor issues, like Tang Jingling, were routinely harassed, beaten, sometimes arrested, and prevented from practicing their profession across the administration of Hu Jintao and Wen Jiabao (Tang was sentenced to five years in prison following his alleged involvement in protests shortly after Xi came to office). As with its concessions, when it coerces organizers, the government is continuing a long - standing tactic. Responsive capacity plus repressive capacity. More of each when the going gets tough for officials, locally and nationally. New administrations matter, but there is plenty of continuity along with the change that leaders bring.

A Shifting Balance

What certainly alters from leader to leader at all levels of government is the *balance* of relying on the state's augmented repressive versus responsive capacities. This is observable in broad sweeps. In the Mao era, although class struggle was celebrated, labor activists and sympathetic trade union leaders came under intense pressure, as happened following the Hundred Flowers Movement strike wave (Perry 1994). During the early years of reform and opening, the right to strike was stripped from the constitution (although striking was also not explicitly forbidden), but the All-China Federation of Trade Unions was revived, along with Staff and Workers Representative Congresses, in a bid to maintain worker support (and head off a Polish-style independent trade union movement). In fact, throughout the 1980s, the union charted an increasingly independent path (China Labour Bulletin 2009b). Workers bore the brunt of the Tiananmen crackdown in 1989 (Walder and Gong 1993). And in the late

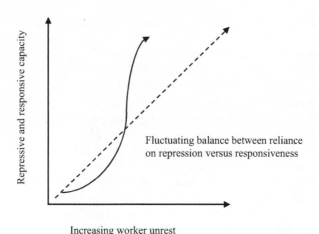

FIGURE 7.1 Long-term change and fluctuating short-term policies.

1990s and early 2000s, under Jiang Zemin and Zhu Rongji, as noted, labor was the subject of intense repression following protests over SOE layoffs. But then, the state also expanded social supports for workers and others in the same era (Cai 2010; Solinger 2009), especially in wealthy areas (Hurst 2009). More recent shifts have already been discussed at length. Over the years, policy has lurched from one emphasis to another. This is not a finely tuned machine. Tacking back and forth to stay ahead of popular pressures, the government makes important advances but simultaneously undoes many of its accomplishments. But it is also worth noting the ambiguities throughout. Maoist workers were encouraged to struggle but repeatedly reined in; early reform-era workers were given new forums but were smashed when they rose up with the student democracy protesters; protesting workers of the later reform era were alternately accommodated and arrested, but welfare and legal frameworks were extended for them. If the "political opportunity structure" for labor has altered, it has often not done so in straightforward ways. As McAdam, Tarrow, and Tilly (2001, 45) note, "Opportunities and threats are not objective categories, but depend on ... collective attribution." How workers have interpreted their options is important. And in the end, what they have then *done* is key. Change ultimately springs from the bottom up. Figure 7.1, building on the figures used in the first chapter of the book, conveys what the process looks like. As unrest rises, there is a general corresponding rise in repressive and responsive capacity. But the government's reliance on one or another policy tool may fluctuate from administration to administration. These shifts are important. They affect the calculations of all actors in Chinese labor politics, as we have seen so far in the Xi era. However, they should not obscure more fundamental trends at work. In fact, not only the continuity between administrations noted above but also the geographical diversity *within* administrations, shown both in my case studies of the Yangtze River Delta and the Pearl River Delta in Chapters 4 and 5 and my statistical work in the previous chapter, speak to this. When and where unrest is more intense, the usual bureaucratic incentives for officials kick in and state changes more, regardless of who is leading the country.

SUMMARY

Worker resistance is clearly shaped in important ways by elite politics. In this chapter, however, I have argued that this top-down dynamic does not fundamentally undercut the bottom-up dynamics that have been the focus of this book. Local politicians, although shaped by the same pressures to keep order, have their own, idiosyncratic approaches to their work. They also vary in their willingness to shake up the system. But whether they direct their energies to labor issues per se, depends on whether workplace conflict is intense in their jurisdictions. This is shown in the case of Chongqing and its successive leaders Wang Yang and Bo Xilai: neither of these dynamic politicians – with different but equally strong ideological reasons for being interested in worker rights – paid much attention to industrial relations while in charge of the city. Instead, they focused on related but distinct issues like the urban-rural divide. I posit that this is explained by the fact that Chongqing has experienced only moderate unrest. In contrast, when Wang was reassigned to contentious Guangdong Province, he initiated important labor reforms. Wang did not pursue the same policies everywhere. Pressure from below determined what he prioritized. The same went for Bo. Nationally, administrations vary in their political openness, and the current Xi Jinping administration has distinguished itself with its extreme intolerance of dissent. I have provided sobering details related to recent arrests of labor leaders. But the ongoing clampdown should not obscure cross-administration continuities: repression under Xi's predecessors or responsiveness today. The Chinese government shifts in its reliance on its tools of coercion versus conciliation, but the shifts contain considerable ambiguity. Much comes down to workers' interpretations of openings and constraints. Variation across time and space in the level of labor resistance is still decisive. There are strong reasons, therefore, to begin analysis with what workers are doing and build from there, incorporating elite politics into our analysis as an important complicating factor – but just that, a complicating factor, not the driver of change. Challenges from the grassroots are decisive. In the next, concluding chapter, I review the argument of the book and ask what these dynamics mean for China going forward – as well as for other, similarly situated countries, especially others with a state socialist past.

8

Conclusion

In the years since the second round of protests at Xing Ang and Xing Xiong described at the outset of this book, the situation in Dongguan has continued to evolve. With revenue slowing, Stella International finally closed Xing Ang in 2016 (while leaving Xing Xiong in operation). The company has since promised to "selectively reduce production capacity in China in order to improve utilization efficiency and deliver margin recovery over the medium term" (World Footwear 2018). This will likely mean more orders being directed to Stella's facilities in Vietnam and Indonesia. And the Taiwanese shoe giant is not alone: with rising Chinese wages, more and more businesses are rerouting their supply chains abroad (Interview 82). Meanwhile, retail and finance are making inroads into the Pearl River Delta's sweatshop wasteland. A scan of Baidu Maps shows that a luxury mall with foreign clothing stores and a Pizza Hut has opened next door to the old Xing Ang plant. Dongguan's train station, previously bustling, can be surprisingly empty now – as can the wide roads around it. Old factories are turning into warehouses for e-commerce companies or standing empty with signs for rent. Migrants are staying in the countryside, waiting for an uptick, or finding jobs in firms that have moved inland, closer to their homes (Group Interview 114). The COVID-19 pandemic has, of course, dampened industrial activity further. There is a feeling that an era of intense movement in Chinese labor relations is drawing to a close, and it is not clear what lies ahead.

Yet, worker resistance in China is not dead. Far from it. As noted throughout this book, protests continue in factories like Stella's, even if employees, after moving in a more aggressive direction, are turning back toward defensive demands for the moment. Workers who have found jobs near where they grew up in the interior vow to draw on protest tactics they learned on the coast – blocking roads, threatening bosses – if their rights are ever infringed again (Group Interview 114). And indeed, riots have occurred in places like a new

Foxconn facility in Shanxi Province in the northwest (Chan, Selden, and Pun 2020, 164–167). Activism is also spreading to new, tech-enabled sectors of the sort that the Chinese government is eager to grow. App-based food delivery drivers have repeatedly struck in recent years (China Labour Bulletin 2018b). Overworked software engineers conspire on Github, a forum that authorities have been loath to censor because of its centrality to domestic innovation (E. Feng 2019). Layoffs in the wake of COVID-19 have spurred protest, particularly in mask-producing factories, which have experienced a rapid boom and then bust (China Labour Bulletin 2020). The previous chapter noted that despite the increased repression of leading labor activists, industrial actions in 2018 featured astonishingly transgressive tactics, including coordinated, nationwide strikes by crane operators and truck drivers (China Labour Bulletin 2018a, 2018c). These actions are building on a cross-provincial network of Wal-Mart employees' pushback against erratic work scheduling a couple of years before (A. Chan 2016).[1] Organizationally, the growth of Marxist student groups in support of workers is similarly boundary-breaking (although repression may be snuffing out this nascent trend for the moment, as discussed) (Y. Yang 2019). Across the border from Shenzhen, in Hong Kong, pro-democracy protests have given a boost to radical union organizers, who have formed, among other things, a new Hospital Authority Employees Alliance, which went on strike over the city's response to COVID-19 in early 2020; dozens of new unions have registered in Hong Kong since the protest movement began (McLaughlin 2020). It is clear that the next era will be one of tremendous ferment of its own, whatever its precise form.

REVIEWING THE PROCESS OF CHANGE

As a result of the conflict that has occurred up to now, my book has documented a broad process of change underway in China. Expanding on the rich existing research on Chinese labor issues, I have shown, first of all, how certain industrial sectors and worker demographics constitute recipes for certain types of worker resistance. These recipes shift. They will likely change again going forward, as some parts of the Chinese economy fade and others rise to prominence. Regardless, unrest of any sort places intense pressure on local officials, who must demonstrate to their superiors that they are on top of things in order to rise in the ranks or, if they are less ambitious, just go about their business without disturbance from higher levels of government. This dynamic is a function of the bureaucratic incentives baked into the Chinese system. Each arm of the state then takes action, and – by accident or design – these actions together generate distinct regional models of control. Where resistance

---

[1] Under a new ultra-flexible system, Wal-Mart abandoned its eight hour day standard for full-time employees and instead scheduled hours as it wished as long as they added up to 174 hours per month.

generally takes a contained or, at most, boundary-spanning form, the model is orthodoxy; where it takes a boundary-spanning to outright transgressive form, the model is risk-taking. I have illustrated these models with the experiences of Jiangsu's portion of the Yangtze River Delta and Guangdong's portion of the Pearl River Delta, respectively. Underneath or alongside these models, as the government grapples with labor, it develops greater repressive and responsive capacity. These capacities can take many shapes. I have shown how, in particular, investment in the People's Armed Police (repressive capacity) and the ability to overcome employer objections and rule fully or partially in workers' favor in formally adjudicated disputes (responsive capacity) have risen in step with unrest. The state is thus growing in a paradoxical way. And it is fundamentally doing so because of popular pressures. My shadow case study of Chongqing and discussion of changes that have occurred since Xi Jinping came to power in 2012 have demonstrated that, although the elite politics matter in labor politics, where particular leaders choose to insert themselves into policymaking is ultimately determined by events on the ground. Some politicians may be more inclined than others to shake things up, but they only shake up labor relations when they feel pressure in this area. Otherwise, they direct their energies elsewhere. At a national level, there can also be wide fluctuations in the balance between reliance on repressive versus responsive capacity between administrations. I have explained how the switch from the Hu Jintao-Wen Jiabao to the Xi Jinping administration, in particular, has coincided with a new intolerance of dissent. But such fluctuations should not lead us to ignore important continuities across governments. Labor activists were harshly repressed at points under Hu and Wen – and Jiang Zemin before them – and there have been glimmers of responsiveness under Xi. As long as conflict exists, the process of change will advance on its contradictory path.

AREAS FOR FURTHER RESEARCH

The book's analysis could be extended further. In particular, its case studies could cover more regions of China, rather than be restricted to a pair of "most similar" but not necessarily typical cases (plus the shadow case of Chongqing and its politicians in the previous chapter). My impression is that the PRD, as the cutting edge of Chinese industrial relations, represents a relatively small sliver of the country. The only place that might conceivably also fit into this sliver would be Zhejiang, one of China's runners-up in strikes, which contains the portion of the YRD not in Jiangsu or Shanghai. Zhejiang experimented with elections for enterprise-level union leaders before Guangdong (Pringle 2011, 160–88). Moreover, at least one labor rights NGO was recently forced to close in Zhejiang's provincial capital, Hangzhou (Interview 2), and an interviewee reported that another Hangzhou group that had managed to establish a partnership with the local trade union was subsequently prevented from even using the word "worker" in its name (Interview 24): more shows of repressive and responsive capacity, in other words. In contrast, the YRD and its orthodox control, stands in for a fairly wide, average swath of places. Chongqing, for instance, matches it in many ways (a labor official I met there said his city had studied the YRD's "harmonious enterprises" program, see Interview 112). Another example: brief visits I made to the northeastern city of Tianjin, which has experienced a similar or slightly lower number of strikes per capita over the past decade as the YRD, revealed many of the same patterns of governance. The city also has a prominent harmonious enterprises program. A Tianjin local labor official was proud of how, after disputes occurred at a prominent Korean electronics firm, his government had organized meetings with representatives of all the Korean companies in the city, nudging them to improve conditions (Interview 49). He further declared, "The union … occupies a middle position between capital and management … The union can't be like foreign ones or the country will be finished" (Group Discussion 95). An enterprise-level union leader in Tianjin explained: "For two months every year, we represent workers in consultations with management. During the other ten months, we help the enterprise" (Group Discussion 95). Another union cadre said of her union, "We go to people's homes and show sympathy, explain the company's policies … There are other things we do. We have an enterprise newsletter. We make dumplings, bring people together to eat" (Group Discussion 95). As an academic explained to me, striking workers there are prodded into line through quiet, individual persuasion in the form of home visits (Interview 74). Then, there are parts of the country that have few worker protests and therefore less predictable responses to the little unrest they nonetheless do have to deal with. As I noted in the previous chapter, in Xining, in the remote southwest, officials reacted with unexpected fierceness to a taxi strike in their city, which might have been treated as routine elsewhere (China Labour Bulletin 2009b). In Taiyuan, in the northwest, authorities responded to a similar industrial action by convening a forum including representatives of the government, drivers, and passengers – a tactic also pursue in places like Hangzhou and Shenyang (TY TX #3, Elfstrom 2019a). But these are just anecdotes and this all deserves more thorough testing. Scholars might do well to return to the rustbelt of Northeast China, especially, which inspired such strong research in the early 2000s (e.g., Cai 2006; Hurst 2009; Lee 2007). A few works, like Cho's (2013) study of a Harbin suburb, suggest that further changes in the heartland of the old Maoist working class deserve attention. Conflict may return to these places and, if it does, it will be interesting to see how it compares to the strikes of the PRD and YRD and elsewhere.

It should also be emphasized that my analysis speaks to the experience of a particular segment of workers in China. Wemheuer (2019) stresses the intersectionality of identity in the Mao era: citizens defined themselves and were formally divided up by the state at the intersection of the rural-urban divide, class categories, gender, and ethnicity. Some of these categories trumped others. This is still the case. I under-sample SOE employees. More importantly, women only make up 21 percent of my interviewees (see again Table 1.2 in Chapter 1). As documented by others, like Lee (1998) and Pun (2005), women's experiences of work – the networks they are a part of on shop floors, the ways that managers attempt to discipline them to the demands of factory life, even the laws that lay out women workers' rights – are different from those of their male counterparts. Few of the strikes in my dataset occur in Tibet or Xinjiang. This is a notable shortcoming, even if it probably accurately reflects the overall distribution of labor unrest. Protesting Tibetan or Uyghur workers are unlikely to be treated as worker-activists first and foremost. Instead, their industrial actions can be expected to be brutally suppressed as a part of the government's long-standing campaign against the national self-determination struggles in "minority" areas. Hillman (2016) argues that even if officials in Tibet, in particular, could accommodate local civil society and in so doing better fulfill central policies, their incentives are to instead always take a hard line against any perceived "separatists," consequences be damned. Mobilization will therefore not necessarily result in greater repressive and responsive capacity on the non-Han Chinese periphery – but rather only greater investment in the security apparatus. In other words, the dynamics described in this book have important scope conditions that need to be explored in greater detail. Such an exploration would greatly enrich our understanding of Chinese labor politics – and contentious politics in China more generally.

Nor do my findings necessarily apply to other protesting groups in China. Parallels to the government's treatment of worker mobilization can be found in how the state has managed environmental activists, for example: cancelling unpopular chemical plants and opening new opportunities for public comment and environmental litigation, while suppressing environmental protests in an increasingly harsh way, as in Chengdu in 2016 or Wuhan in 2019. Similar dynamics might also have been found in the area of rights lawyering – at least until recently – or in the media. But religious minorities like Christians in underground "house churches" have not received the same give and take. Nor have political dissidents. These contrasts have been studied by others (e.g., Y. Li 2019; Wright 2018). But they deserve further examination. By the same token, the changes in state policy documented in this book are the result of not only worker protest, but pressures from numerous directions. My argument has not been that workers are the only group that matters in China, but instead that they are having a distinct and important effect on policy, alongside the effects wrought by others.

Rather than delve superficially into these other regions of China, other groups of workers, and parts of society, however, in this final, concluding chapter of the book, I will instead reflect on some of the broader implications of what I *have* been able to document. Specifically, I will draw on a rich body of literature about Beijing's adaptability to raise the possibility that labor unrest is not just building the state's repressive and responsive capacity but perfecting the machinery of control to the point that a system is being created that will be nigh on impossible for workers to overcome in the future. Rejecting this possibility, however, I will posit that unrest is likely to instead end up *warping* the state over the long haul, in the sense that authorities will be forced into spiraling suboptimal choices. Focusing on building up repressive and responsive capacity has up to now led to the neglect of other important forms of capacity-building, has alienated capital without winning over labor, and, at any rate, will be difficult to continue to coordinate effectively in the future. Of course, there are promising elements in the models of control of places like Guangdong, but these will be hard to deepen and spread, in part because other areas of China actively anticipate and try to head off the dynamics seen in such hotspots of contention and in part because of central government vacillation. Finally, I will consider how well China's experience with labor activism "travels." What – if any – global trend does the country represent? Today's People's Republic has been compared to early, *laissez faire* industrializers like the turn-of-the-century United States, to China's authoritarian developmental state neighbors of the mid-twentieth century like the South Korean and Taiwanese regimes, and to stagnant and economically divided countries like those of late-twentieth-century Latin America (the "Latin American-ization" debate). I will instead suggest that Chinese workers' struggles are most closely mirrored by those of their counterparts in other post-state socialist authoritarian regimes, a broad but diverse group of countries united by shared challenges and opportunities. Similar to China, states like Vietnam, Egypt, and Russia likely face neither a dramatic democratic transition nor unblemished authoritarian resilience for the foreseeable future, but rather constant switchbacks. China has proven that worker-led change can occur in unlikely places. However, if labor is gradually altering Chinese governance from below – as it is the governance of other post-state socialist authoritarian regimes – it is doing so in an iterative, not linear, manner.

THE CHINESE STATE ADAPTS AND REBUILDS

There is a rich body of literature highlighting the CCP's ability to continually adapt itself to changed circumstances. For example, Heilmann (2008) explores authorities' practice of "experimentation under hierarchy" and Heilmann and Perry (2011) identify a "guerilla policy style" that they attribute to lessons learned by the Party during its long period of revolutionary struggle before seizing power. China's early market reforms, in particular, have frequently been interpreted with a phrase coined by Chen Yun (but frequently attributed to Deng Xiaoping): "Crossing the river by feeling the stones." In the 1980s, as Naughton (1995) explains, one change to the country's economic system naturally set up the next, yielding the unplanned but fortuitous result of China "growing out of the plan" without the level of social disruption experienced by eastern Europe and the Soviet Union. Recently, Ang (2016) has argued that China escaped the "poverty trap" through an iterative process of "coevolution" between market forces and the state. Investigating one representative county, she shows how local authorities used pre-existing, Mao-era institutions to crudely build markets where there had been none, how those markets next stimulated better institutions, and how those improved institutions then preserved markets (Ang 2016, chap. 2). Whiting (2001) documents a similar process with regard to rural industries, in particular. In a very different realm, Cheek (2014) muses about how the government has, through its continual loosening of propaganda control (at least until recently), settled into a sustainable pattern of "managing" if not fully controlling its public intellectuals. The basic takeaway of all this work: the Chinese state can learn from challenges and grow.

One possible end result of the continual adjustments by authorities documented in this book with regard to labor relations is thus conceivably a balanced, fine-tuned machine, expertly doling out punishments and prizes for good behavior. Some scholars have argued that this is more or less where the state is headed already, if not because of labor unrest then because of its responses to other pressures. Dickson (2016), for instance, believes that, since Tiananmen, the CCP has begun to adopt a more balanced approach to perpetuating its rule, consisting of "the heavy hand of the state" paired with various legitimacy-boosting measures: economic growth, but also local political reforms, public goods via an expanded welfare state, new values (neo-Confucianism, nationalism), and the co-optation of elites (although he also identifies the dangers of the approach, especially the possibility of resentment born of repression and raised expectations born of fresh state commitments, which we will return to shortly). Studies of Chinese web control, in particular, have provided evidence that, after a rocky start in the early internet age, the state has become quite sophisticated at controlling popular debate – not by crudely blocking everything undesirable but, as Roberts (2018) describes the dynamic, by selectively creating "fear" of the consequences of voicing dissent, generating just enough "friction" to dissuade people from pursuing alternative information, and "flooding" the public with regime-friendly commentary. Other scholars have gone further in envisioning the rise of a techno-state uniquely empowered to organize China as it sees fit, unconstrained by any popular pushback. For example, in his provocative book, *The Perfect Dictatorship: China in the 21st Century*, Ringen (2016, 60, 138) describes the CCP as dealing with society "through an intricate good-cop, bad-cop act" and argues:

China is now a dictatorship in which dictate is restrained and in which, except in last resort, indirect control is substituted for direct command. This mode of control, hard in effect but soft in execution, is being developed to perfection and makes the Chinese state a kind of dictatorship never seen before … It is not an autocracy; that is too benevolent. It is not a dictatorship like others; that is too crude. I give it the name *controlocracy*.

Worker resistance might, therefore, be calling forth a leviathan of a sort that it cannot possibly contend with.

WARPED DEVELOPMENT

Yet, despite the government's clear progress in social control, some of which I have documented in previous chapters, I submit that a "controlocracy" is unlikely to ever be more than a dream. As Shue and Thornton (2017, 8) argue, an overemphasis on new "pillars of order" in places like China has the effect of exaggerating "the fixity of political institutions, while eliding the inherent systemic fragilities, maladaptive responses, and 'patterned anarchy' that actually compromise the core of much of political life." Change does not stop with the government's first reactions to the challenges it faces – or its second or third or fourth reactions. In fact, the reactions themselves have complex repercussions. To quote Shue and Thornton again, evolutionary biologists have shown us that "accommodations in one realm of activity that appear positively adaptive in response to pressures or shifts in the short term may prove maladaptive over a longer time frame," and, for politics, this means that we require an "approach attuned to recognizing the internal strains of criss-crossed and intersecting trends within political systems" (Shue and Thornton 2017, 11, 13). When it comes to the CCP's handling of worker resistance, adaptive as the Party might be, it seems to be adapting itself out of shape in the long run. It is *warping* itself in the sense that it is constantly making suboptimal choices, and these choices have the potential to add up, to interact, and to throw plans off course. Shue and Thornton suggest that a "braided stream," with its implications of sequential advancement across multiple dimensions, is a better analogy for how governance evolves than a branching tree (Shue and Thornton 2017, 20). This makes sense. But perhaps a tree surviving and growing but twisted out of shape – bulging around irritants in its bark, ducking under power lines, and struggling to get a grip on loose soil – better captures how the Chinese government has handled the pressure of industrial conflict. The tree may not break anytime in the foreseeable future, although this is always possibility, but it will probably not loom straight and tall over the forest either. It will continue to struggle to endure in inhospitable conditions.

There are several reasons to believe this warping – or twisting, bulging, ducking, and struggling to get a grip – will become only more pronounced as the years and decades pass. Most basically, Chinese authorities are putting tremendous fiscal resources into cajoling and coercing their citizens that could be used much more productively in other areas. As shown in Figure 8.1, spending on public security in China (local and central combined) has closely tracked spending on national defense over the past decade-plus, overtaking defense spending in 2010 and staying narrowly ahead ever since. Of course, as noted in Chapter 6, the category of "public security" includes a wide range of expenses. A significant – if still minor – portion of this increase has been devoted to the People's Armed Police (the focus of my statistical analysis in Chapter 6). Given that courts, too, seem to be counted in the public security line item, responsiveness also has a very real price tag. It is no wonder that military

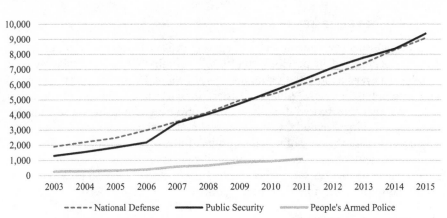

FIGURE 8.1 Spending on public security versus national defense (100 million RMB).
Source: *China Statistical Yearbooks* 2004–16.

analysts view China's foreign policy ambitions as constrained by domestic
insecurities (Ross 2009). Less discussed are the ways that its social ambitions,
too, are constrained. Y. Xie (2013) argues that "stability maintenance" has
exerted a particular squeeze on poorer areas of the country, despite early 2000s
fiscal reforms. In a piece describing what this squeeze looks like in practice,
dissident journalist He (2012) notes how in 2009, the Pearl River Delta city of
Huizhou spent 36.64 million RMB on leasing security monitors while the city's
fund for eleven social services totaled only somewhat more, 50.4 million RMB,
and Guangdong as a whole spent 4.4 billion RMB on stability maintenance
compared to just 3.52 billion RMB on social insurance. J. Pan (2020) demonstrates that the Minimum Livelihood Guarantee Scheme (or *dibao*) has been
used by local authorities to monitor and discipline potential protesters, i.e., that
assistance itself has, in some instances, been turned repressive. This redirection
of *dibao* to "troublemakers," she shows, has caused a backlash from other
people who are being denied the benefits they deserve. Worker resistance is not
the only cause of this imbalance in priorities. Other groups are straining and
misdirecting budgets with their protests.[2] But as Chapter 6 showed, labor is
having a distinct impact. There are also non-political reasons for funds to go
where they go, including the need to train a modern crime-fighting force and
strengthen the rule of law (Liebman 2007; Scoggins and O'Brien 2015). But the
focus on stability maintenance undermines these goals, too. Vladimir Putin's
Russia provides a cautionary example of where this focus can lead: increased
attention to "exceptional" law enforcement tasks have come at the expense of

---

[2] S. Wang (2010), for example, has shown how border regions tend to spend more on armed police
and militias.

improvements in handling "routine" tasks in Russia (B. D. Taylor 2011). In this way, the politicization of policing in China continues to hamper the sort of "order" prized by ordinary citizens, causing discontent (Trevaskes 2010). One counterpoint to Ringen's (2016) argument then is this: what could China accomplish if it was not trying to control everything? Would it not be stronger?

Meanwhile, the government is being forced to reorganize its class alliances – but in an incomplete manner that leaves no one satisfied. In the face of workplace unrest, the Party has swung from welcoming entrepreneurs into its ranks to doing the same while *also* hesitantly seeking the support of workers. Outreach to new groups builds a valuable nimbleness. But it also entails strains. Capitalists grumble that the workers' needs are prioritized over theirs. A manager at an IT company in Shanghai complained to me: "It is hard to win lawsuits against workers. The courts mostly side with employees" (Interview 11). One of his colleagues similarly said, "The government protects workers much, much more. Today, in over 90 percent of [legal] cases, the company will lose" (Interview 10). Someone employed in human resources at a firm in Wuxi commented, "The government intervenes in things that it should leave to the market and leaves to the market things that are its responsibility. Some things could be worked out by bosses and workers and do not need to be decided at the top" (Interview 24).[3] These are just anecdotes. It is difficult to obtain a good overall sense of the perceptions of domestic businesses. However, the American Chamber of Commerce in Shanghai, which vociferously opposed the 2008 Labor Contract Law, produces an annual report on China's investment climate based on a survey of foreign firms. It is not a perfect guide to the opinion of domestic capitalists, of course. But the report's findings are intriguing: its 2008–9 version found that companies listed the following among their top "issues" in China: wage increases (34 percent of respondents and the third-rated issue), poor employee retention (19 percent), shortages of adequate personnel (17 percent) and the difficulties of "social compliance" (3 percent) (The American Chamber of Commerce in Shanghai and Booz & Company 2009). The Chamber's 2018 report, meanwhile, found that the leading reason that the companies surveyed were leaving the country or slowing their investment in it was "rising costs, including labor" (33 percent and 25 percent, respectively) (American Chamber of Commerce China, and Bain & Company 2018). Naturally, companies realize that wages and labor shortages are to some extent beyond the government's control. But to the degree that these developments are seen (rightly or wrongly) as resulting from authorities favoring workers, businesspeople are becoming disillusioned with the Chinese government. This weakens a core base of support cultivated by the regime and

---

[3] Notably, there were also businesspeople who felt the government should take more proactive measures to protect workers' rights. See sections of Interviews 24, 36, and 32. This was in part seen as a way of leveling the playing field for those businesses that played by the rules.

prevents Beijing from assembling the sort of counterrevolutionary coalition described by Slater and Smith (2016).[4] In fact, we can perhaps think of China as an example of failed "counterrevolutionary conversion," to use these scholars' term or, perhaps, a missed opportunity at what Kohli (2004) calls a "cohesive-capitalist" state. Rather than consolidating elites around it, the Party must continually intimidate and bribe its entrepreneurs into line. None challenge the CCP, but their enthusiasm for it is diminished.

At the same time, the state has not brought labor into its fold by a long shot. In an influential study of Tianjin, Blecher (2002) found that the state's new market ideology exercised a powerful influence over workers, especially younger ones. Other scholars have argued explicitly or implicitly that China's new labor laws are intended to build state hegemony and have succeeded in this project to some degree (E. Friedman and Lee 2010; Hui 2018; Lee and Shen 2011; Stockmann and Gallagher 2011; in the somewhat different context of rural politics, see Whiting 2017). Yet, survey research by Gallagher (2006, 2017, chap. 5) finds that workers who actually use the legal system become disenchanted with the law, even if their own confidence in navigating the system increases (she calls this "informed disenchantment"). In 2010, the Chinese General Social Survey (CGSS) conducted by Renmin University asked how much citizens trusted courts, the national government, and the central government, and in 2011, it asked about local governments only (Renmin University 2015). People without local household registration, i.e., migrants, were less likely to express trust than the national average in each instance. See Figure 8.2. Between 2010 and 2015, the CGSS further asked: "In general, do you think society is currently fair or not?" Again, migrants consistently lagged six to eight points behind the national average in their evaluation of fairness. See Figure 8.3. These are not encouraging figures for the government. In a qualitative study, Hui (2018, 28) identifies three groups of workers: those who "actively grant consent" to legal hegemony, those who are indifferent, ambivalent, or critical and give only passive consent, and radicals who challenge "both the capitalist economy and the party-state." The potential growth of the final group represents a vulnerability for the system. Making yet more state commitments to fairness but failing to follow through on them could further swell the ranks of both the second and third groups. Dickson (2016) and Gallagher (2017, chap. 6) make this point in different ways in their recent books. If China's constitution declares that the country is "a socialist state under the people's democratic dictatorship led by the working class and based on the alliance of workers and peasants" and the Party was entrusted with representing the "most advanced forces of production" in the 1990s, then who does it now represent? Pepinsky (2009) shows that whereas Suharto's regime collapsed

---

[4] For more on the importance and challenges of maintaining elite cohesion, see Reuter and Szakonyi (2019).

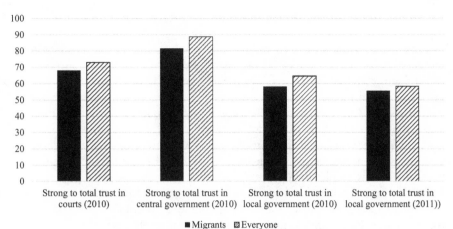

FIGURE 8.2 Levels of trust in different government institutions.
Above: Percentages of respondents who answered that they have "strong" or "total" trust in various government institutions in the 2010 and 2011 rounds of the Chinese General Social Survey (questions d301–303 in 2010 and a34a1 in 2011). Migrants are defined as people who say they do not have local household registration (question a21).

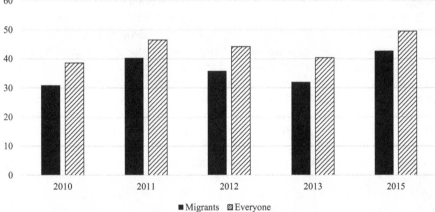

FIGURE 8.3 Beliefs that society is fair.
Above: Percentages of respondents who responded that society is "relatively fair" or "completely fair" (combined) in the 2010, 2011, 2012, 2013, and 2015 rounds of the Chinese General Social Survey (question a34a1). Migrants are, again, defined as as people who say they do not local household registration (question a21).

following the 1997 East Asian Financial Crisis, divided by clashing interests, namely fixed versus mobile capital, Mahatir's Malaysia weathered the same economic headwinds successfully because of its robust alliance of fixed capital and labor. What groups will rally to the CCP's aid in a crisis?

Finally, and relatedly, perfectly coordinating carrots and sticks is difficult, especially over an extended period, even when just labor is concerned. Increased use of the state's repressive capacity can destroy the trust built by increased responsive capacity. Thus, one of the striking workers I interviewed at a handbag factory in Zhongshan mentioned in Chapter 6 said of the local government's detentions of her co-workers, "Before this happened, this was only the sort of thing I saw in television shows about the [pre-revolutionary] past. Who would think this kind of thing could still happen today? The government here is too black" (Interview 60). Meanwhile, increased responsive capacity may encourage the very activism that repression is meant to deter. It is no accident that employment lawsuits doubled in 2008, the same year that the Labor Contract Law and Labor Dispute Mediation and Arbitration Law went into effect – or that more boundary-spanning activism in the streets soon followed suit (although the global financial crisis likely also played a role in the spike) (see again Elfstrom and Kuruvilla 2014). Pfaff (2006) argues that East Germany's combination of an extraordinarily comprehensive surveillance system in the form of the Stasi and massive outlays for improved quality of life – community gardens and dachas, etc. – far from nipping dissent in the bud, had the effect of pushing it out of the public sphere and into "niche" communities that the enhanced welfare state made possible, where it awaited the right spark to explode into resistance. The decision by East German authorities to essentially pursue bread and guns at once and not acknowledge a trade-off, also, of course, severely strained the state's budget (Pfaff 2006). Although China has not made the same investments as Eastern Germany, one can imagine a similar dynamic playing out. For repressive and responsive capacity to be deployed in a complementary not mutually undermining manner may take more skill than even China's technocrats can muster for long.

The country's regional models of control offer promising paths forward. More risk-taking in terms of government responsiveness, such as that seen in the Pearl River Delta but much, much more ambitious in scope and without an accompanying crackdown, might ultimately the best route for authorities, helping them institutionalize their various bids for worker support and get over the hump of entrenched worker skepticism (as argued by Estlund 2017; E. Friedman 2014b). But it would take a special leader to be ready to double down on worker needs, place business concerns to the side, and weather high levels of unrest on the road to a more comprehensive solution to pressing social issues. Meanwhile, officials in areas like the Yangtze River Delta are unlikely to quickly take up the cause of their counterparts in hotspots. Instead, they will probably engage in what Koesel and Bunce (2013) call "diffusion proofing" or exercise what Gibson (2013) dubs "border control" to prevent the contagion of resistance from spreading to their jurisdictions. As a Shenzhen-based corporate social responsibility officer observed to me, "The logic in Zhejiang and Jiangsu is this: if there are strikes in Guangdong, then this shows that there are problems with management in Guangdong. People [in the north] don't see the worker's voice as something to strive for" (Interview 67). Indeed, a Jiangsu labor bureau officer said, "So, regarding Guangdong's issues ... I can't say they definitely won't crop up here. But we do a lot to prevent them from occurring. If one day we come to have the same problems as they do, this shows we have not done our work well" (Interview 113). Thus, new approaches like the Pearl River Delta's, can certainly spread, but they do so slowly and unevenly, distorting their effect. There is no rapid, straight route onward.

INTERNATIONAL COMPARISONS

What does the Chinese experience described in this book represent more broadly? How far do my findings travel? One line of thinking is that the country is in the same situation as *laissez faire* industrializing countries in North America and Europe were a century or more ago, with their brutal working conditions and open class conflict. But the Chinese leadership clearly sees its policy options as more limited than than the choices those capitalist trailblazers eventually conceived. It has showed no signs, in particular, of being open to a New Deal–like institutional accommodation of worker power (Estlund 2017), let alone a full-scale social democratic de-commodification of services like healthcare, as in Scandinavia (Esping-Andersen 1990). Another common line of comparison is with China's authoritarian developmental state neighbors, particularly mid-twentieth-century Taiwan and South Korea. In Korea, especially, militant worker mobilization, aided by networks of students, churchgoers, and dissidents helped usher in democracy in the face of harsh repression (Koo 2001). Taiwan went from dependent but closely state-coordinated economic growth and relative political quiescence to international isolation and contending with an increasingly rowdy opposition and, like Korea, eventual democratization (Gold 1986). But Beijing appears to be actively stifling any initiatives that might lead it down the trail of political liberalization blazed by these countries (Minzner 2018, chap. 5). It is also much more unequal than they were decades ago, when they began to democratize – and it has the potential to get worse on this score (Alvaredo et al. 2017; WID – World Inequality Database n.d.). For a period, in the 1990s and early 2000s, there was considerable concern about what was described as the potential "Latin Americanization" of the country, meaning that China might continue to develop along some dimensions but be held back by sharp cleavages: between the countryside and city and, within cities, between haves (the new middle class) and have-nots (migrant workers) (Gilboy and Higenbotham 2004; The Jamestown Foundation 2006). This discussion has died down with China's rise on the world stage. However, as the economy now begins to slow again, even as the country races ahead technologically, and, crucially, as the country's system becomes more open to certain popular demands even as it reacts more harshly than any time in recent memory to organized opposition and puts off more far-reaching social changes, this debate may deserve revisiting – but with a different group of international comparisons in mind. The best group to situate the People's Republic within is arguably that of *post-state socialist authoritarian regimes*. In the next section, I turn to these countries and China's place among them. I begin with the dilemmas faced by authoritarian regimes in general when they seek to control worker resistance (compared to their democratic counterparts), but I quickly focus on the particular difficulties – and opportunities – experienced by autocrats trying to bring labor into line after their governments have abandoned egalitarian projects.

DYNAMICS OF POST-STATE SOCIALIST AUTHORITARIAN REGIMES

If every kind of regime is pressured by worker resistance, none feels this pressure in the same way. In authoritarian regimes like China's, critiques of society, once developed and articulated in public, cannot be safely channeled through ostensibly "neutral" institutions. A whole body of work examines the ways in which the post war industrial relations system in the United States, which treated workplaces as societies in miniature, with collective bargaining serving as a sort of "legislature" for resolving issues between purportedly "equal" parties, directed the energies of unions toward narrow procedural issues and away from disruption (e.g., Klare 1978; Stone 1981). Elections can play a similar role. Thus, Teitelbaum (2011) shows how India and Sri Lanka both successfully "mobilize restraint" from workers today by cultivating strong ties between unions and political parties. Robertson and Teitelbaum (2011), meanwhile, demonstrate that foreign direct investment places strains on all kinds of societies, but results in more protests in autocracies than democracies. Dictators lack processes that can co-opt labor at arm's length. Tensions in society are therefore absorbed directly into the body of the state.[5]

But China is not just authoritarian. It is a *post-state socialist* authoritarian regime, meaning, specifically, that its ruling party *once* led in the name of the working class and economic decisions were *once* made in large part through "bureaucratic coordination" but are now made through market coordination[6] – and, of course, the minimal prerequisites of democracy are absent on top of all this. The economies of many such regimes are today popularly dubbed "state capitalist," meaning that their governments still control key

---

[5] What have become known as "competitive authoritarian regimes" or "hybrid" regimes may constitute a partial exception (Diamond 2002; Levitsky and Way 2010; Robertson 2011). China, however, is most definitely not such a regime. Its representative institutions have received new attention as sources of interest aggregation (e.g., Truex 2016), but they are by no means competitive or capable of attracting the energies of workers and others.

[6] Here and throughout the book, I use the terms "state socialist" and "post-state socialist" to acknowledge that the centrally planned, undemocratic "socialism" these governments once practiced does not exhaust the possibilities of socialist governance. Other, more participatory,

corporations directly or indirectly, even if those corporations compete and accumulate profits in a manner not possible under the countries' old, planned economies.[7] Because of the extraordinary spread of state socialist experiments during the twentieth century and the difficulty their successor states have frequently experienced establishing liberal institutions, the world is littered with governments of this type (for discussions, see Bunce 1999; Bunce and Wolchik 2011; Kornai 1992). If we leave out the Democratic People's Republic of Korea and Cuba for still being essentially state socialist, twenty-nine states were listed as "socialist" in 1987 by Kornai (1992) and were *also* listed as "not free" or only "partly free" by the 2018 Freedom House rankings (see Freedom House 2018). Examples include Russia, Belarus, Egypt, Algeria, Vietnam, Ethiopia, and Zimbabwe.

Post-state socialist authoritarian regimes like China's and those listed above fuse economic and political power in an especially transparent manner. Note that I say *transparent*: long-standing capitalist governments, both authoritarian and democratic, mix business and politics, too, and with equally socially destructive results. However, they rarely do so in such an upfront manner, as it was never part of their very *raison d'être*. The openness of post-state socialist regimes in this regard is a significant vulnerability. Under the state socialism of the past, as Burawoy and Lukács (1992, 20–22) note, when enterprise bosses appropriated surpluses from producers by virtue of being planners responsible for the "collective interest" (rather than simply by virtue of owning the means of production), ideological justifications for appropriation were more easily exposed as just that. Moreover, every protest against a firm became a protest against the government. Given that even after state socialism has been replaced by post-state socialism, many firms continue to be directly owned by the state ("state capitalism" again) or, if state assets have been sold, by officials-turned-businesspeople, the standoff remains the same as it was. Although much in such societies has been marketized, workers and the state clash with less of a private sector buffer than their counterparts in regimes without the same legacies.

The success of state socialist and post-state socialist governments in heading off the establishment of independent trade unions also presents a paradoxical challenge for leaders. Non-democracies vary widely in their treatment of unions, from the blatantly exclusionary approaches of right-wing dictatorships to the more inclusionary corporatist ones of their left-populist counterparts (for

---

paths are available. Given that "communism" is a theoretical end goal that few states claim to have reached even at their most utopian moments, the terms "communist" and "post-communist" seem inappropriate as substitutes. For more on bureaucratic coordination, market coordination, and coordination through institutions like family ties, see Kornai (1992).

[7] For a seminal discussion of "state capitalism," see The Economist (2012). This definition of state capitalism, it should be noted, is distinct from the use of the term by some Marxists as a criticism of the economy of the Soviet Union, as in the writings of people, such as Mandel (1951) and Pannekoek (1936).

a review, see Caraway, Crowley, and Cook 2015). However, under state socialism, with a few important exceptions like Yugoslavia (see, for example, Grdešić 2015), autocrats generally prefer to maintain industrial "preemptive organizations" (Johnson 1970b). In China, this took the form of the ACFTU, the official successor to radical unions that supported the 1949 revolution. Besides distributing welfare benefits, organizations like this were effective at "serving the regime's mobilization goals and ... inhibiting the formation of private loyalties" (Johnson 1970b, 19). *Post*-state socialist successor states have frequently retained such groups (this is especially well documented in the case of Russia, see Pringle and Clarke 2011; Robertson 2011). As their name suggests, preemptive organizations occupy the space that worker-led unions might otherwise, signing collective contracts, attending international conferences, etc. – and thereby making it difficult for more representative groups to do so (Gallagher 2015). In fact, old "legacy unions" have been described as "some of the most tenacious actors from an authoritarian past that survive transitions to democracy" – and they do even better under new nondemocratic regimes (Caraway 2012, 278). The catch is that government-controlled bodies are woefully ineffective at redirecting workplace conflict once it breaks out, because they do not have the workers' trust, something we have already discussed at length in the Chinese context (for more on this, see again E. Friedman 2014b). Authorities save themselves the headache of independent organizations but experience a worse headache in the form of uncontrolled and unpredictable contention – as witnessed, again, in China today.

Finally, and most basically, workplace mobilization in the aftermath of state socialism highlights a sharp disconnect between the regime's founding promises to workers and the country's current inequities. Whatever the frustrations felt by workers under the old system, the "radiant future" promised by radical efforts at social reform becomes the "radiant past" against which the present is judged (Burawoy and Lukács 1992). This is especially true for those governments that retain a nominally "communist" or "workers" or "socialist" party in power after the transition. Based on surveys conducted in several long-standing capitalist countries and several post-state socialist countries, Whyte (2010, chap. 4) finds that people in the latter group are more likely to find economic inequality undesirable and to link it to structural problems rather than individual merit. The same surveys show that China as a whole is something of a post-state socialist outlier: its citizens tolerate the concentration of wealth to a remarkable extent – more so even than some long-standing capitalist countries – and are skeptical of redistributionist measures (Whyte 2010, chap. 3). However, similar to the China General Social Survey findings cited above, Whyte notes China's urban unemployed and migrant workers are an exception to the exception and are deeply bitter about growing disparities (Whyte 2010, 107–14). And it is *these* people's discontent that is the focus of this book. Perry (2012, 292–93) argues that the "legitimacy of Chinese Communism rests ... not simply on alleged connections to an ancient civilization, but also on a revolution that promised dignity for its most down-trodden citizens." This promise is a double-edged sword; failing to fulfill it means loss of legitimacy with the Party's original constituency.

Post-state socialist authoritarian governance is thus marked by distinctive vulnerabilities to worker resistance – not necessarily more powerful than the challenges facing authorities in other contexts, but distinctive. At the same time, such regimes have advantages, too. They have often inherited from their old, planned economies a party and state structure that can pass down directives to its lower layers and monitor its agents up to a point, as China does. They have organs intact for delivering (imperfect) justice and (incomplete) coercion. And they frequently have some basic workplace protections in place to build upon. In fact, post-state socialist authoritarian regimes score marginally better than the world average on the four of the most consistently collected indicators relating to labor regulations in the World Bank's "Doing Business" survey, namely required additional overtime pay as a percentage of normal pay, premiums for weekend work, mandated paid annual leave for people with one year of tenure with a firm, and a minimum number of days of maternity leave (World Bank 2017). Resistance hits particular sore points for such governments, but they have the resources necessary to evolve. How they evolve, though, as in China, may make sense in the short term but be sub-optimal over time.

POST-STATE SOCIALIST AUTHORITARIAN REGIMES REACT TO WORKER RESISTANCE

Like China, other post-state socialist authoritarian regimes have both increased their repressive and responsive capacities in the face of worker resistance in recent years, confounding observers' expectations. In Egypt, for example, a country with a long history of labor mobilization under colonial rule, Gamal Abdel Nasser's revolutionary government came to a compromise with labor radicals in the 1950s: a jobs guarantee paired with a monopoly by the party-controlled Egyptian Trade Union Federation (ETUF) – an institution Nasser had originally avoided creating because it would grant *too much* power to workers (Beinin and Lockman 1998; Posusney 1997). As labor began to come under pressure from successive rounds of market reforms starting in the 1970s and accelerating in the 1980s and 1990s, the ETUF began to act with some limited autonomy from its state sponsors, stalling new enterprise privatization laws and labor legislation until better employment protections were included and the right to strike was expanded (Paczynska 2006; Taha 2014). Then, in the lead-up to the 2011 Tahrir Square protests, as strikes grew, sometimes aided by student activists, the government finally agreed to the formation of unions altogether independent of the ETUF, starting with a union of tax collectors (Bishara 2018). This showed remarkable state flexibility – more than can be imagined from China in the near future. At the same time, Egyptian authorities brought the full weight of their repressive apparatus to bear on activists in working class areas during the uprising in 2011, killing scores (A. Alexander and Bassiouny 2014). Through the short-lived democratically elected government of Mohamed Morsi and the new authoritarianism of Abdel Fattah el-Sisi, labor groups have persisted, but their allies have disappeared into prison and employees have frequently been exhorted to rein in their demands (Sabea 2014). Compared to worker-activists in nearby Tunisia, Egypt's remain weak and divided (Hartshorn 2018). Importantly, the ETUF has been remarkably resilient (if dull) and has drawn only closer to the regime, while Tunisia's legacy union has carved out an autonomous and powerful role for itself (Hartshorn 2018). Vietnamese workers, meanwhile, appear to be on the cusp of major union reforms, including the breakup of the country's official, party-controlled union federation into competing unions (or at least union-like shop floor organizations) (Bradsher 2015). If these changes come to pass, a milestone will have been reached. And the very discussion of this possibility shows considerable confidence on the part of authorities. But the last time Vietnam had a major strike wave, in 2006, the result was labor legislation that opened new channels for striking legally – but also brought with it a severe clampdown directed at labor-allied lawyers and others (Clarke 2006; Human Rights Watch 2009a; Kerkvliet 2011; Mantsios 2010; Trần 2013). For a period, Russian workers allied with local political elites to pressure central authorities (Evans 2016; Robertson 2011). Moscow has now largely managed to tame its independent unions, handing the state-dominated bodies it inherited from the Soviet Union the upper hand, but it still scrambles to stay ahead of incidents like a recent truck strike, watering down rules loathed by workers while detaining organizers (Coalson 2016; Pringle and Clarke 2011; Robertson 2011). Some see Russian workers moving from "defensive" demands to more offensive claims in the much the same manner as their Chinese counterparts, along with the same backsliding in recent years (Vinogradova, Kozina, and Cook 2012). But in pursuing these demands, the Russians will have few organizational resources. Wrangling with labor has been a persistent headache for Zimbabwean authorities. When, in 2015, leaders of the opposition-aligned Zimbabwe Congress of Trade Unions criticized a new law making it easier to fire workers, they were arrested before they could lead a planned demonstration, but the law was amended all the same (Dzirutwe 2015; ITUC 2015). And finally, Belarus, which has embraced the rhetoric if not the substance of its state socialist past more than many of its neighbors, had to back down on unpopular plans to reduce its social safety net and charge a "social parasite tax" in 2017 after unions (and eventually rightist groups) took to the streets of Minsk – though the government hunted down and arrested its proletarian critics, too (the Belarusian government's ability to withstand worker activism following disputed elections in 2020 remains to be seen at the time of this writing) (BBC 2017; Erickson 2017; Liasheva 2017). In all these instances, we observe states that are able to adapt. These governments do not, for the most part, wantonly open fire on protesters or assassinate union leaders as they do in, say, Colombia (Rochlin

2016), though instances like violence against Tahrir Square demonstrators mark exceptions (Alexander and Bassiouny 2014). Nor do they anxiously cede ground in every instance. Instead, they show a remarkable capacity both to rearrange their systems in modest ways in line with grievances and to hold the line on broader participation by workers in affairs of state, punishing activists who go too far. In fact, many post-state socialist authoritarian regimes have advanced further than China in both dimensions – greater displays of repressive and responsive capacity – providing valuable clues to where the People's Republic might go in the not-too-distant future. But few of these countries can be described as stable societies. None has come close to "solving" the issue of worker resistance. And some of their alterations may worsen the situation over the long haul. Given that they represent such a wide swath of the world, these regimes will powerfully influence the impact that working-class mobilization has in the twenty-first century.

FORGING AHEAD

The precedents of North America and Europe or certain of China's East Asian neighbors suggest that, when faced with labor unrest, countries may embark upon dramatic reforms of existing institutions, while the experience of Latin American nations in the 1990s points instead to backsliding and splitting as a likely outcome. Events in China and other post-state socialist authoritarian regimes highlight another path: steadily deepening contradictions and real change – but of a sort that is slow-moving and snaking from a long perspective, turning back on itself as much as it moves forward. More generally, the dynamics explored in this book and noted above in countries like Egypt and Vietnam remind us how in *all* societies seemingly opposite state responses to contention can occur at once and interact with each other. We need not restrict our analysis to the determinants of openings *versus* closures. Both may speed up and slow down in tandem. Moreover, alongside broad national trends in movement-building and state capacity-building, clashes between activists and authorities can generate complex forms of governance at various levels that mix progressive with reactionary elements and defy easy categorization. Today's Chinese political arrangements, like those of the other countries described above, are not an endpoint – a perfection of something or a sign of something's imminent failure – but merely a stop along the way. Examining *how* change occurs can be at least as illuminating as making predictions about its final destination. This book has set out to trace the process of change in Chinese labor politics up to this point, from grievances and opportunities for collective action in particular economic sectors to varying strike activity in different sorts of companies and areas of the country, to bureaucratic incentives for certain state reactions, to regional models of control, to national patterns of capacity-building and elite politics. But the situation is dynamic. Others should take the analysis further, revisiting the Chinese case with updated information or digging into other, similar cases in greater detail.

REASONS FOR OPTIMISM AND PESSIMISM

In 2017, nearly two years after completing most of my fieldwork for this book, I made a brief trip back to the Pearl River Delta. The crackdown of December 2015, when dozens of labor NGO leaders were detained and two were put on trial, had just passed. In less than a year, the next big round of repression would commence, ensnaring many more people. Meeting with me in the lobby of a once high-end but now deserted and dusty hotel, the head of one group commented, "I don't dare gather people together ... Recently, I was invited to a conference. But authorities forced the conference to be cancelled. I had to cancel my tickets. Two people came to my office and said I had to register before I did any further activities" (Interview ACT #3-1 March 2017). Regarding other activists in the region, he continued, "There are no NGOs taking part in strikes now ... People still talk about collective bargaining on WeChat [a popular social media application]. But nobody is *doing* this kind of programming" (Interview ACT # 3-1 March 2017). After our conversation, we each exited the hotel separately to avoid notice. One could be forgiven for taking a dim view of the future of China's nascent labor movement. Yet, the same activist quoted above also said, "Sometimes this is very tiring, this work. But then I interact with people at the bottom rungs of society, and [I feel that] I am really lucky that what I do has meaning" (Interview ACT #3-1 March 2017). He had not folded up his organization yet. Meanwhile, another activist noted to me the same year that "others have changed their programming, become essentially service workers" (Interview ACT #2-2 March 2017). But he said, "We still do a lot of collective bargaining ... We just do it more quietly than before" (Interview ACT #2-2 March 2017). Why the continued engagement on collective bargaining, I asked? He made a familiar argument: "It's faster. You can get more than the courts will give ... Workers don't believe in the law. It still makes sense to launch lawsuits over work injuries and stuff like that. But not other stuff" (Interview ACT #2-2 March 2017). This combative spirit holds a lot of promise for the future. Based on their continued mobilization, it seems that Chinese workers judge the rewards of taking action to be higher than the risk – at least for now. But they face a very challenging path ahead, as does the state that tries to manage them. How these contending forces evolve in response to each other is worthy of close attention from all concerned with China, with labor, and with social justice.

Appendices

Appendix 1
Interview Details

September–December 2014

1. Cab drivers and shop owners	Zhenjiang, Jiangsu
2. CSR activist	Hong Kong
3. Construction worker	Zhenjiang, Jiangsu
4. Class discussion	Beijing
5. Factory guards and others	Zhangjiagang, Jiangsu
6. Academic conference attendees	Beijing
7. Professor (phone call)	Chengdu, Sichuan
8. Professor	Hong Kong
9. Professor	Nanjing, Jiangsu
10. Technology company management	Shanghai
11. Technology company management	Shanghai
12. Labor NGO activist	Nanjing, Jiangsu
13. Job market security guard	Kunshan, Jiangsu
14. Job market employee	Kunshan, Jiangsu
15. Job market employee	Kunshan, Jiangsu
16. Job market employee	Kunshan, Jiangsu
17. Job market employee	Kunshan, Jiangsu
18. Professor	Shanghai
19. Apparel factory managers	Lianshui, Jiangsu
20. Labor NGO activist	Beijing
21. Migrant workers at job market	Nanjing, Jiangsu
22. Migrant workers at job market	Nanjing, Jiangsu
23. Academic and Party School instructor	Beijing
24. Factory manager from Wuxi	Suzhou, Jiangsu

25. Factory manager from Wuxi	Wuxi, Jiangsu
26. Foreign rule of law program manager	Shanghai
27. Trade union leader at SOE	Nanjing, Jiangsu
28. Professor	Suzhou, Jiangsu
29. Taxi driver	Kunshan, Jiangsu
30. Taxi driver	Nanjing, Jiangsu
31. Textile manufacturers assn. leader	Beijing
32. Apparel co. CSR manager (phone call)	Guangdong
33. Taxi driver	Zhangjiagang, Jiangsu
34. Taxi drivers	Zhangjiagang, Jiangsu
35. Taxi drivers	Shuyang, Jiangsu
36. Apparel co. CSR managers	Shanghai
37. Government think tank researcher	Nanjing, Jiangsu
38. Class discussion	Beijing
39. Workers at factory with runaway boss	Zhangjiagang, Jiangsu
40. Professor	Beijing
41. Professor	Beijing
42. Collector of migrant worker poetry	Suzhou, Jiangsu
43. Professor	Nanjing, Jiangsu
44. Discussion with students	Tianjin
45. Foreign CSR activist	Suzhou, Jiangsu
46. Labor NGO activist	Suzhou, Jiangsu
47. Professor	Nanjing, Jiangsu
48. NGO activist	Nanjing, Jiangsu
49. Professor and labor bureau official	Tianjin
50. Labor NGO activist	Nanjing, Jiangsu
51. Professor	Yangzhou, Jiangsu
52. Professor & govt. think tank researcher	Nanjing, Jiangsu
53. Professor & govt. think tank researcher	Yangzhou, Jiangsu
54. Labor bureau official, professors	Yangzhou, Jiangsu

January–April 2015

55. Labor NGO activists	Hong Kong
56. Labor NGO activist	Shenzhen, Guangdong
57. Professor	Hong Kong
58. Labor NGO activists	Hong Kong
59. Construction workers	Shenzhen, Guangdong
60. Striking handbag factory workers	Zhongshan, Guangdong
61. Striking handbag factory workers and local police	Zhongshan, Guangdong
62. Former union leader	Guangzhou, Guangdong
63. Labor NGO activists	Shenzhen, Guangdong
64. Labor lawyer	Shenzhen, Guangdong

65. Electronics factory CSR meeting — Shenzhen, Guangdong
66. Job market employee — Shenzhen, Guangdong
67. CSR activist — Shenzhen, Guangdong
68. Union staffers — Shenzhen, Guangdong
69. Union staffer — Shenzhen, Guangdong
70. Union staffer — Shenzhen, Guangdong
71. Professor — Nanjing, Jiangsu
72. Human rights activist — Hong Kong
73. Labor/rural activist — Beijing
74. Professor — Beijing
75. NGO activists — Guangzhou, Guangdong
76. Injured workers and NGO activist — Suzhou, Jiangsu
77. Labor NGO activist — Dongguan, Jiangsu
78. Labor NGO activist — Shenzhen, Guangdong
79. Labor NGO activist — Shenzhen, Guangdong
80. Labor NGO activist — Shenzhen, Guangdong
81. Electronics factory staff — Shenzhen, Guangdong
82. CSR activist — Hong Kong
83. Academic discussion — Guangzhou, Guangdong
84. Taxi driver — Guangzhou, Guangdong
85. Taxi driver — Nanjing, Jiangsu
86. Taxi driver — Shenzhen, Guangdong
87. Taxi driver — Nanjing, Jiangsu
88. Taxi driver — Nanjing, Jiangsu
89. Taxi driver — Shenzhen, Guangdong
90. Taxi driver — Nanjing, Jiangsu
91. Taxi driver — Nanjing, Jiangsu
92. Taxi driver — Nanjing, Jiangsu
93. Taxi driver — Nanjing, Jiangsu
94. Taxi driver — Shenzhen, Guangdong
95. Enterprise trade union leaders — Tianjin
96. Worker with injury — Shenzhen, Guangdong
97. Injured worker and NGO activist — Shenzhen, Guangdong
98. Injured worker and NGO activist — Shenzhen, Guangdong
99. Injured workers and NGO activist — Dongguan, Guangdong
100. Injured workers and NGO activist — Shenzhen, Guangdong
101. Trade union leader — Shenzhen, Guangdong
102. Professor — Shenzhen, Guangdong
103. Professor — Macau
104. Labor NGO activist — Panyu, Guangdong
105. People around electronics factory — Shenzhen, Guangdong
106. Striking workers at electronics factory — Shenzhen, Guangdong

July–August 2015

107. Labor arbitrators	Chongqing
108. Professor	Chongqing
109. Local official	Nanchong, Sichuan
110. Foxconn factory workers and taxi driver	Chongqing
111. NGO activist	Chongqing
112. Labor bureau official	Chongqing
113. Labor bureau official	Nanjing, Jiangsu
114. Returned migrant workers	Nanchong, Sichuan
115. Party School instructor	Beijing
116. Real estate developer	Nanchong, Sichuan
117. Statistics bureau employee	Nanchong, Sichuan
118. Taxi driver	Chengdu, Sichuan
119. Taxi driver	Chongqing
120. Taxi driver	Nanjing
121. Taxi driver	Chengdu, Sichuan
122. Taxi driver	Chongqing
123. Taxi driver	Chongqing
124. Taxi driver	Chongqing
125. Taxi driver	Chongqing
126. Taxi driver	Chongqing
127. Taxi driver	Chongqing
128. Taxi driver	Chongqing
129. Taxi driver	Chongqing
130. Taxi driver	Chongqing
131. Taxi driver	Chongqing
132. Taxi driver	Chongqing
133. Taxi driver	Chongqing
134. Taxi driver	Chongqing
135. Taxi driver	Chongqing
136. Taxi driver	Chongqing
137. Taxi driver	Chongqing
138. Professor	Chongqing
139. Professor	Chongqing
140. Taxi activist (phone call)	Chongqing
141. Labor lawyer	Chongqing

Additional Interviews: June–July 2011

TY TX #3. Taxi driver	Taiyuan, Shanxi
CQ TX #12. Taxi activist	Chongqing
XN TX #1. Taxi driver	Xianning, Hubei

XN TX #11. Taxi driver   Xianning, Hubei
GY TX #21. Taxi driver   Guiyang, Guizhou
GY TX #25. Taxi driver   Guiyang, Guizhou

Additional Interviews: March 2017

ACD #1 Beijing March 2017   Beijing
ACT #2-2 Shenzhen March 2017   Shenzhen, Guangdong
ACT #3 Shenzhen March 2017   Shenzhen, Guangdong
ACT #3-1 Guangzhou March 2017   Guangzhou, Guangdong
GOV #1 Beijing March 2017   Beijing
POS #1 Beijing March 2017   Beijing
POS #2 Shanghai March 2017   Shanghai
UOS #1 Shenzhen March 2017   Shenzhen, Guangdong

Appendix 2

Government Sources

Note: Multiple years of most of the yearbooks are used, so rather than list each year of each yearbook separately, a spread for each is indicated below. Publishing houses for local almanacs may alter from year to year. Sample publishing houses are listed.

NATIONAL STATISTICAL YEARBOOKS

Department of Population and Employment Statistics, National Bureau of Statistics. 2004–2013. *China Labour Statistical Yearbook*. Beijing: China Statistics Press.

Ministry of Finance of the People's Republic of China. 2003–2009. *Quanguo dishixian caizheng tongji ziliao [Financial statistics of cities and counties]*. Beijing: Zhongguo Caizheng Jingji Chubanshe.

National Bureau of Statistics. 1997–2014. *China Statistical Yearbook*. Beijing: China Statistics Press.

Research Department of All-China Federation of Trade Unions. 2004–2013. *China Trade Unions Statistical Yearbook*. Beijing: China Statistics Press.

PROVINCIAL AND PREFECTURAL YEARBOOKS

Changzhou Yearbook Compilation Committee. 2003–2012. *Changzhou Yearbook*. Changzhou, Jiangsu: Changzhou Nianjian She.

Dongguan Yearbook Compilation Committee. 2003–2012. *Dongguan Yearbook*. Guanzhou, Guangdong: Guangdong Renmin Chubanshe.

Foshan Yearbook Compilation Committee. 2003–2012. *Foshan Yearbook*. Guanzhou, Guangdong: Guangdong Renmin Chubanshe.

Guangdong Yearbook Compilation Committee. 2003–2012. *Guangdong Yearbook*. Guangzhou, Guangdong: Guangdong Nianjian She.

Guangzhou Yearbook Compilation Committee. 2003–2012. *Guangzhou Yearbook*. Guangzhou, Guangdong: Guangzhou Nianjian Chubanshe.

Huai'an People's Government. 2003–2012. *Huai'an Yearbook*. Beijing: Fangzhi Chubanshe.

Huizhou People's Government. 2003–2012. *Huizhou Yearbook*. Guangzhou, Guangdong: Guangdong Renmin Chubanshe.

Jiangmen Yearbook Compilation Committee. 2003–2012. *Jiangmen Yearbook*. Beijing: Fangzhi Chubanshe.

Jiangsu Yearbook Compilation Committee. 2003–2012. *Jiangsu Yearbook*. Nanjing, Jiangsu: Jiangsu Nianjian Zazhi Chubanshe.

Nanjing Yearbook Compilation Committee. 2003–2012. *Nanjing Yearbook*. Nanjing, Jiangsu: Nanjing Nianjian Bianji Bu.

Nantong Yearbook Compilation Committee. 2003–2012. *Nantong Yearbook*. Beijing: Fangzhi Chubanshe.

Shenzhen Yearbook Compilation Committee. 2003–2012. *Shenzhen Yearbook*. Shenzhen, Guangdong: Shenzhen She.

Suzhou Yearbook Compilation Committee. 2003–2012. *Suzhou Yearbook*. Suzhou, Jiangsu: Suzhou Daxue Chubanshe.

Taizhou Yearbook Compilation Committee. 2003–2012. *Taizhou Yearbook*. Beijing: Fangzhi Chubanshe.

Wuxi Yearbook Compilation Committee. 2003–2012. *Wuxi Yearbook*. Beijing: Fangzhi Chubanshe.

Zhaoqing Yearbook Compilation Committee. 2003–2012. *Zhaoqing Yearbook*. Beijing: Guangming Ribao Chubanshe.

Zhenjiang Yearbook Compilation Committee. 2003–2012. *Zhenjiang Yearbook*. Beijing: Fangzhi Chubanshe.

Zhongshan Yearbook Compilation Committee. 2003–2012. *Zhongshan Yearbook*. Shenyang, Liaoning: Liaoning Minzu Chubanshe.

Zhuhai Yearbook Compilation Committee. 2003–2012. *Zhuhai Yearbook*. Guangzhou, Guangdong: Guangdong Jiaoyu Chubanshe.

Appendix 3

Websites and Search Terms for China Strikes Dataset

In 2017, a research assistant double-checked the completeness of the China Strikes dataset using a fixed set of search terms and sites. This had the result of adding over 400 incidents. The following websites, which include dissident sources and foreign and domestic media, were analyzed: Baidu News (first five pages of results), Boxun, Epoch Times, Google News (first five pages), Ming Pao, Southern Media Group (Nanfang Wang), Xinhua News Agency, and Zhongguo Molihua Geming (after 2011). Each source was searched for the same set of keywords for each year between 2003 and 2012: [year] + (工人, 农民工, or 员工) + (罢工、聚集、抗议、静坐、示威、拘留、警察、血汗钱、横幅、维权、封路、拖欠、堵塞交通、赔偿、政府、裁员、or 工伤). The websites of the Associated Press, Agence France Presse, and Reuters, and other sources were used to confirm stories where possible.

Appendix 4

Dictionary of Words Used in Yearbook Content Analysis

SOCIAL CONFLICT

上访
不稳定
信访
冲突
抗议
政治事件
敏感
矛盾
示威
纠纷
维稳
群体事件
群体性事件
调解
邪教
重点人

COMPANIES

企业
公司
单位

LABOR ISSUES

下岗
农民工
劳动者
劳资
劳资争议
劳资纠纷
外来人
失业
工人
拖欠
拖薪
流动人口
集体协商
集体合同

POLICING INNOVATION

信息化
创新
协调
安全感
新社会管理
满意度
监督
综合治理
综合管理
风险评估

ROUTINE POLICING

事故
交通
刑事
吸毒
打黑
暴力
杀人
毒品
消防
灭火
盗窃
破案

禁毒
赌博
酒后开车
醉酒驾车
黑社会
黄赌毒
黑恶犯罪

Appendix 5

Variation in Claims Made in Mediation, Arbitration, and Court Cases

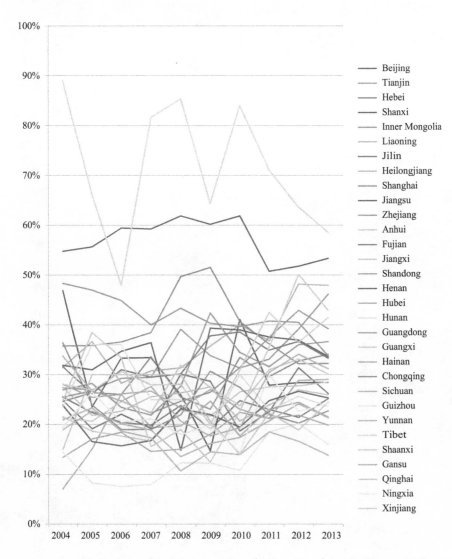

FIGURE A5.1 (a) Cases involving remuneration. (b) Cases involving insurance. (c) Cases involving lay-offs.

Above: the percentages of total disputes in different provinces featuring different claims. Lines represent individual provinces. In one instance, Guangxi in 2008, the number of cases recorded as featuring insurance issues exceeded the total number of "accepted cases." This observation was dropped, as it likely reflected a reporting error.

Source: *China Labour Statistical Yearbooks* 2004–13.

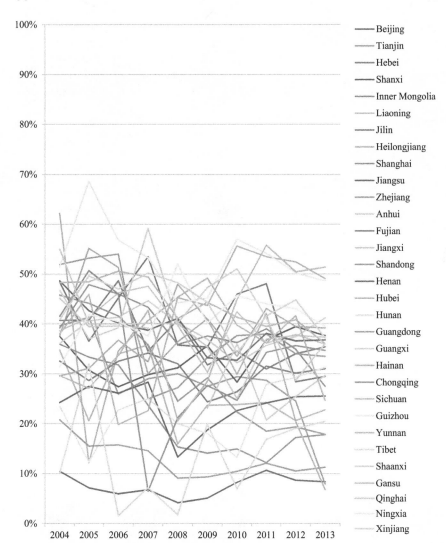

FIGURE A5.1 *(cont.)*

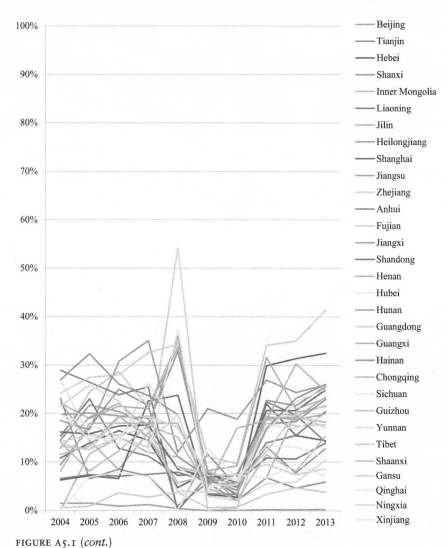

FIGURE A5.1 *(cont.)*

Appendix 6

Strikes, Protests, and Riots and People's Armed Police Spending 2003–2009

	(1) Δ PAP Spending (1M RMB)	(2) Δ PAP Spending (1M RMB)
Δ Strikes	4.698[*]	4.806[*]
	(0.656)	(0.706)
Log GDP per Capita		53.95
		(27.56)
% Migrant		−0.319
		(1.675)
% SOE		−0.419
		(4.076)
Labor NGOs		10.74[*]
		(2.266)
Collective Contracts		0.000247
		(0.000391)
Population		0.00530
		(0.00402)
% Urban		−0.206
		(0.919)
Constant	88.22[*]	−462.9
	(12.31)	(239.1)
N	176	172
R^2	0.0426	0.3816

Robust standard errors in parentheses. [*] $p < 0.05$.
Sources: *Quanguo dishixian caizheng tongji ziliao [Financial statistics of cities and counties]* collections from 2003 to 2009 for PAP spending, China Strikes (2017) for strikes, *China Labour Statistical Yearbooks* from 2004 to 2013 for dispute outcomes, *China Trade Unions Yearbooks* 2004 to 2013 for collective contracts, a list of NGOs and their founding dates provided to the author by China Labour Bulletin for labor NGOs, and *China Statistical Yearbooks* from 2004 to 2013 for everything else.

Appendix 7

Strikes, Protests, and Riots and Formally Adjudicated Employment Dispute Outcomes 2003–2012

	(1) Δ Pro-Worker	(2) Δ Split	(3) Δ Pro-Business	(4) Δ Pro-Worker	(5) Δ Split	(6) Δ Pro-Business
Δ Strikes	79.73* (25.96)	110.1* (12.96)	3.809 (5.746)	129.8* (43.45)	66.19* (20.47)	2.087 (7.034)
Log GDP per Capita				-283.2 (313.9)	-300.0 (297.9)	-252.3 (166.9)
% Migrant				-32.73* (11.65)	-55.75 (39.05)	-5.441 (4.146)
% SOE				-12.27 (96.38)	-183.9 (131.9)	-75.33 (42.86)
Labor NGOs				-106.4 (68.97)	137.6* (49.07)	9.431 (20.11)
Collective Contracts				-0.00767 (0.00505)	-0.00779 (0.00554)	-0.00309 (0.00182)
Population				0.0934 (0.0663)	0.0941 (0.0718)	0.0135 (0.0231)
% Urban				41.85* (17.87)	83.01* (32.30)	28.81* (9.542)
% Remuneration				-509.1 (2,103.5)	4,779.0 (2,974.5)	904.3 (624.2)
Constant	234.7* (92.03)	810.4* (210.9)	148.4* (57.50)	1,761.8 (2,090.3)	75.12 (2,633.7)	1,597.8 (1,273.1)
N	279	279	279	275	275	275
R^2	0.0349	0.0329	0.0006	0.0858	0.1209	0.0780

Robust standard errors in parentheses. * $p < 0.05$.

Sources: *China Strikes* (2017) for strikes, *China Labour Statistical Yearbooks* from 2004 to 2013 for dispute outcomes and the percent of disputes focused on remuneration, *China Trade Unions Yearbooks* 2004 to 2013 for collective bargaining agreements, and a list of NGOs and founding dates provided to the author by China Labour Bulletin, and *China Statistical Yearbooks* from 2004 to 2013 for everything else.

Appendix 8

Formally Adjudicated Employment Disputes as the Independent Variable

	(1) Δ PAP Spending	(2) Δ Pro-Worker	(3) Δ Split	(4) Δ Pro-Business
Δ Disputes	5.022*	150.7*	85.50*	4.010
	(0.736)	(43.83)	(24.40)	(9.375)
Log GDP per Capita	85.53*	96.81	788.1*	−1.512
	(32.98)	(461.4)	(378.4)	(184.1)
% Migrant	−2.049	−39.67	−132.3*	−28.34*
	(3.484)	(27.98)	(52.28)	(9.849)
% SOE	2.386	80.36	−574.2	−269.1
	(27.52)	(591.9)	(621.8)	(256.8)
Labor NGOs	10.57	24.44	454.7	44.74
	(6.309)	(180.4)	(390.9)	(92.98)
Collective Contracts	−0.000406	−0.00703	−0.00474	−0.000439
	(0.000615)	(0.00536)	(0.00539)	(0.00264)
Population	0.0305	−5.272	−6.706	−1.330
	(0.0963)	(4.736)	(7.627)	(2.141)
% Urban	1.509*	42.13	40.39	19.70
	(0.726)	(37.02)	(34.44)	(14.91)
% Remuneration		−6,499.3	7,502.7	33.29
		(6,088.3)	(6,120.7)	(1,294.7)
Provincial FE	Yes	Yes	Yes	Yes
Constant	−937.3	21,978.5	22,215.4	6,801.0
	(601.0)	(23,368.3)	(33,721.8)	(9,934.0)
N	172	275	275	275
R^2	0.246	0.146	0.081	0.053

Standard errors in parentheses. *$p < 0.05$.
Sources: *Quanguo dishixian caizheng tongji ziliao [Financial statistics of cities and counties]* collections from 2003 to 2009 for PAP spending, *China Labour Statistical Yearbooks* from 2004 to 2013 for dispute outcomes and the percent of disputes focused on remuneration, *China Trade Unions Yearbooks* 2004 to 2013 for collective contracts, a list of NGOs and their founding dates provided to the author by China Labour Bulletin for labor NGOs, and *China Statistical Yearbooks* from 2004 to 2013 for everything else.

Appendix 9

Using the Arellano Bond Estimator

	(1) PAP Spending	(2) Pro-Worker	(3) Split	(4) Pro-Business
PAP Spending (L1)	0.469* (0.0872)			
Pro-Worker (L1)		0.227 (0.118)		
Split (L1)			0.240 (0.144)	
Pro-Business (L1)				0.222 (0.137)
Δ Strikes (Instrumented)	4.594* (2.182)	−41.65 (27.54)	−32.12 (31.99)	−53.78* (12.94)
Log GDP per Capita	246.0* (53.81)	1,612.4* (480.1)	1,343.3* (599.4)	405.1 (217.9)
% Migrant	4.163 (4.255)	−108.8* (37.47)	−48.11 (70.15)	−24.66 (14.31)
% SOE	−14.10 (66.47)	−312.2 (615.7)	−2,696.1* (1,094.1)	−794.9 (474.2)
Labor NGOs	35.59* (12.52)	754.7* (317.7)	1,991.1* (613.4)	517.6* (198.0)
Collective Contracts	0.00119 (0.000910)	0.00840 (0.00688)	0.0102 (0.00668)	0.00657 (0.00590)
Population	0.113 (0.160)	−8.303 (5.978)	0.103 (7.363)	−0.609 (2.538)
% Urban	0.152 (1.226)	67.63* (33.98)	−12.01 (28.46)	−3.144 (10.29)
% Remuneration		−2,765.5 (6,336.8)	1,0448.2 (7,120.4)	761.5 (1,361.0)
Constant	−2,702.4* (1,106.9)	23,982.6 (28,428.0)	1,903.0 (31,854.4)	4,147.0 (10,781.4)

Robust standard errors in parentheses. $^{*}p < 0.05$.

Sources: *Quanguo dishixian caizheng tongji ziliao [Financial statistics of cities and counties]* collections from 2003 to 2009 for PAP spending, *China Labour Statistical Yearbooks* from 2004 to 2013 for dispute outcomes and the percent of disputes focused on remuneration, *China Trade Unions Yearbooks* 2004 to 2013 for collective contracts, a list of NGOs and their founding dates provided to the author by China Labour Bulletin for labor NGOs, and *China Statistical Yearbooks* from 2004 to 2013 for everything else.

Appendix 10

Accounting for Regional Biases in Reporting with Provincial Fixed Effects

	(1) Δ PAP Spending	(2) Δ Pro-Worker	(3) Δ Split	(4) Δ Pro-Business
Δ Disputes	0.000652	0.299*	0.368*	0.0820*
	(0.00147)	(0.0372)	(0.0324)	(0.00589)
Log GDP per Capita	53.62	−0.367	139.5	−142.2
	(27.37)	(248.3)	(325.6)	(110.6)
% Migrant	−0.136	−16.33*	−34.59	−0.598
	(1.630)	(8.202)	(41.36)	(3.737)
% SOE	0.0577	29.67	−136.9	−65.48
	(4.113)	(49.69)	(90.82)	(36.48)
Labor NGOs	9.957*	−59.54*	130.3*	−0.989
	(3.140)	(13.35)	(16.62)	(11.54)
Collective Contracts	0.000293	−0.000210	−0.00348	−0.00278*
	(0.000386)	(0.00204)	(0.00349)	(0.00140)
Population	0.00549	0.00714	0.0177	0.000494
	(0.00403)	(0.0226)	(0.0425)	(0.0197)
% Urban	−0.332	−2.567	31.88	17.91*
	(0.905)	(10.93)	(25.47)	(6.813)
% Remuneration		−1,631.1	3,724.4	713.7*
		(996.7)	(2,298.3)	(353.6)
Constant	−459.1	648.7	−2,429.6	886.8
	(237.0)	(1,962.1)	(2,840.4)	(876.2)
N	172	275	275	275
R^2	0.3403	0.7116	0.6307	0.4568

Standard errors in parentheses. $^*p < 0.05$.

Sources: *Quanguo dishixian caizheng tongji ziliao [Financial statistics of cities and counties]* collections from 2003 to 2009 for PAP spending, *China Labour Statistical Yearbooks* from 2004 to 2013 for dispute outcomes and the percent of disputes focused on remuneration, *China Trade Unions Yearbooks* 2004 to 2013 for collective contracts, a list of NGOs and their founding dates provided to the author by China Labour Bulletin for labor NGOs, and *China Statistical Yearbooks* from 2004 to 2013 for everything else.

References

ACFTU. 2006. "Zhonghua Quanguo Zonggonghui Zhuya Zeren [Main Responsibilities of the All China Federation of Trade Unions]." www.acftu.net/template/10041/file.jsp?cid=61&aid=42616 (accessed September 17, 2020).

Alexander, Anne, and Mostafa Bassiouny. 2014. *Bread, Freedom, Social Justice: Workers and the Egyptian Revolution*. London: Zed Books.

Alexander, Peter, and Anita Chan. 2004. "Does China Have an Apartheid Pass System?" *Journal of Ethnic and Migration Studies* 30(4): 609–29.

Almond, Gabriel Abraham, and G. Bingham Powell. 1966. *Comparative Politics: A Developmental Approach*. Boston: Little Brown and Company.

Alvaredo, Facundo et al. 2017. "Global Inequality Dynamics: New Findings from WID.World." *American Economic Review* 107(5): 404–9.

Amenta, Edwin, Neal Caren, Elizabeth Chiarello, and Yang Su. 2010. "The Political Consequences of Social Movements." *Annual Review of Sociology* 36(1): 287–307.

Amenta, Edwin, and Drew Halfmann. 2000. "Wage Wars: Institutional Politics, WPA Wages, and the Struggle for U.S. Social Policy." *American Sociological Review* 65 (4): 506–28.

American Chamber of Commerce China, and Bain & Company. 2018. *2018 China Business Climate Survey Report*. Shanghai, China: American Chamber of Commerce.

The American Chamber of Commerce in Shanghai and Booz & Company. 2009. *China Manufacturing Competitiveness 2008–2009*. Shanghai.

Andreas, Joel. 2019. *Disenfranchised: The Rise and Fall of Industrial Citizenship in China*. New York: Oxford University Press.

Ang, Yuen Yuen. 2016. *How China Escaped the Poverty Trap*. Ithaca, NY, and London: Cornell University Press.

Anner, Mark, and Xiangmin Liu. 2015. "Harmonious Unions and Rebellious Workers: A Study of Wildcat Strikes in Vietnam." *Industrial and Labor Relations Review* 69 (1): 3–28.

Areddy, James T. 2014. "One Legacy of Tiananmen: China's 100 Million Surveillance Cameras." *WSJ*. https://blogs.wsj.com/chinarealtime/2014/06/05/one-legacy-of-tiananmen-chinas-100-million-surveillance-cameras/ (accessed January 10, 2018).

Arellano, Manuel, and Stephen Bond. 1991. "Some Tests of Specification for Panel Data: Monte Carlo Evidence and an Application to Employment Equations." *The Review of Economic Studies* 58: 277–97.

Art, David. 2012. "Review Article: What Do We Know about Authoritarianism after Ten Years?" *Comparative Politics* 44(3): 351–73.

Ashenfelter, Orley, and George E. Johnson. 1969. "Bargaining Theory, Trade Unions, and Industrial Strike Activity." *The American Economic Review* 59(1): 35–49.

Au, Loong-Yu, and Ruixue Bai. 2010. "Contemporary Labor Resistance in China, 1989–2009." *WorkingUSA* 13: 481–505.

Baum, Richard. 1994. *Burying Mao: Chinese Politics in the Age of Deng Xiaoping.* Princeton, NJ: Princeton University Press.

BBC. 2011. "Zengcheng Riot: China Forces Quell Migrant Unrest." *BBC News.* www .bbc.com/news/world-asia-pacific-13763147 (accessed February 2, 2018).

2014. "China Village Clash: Four Workers Burned to Death." *BBC News.* www.bbc .com/news/world-asia-china-29644225 (accessed September 18, 2020).

2017. "Hundreds Arrested in Belarus Protests." *BBC News.* www.bbc.com/news/ world-us-canada-39393351 (accessed March 15, 2018).

Becker, Jeffrey. 2014. *Social Ties, Resources, and Migrant Labor Contention in Contemporary China: From Peasants to Protesters.* London: Lexington Books.

Becker, Jeffrey, and Manfred Elfstrom. 2010. The Impact of China's Labor Contract Law on Workers. Washington, DC. https://laborrights.org/sites/default/files/publica tions-and-resources/ChinaLaborContractLaw2010_0.pdf (accessed September 18, 2020).

Beijing Commission of Housing and Urban-Rural Development. 2013. "Beijingshi Jianzhuye Nongmingong Quntixing Shijian Yingji Yu'an [Beijing City Contingency Plan for Responding to Mass Incidents Involving Migrant Construction Workers]." *Shoudu zhi chuang.* http://zhengce.beijing.gov.cn/ library/192/33/50/438650/76367/index.html (accessed March 9, 2018).

Beinin, Joel, and Zachary Lockman. 1998. *Workers on the Nile: Nationalism, Communism, and the Egyptian Working Class, 1882–1954.* Cairo: The American University in Cairo Press.

Bell, Daniel A. 2015. *The China Model: Political Meritocracy and the Limits of Democracy.* Princeton, NJ: Princeton University Press.

Bellin, Eva. 2004. "The Robustness of Authoritarianism in the Middle East: Exceptionalism in Comparative Perspective." *Comparative Politics* 36(2): 139–57.

Bernard, H. Russell. 2006. *Research Methods in Anthropology: Qualitative and Quantitative Approaches.* 4th ed. New York: AltaMira Press.

Bernstein, Thomas P., and Xiaobo Lü. 2003. *Taxation without Representation in Contemporary Rural China.* New York: Cambridge University Press.

Bian, Yanjie. 1994. *Work and Inequality in Urban China.* Albany: State University of New York Press.

Bishara, Dina. 2018. *Contesting Authoritarianism: Labor Challenges to the State in Egypt.* New York: Cambridge University Press.

Blasko, Dennis J. 2012. "Politics and the PLA: Securing Social Stability." *China Brief* 12 (7): 5–8.

Blecher, Marc. 2002. "Hegemony and Workers' Politics in China." *The China Quarterly* 170: 283–303.

2008. "When Wal-Mart Wimped Out: Globalization and Unionization in China." *Critical Asian Studies* 40(2): 263–76.

2010. "Globalization, Structural Reform, and Labour Politics in China." *Global Labour Journal* 1(1): 92–111.

BLS. 2016. "Major Work Stoppages in 2015." *Bureau of Labor Statistics*. www.bls.gov/news.release/archives/wkstp_02102016.pdf (accessed January 9, 2019).

Bradsher, Keith. 2015. "Labor Reform in Vietnam, Tied to Pacific Trade Deal, Depends on Hanoi's Follow-Up." *New York Times*. www.nytimes.com/2015/11/06/business/international/vietnam-tpp-trade-agreement-labor-reaction.html (accessed April 16, 2019).

Branigan, Tania. 2010. "China Removes Xinjiang Province Leader." *The Guardian*.

Braverman, Harry. 1998. *Labor and Monopoly Capital: The Degradation of Work in the Twentieth Century*. 25th Anniv. New York: Monthly Review Press.

Brodsgaard, Kjeld Erik. 2006. "Bianzhi and Cadre Management in China: The Case of Yangpu." In *The Chinese Communist Party in Reform*, eds. Kjeld Erik Brodsgaard and Yongnian Zheng. London and New York: Routledge.

2012. "Cadre and Personnel Management in the CPC." *China: An International Journal* 10(2): 69–83.

Brown, Earl V., and Kyle A. deCant. 2013. "Exploiting Chinese Interns As Unprotected Industrial Labor." *Asian-Pacific Law & Policy Journal* 15(2): 150–94.

Bulman, David J. 2016. *Incentivized Development in China: Leaders, Governance, and Growth in China's Cities*. New York: Cambridge University Press.

Bunce, Valerie J. 1980. "The Succession Connection: Policy Cycles and Political Change in the Soviet Union and Eastern Europe." *The American Political Science Review* 74 (4): 966–77.

1999. *Subversive Institutions: The Design and the Destruction of Socialism and the State*. New York: Cambridge University Press.

Bunce, Valerie J., and Sharon L. Wolchik. 2011. *Defeating Authoritarian Leaders in Postcommunist Countries*. New York: Cambridge University Press.

Burawoy, Michael. 1979. *Manufacturing Consent: Changes in the Labor Process under Capitalism*. Chicago: The University of Chicago Press.

Burawoy, Michael, and János Lukács. 1992. *The Radiant Past: Ideology and Reality on Hungary's Road to Capitalism*. Chicago and London: The University of Chicago Press.

Butollo, Florian. 2014. *The End of Cheap Labour? Industrial Transformation and "Social Upgrading" in China*. Frankfurt and New York: Campus Verlag.

2015. "Industrial Upgrading and Work: The Impact of Industrial Transformation on Labor in Guangdong's Garment and IT Industries." In *Chinese Workers in Comparative Perspective*, ed. Anita Chan. Ithaca, NY: Cornell University Press.

Butollo, Florian, and Tobias ten Brink. 2012. "Challenging the Atomization of Discontent." *Critical Asian Studies* 44(3): 419–40.

Cai, Yongshun. 2002. "The Resistance of Chinese Laid-off Workers in the Reform Period." *The China Quarterly* 170: 327–44.

2006. *State and Laid-Off Workers in Reform China: The Silence and Collective Action of the Retrenched*. Abingdon: Routledge.

2010. *Collective Resistance in China: Why Popular Protests Succeed or Fail*. Stanford, CA: Stanford University Press.

Caraway, Teri L. 2012. "Pathways of Dominance and Displacement: The Varying Fates of Legacy Unions in New Democracies." *World Politics* 64(2): 278–305.

Caraway, Teri L., Stephen Crowley, and Maria Lorena Cook. 2015. "Introduction: Labor and Authoritarian Legacies." In *Working Through History: Labor and Authoritarian Legacies in Comparative Perspective*, eds. Teri L. Caraway, Maria Lorena Cook, and Stephen Crowley. Ithaca, NY: Cornell University Press.

Cartier, Carolyn, and Luigi Tomba. 2012. "Symbolic Cities and the 'Cake Debate.'" In *The China Story Yearbook 2012: Red Rising Red Eclipse*, ed. Geremie R. Barmé. Canberra: The Australian National University.

Chan, Anita. 1993. "Revolution or Corporatism? Workers and Trade Unions in Post-Mao China." *The Australian Journal of Chinese Affairs* 29: 31–61.

  2001. *China's Workers Under Assault: The Exploitation of Labor in a Globalizing Economy*. London: M. E. Sharpe.

  2016. "The Resistance of Walmart Workers in China: A Breakthrough in the Chinese Labour Movement." *Made in China: A Quarterly on Chinese Labour, Civil Society, and Rights* 1(2): 11–15.

Chan, Chris King-Chi. 2010. *The Challenge of Labour in China: Strikes and the Changing Labour Regime in Global Factories*. Abingdon: Routledge.

Chan, Chris King-Chi, and Elaine Sio-Ieng Hui. 2013. "The Development of Collective Bargaining in China: From 'Collective Bargaining by Riot' to 'Party State-Led Wage Bargaining.'" *The China Quarterly* 217: 221–42.

Chan, Chris King-Chi, and Ngai Pun. 2009. "The Making of a New Working Class? A Study of Collective Actions of Migrant Workers in South China." *The China Quarterly* 198: 287–303.

Chan, Jenny, and Ngai Pun. 2010. "Suicide as Protest for the New Generation of Chinese Migrant Workers: Foxconn, Global Capital, and the State." *The Asia-Pacific Journal* 8(37): 1–33.

Chan, Jenny, Ngai Pun, and Mark Selden. 2013. "The Politics of Global Production: Apple, Foxconn and China's New Working Class." *New Technology, Work and Employment* 28(2): 100–15.

Chan, Jenny, Mark Selden, and Ngai Pun. 2020. *Dying for an iPhone: Apple, Foxconn, and the Lives of China's Workers*. London: Pluto Press.

Chan, John. 2012. "Top Official Bo Xilai Dismissed by Chinese Communist Party." *World Socialist Web Site*. www.wsws.org/en/articles/2012/03/chin-m20.html (accessed September 18, 2020).

Chan, Kam Wing, and Will Buckingham. 2008. "Is China Abolishing the Hukou System?" *The China Quarterly* 195: 582–606.

Chang, Gordon G. 2002. *The Coming Collapse of China*. London: Arrow.

Chang, Kai. 1995. *Laodong Guanxi, Laodongzhe, Laoquan: Dangdai Zhongguode Laodong Wenti [Labor Relations, Laborers, and Labor Rights: Contemporary Chinese Labor Issues]*. Beijing: China Labor Press.

  2009. *Laoquan Baozhang Yu Laozi Shuangying [Labor Rights Guarantees and Capital-Labor Joint Benefits]*. Beijing: Zhongguo Laodong Shehui Baozhang Chubanshe.

Chang, Kai, and William Brown. 2013. "The Transition from Individual to Collective Labour Relations in China." *Industrial Relations Journal* 44(2): 102–21.

Checkel, Jeffrey T. 2008. "Process-Tracing." In *Qualitative Methods in International Relations: A Pluralist Guide*, eds. Audie Klotz and Deepa Prakash. New York: Palgrave MacMillan.

Cheek, Timothy. 2014. "Citizen Intellectuals in Historical Perspective: Reflections on Callahan's 'Citizen Ai.'" *The Journal of Asian Studies* 73(04): 921–25.

Chen, Chih-Jou Jay. 2009. "Growing Social Unrest and Emergent Protest Groups in China." In *Rise of China: Beijing's Strategies and Implications for the Asia-Pacific*, eds. Hsin Huang Michael Hsiao and Cheng-Yi Lin. New York and London: Routledge, 87–106.

2018. "Demanding Justice: Popular Protests in China." In *Facing an Unequal World: Challenges for Global Sociology*, ed. Raquel Sosa Elizaga. New York: Sage Publications, 250–63.

Chen, Feng. 2000. "Subsistence Crises, Managerial Corruption and Labour Protests in China." *The China Journal* 44: 41–63.

2010. "Trade Unions and the Quadripartite Interactions in Strike Settlement in China." *The China Quarterly* 201: 104–24.

Chen, Feng, and Xuehui Yang. 2017. "Movement-Oriented Labour NGOs in South China: Exit with Voice and Displaced Unionism." *China Information* 32(2): 155–74.

Chen, Frank. 2014. "Factory Blast Ends Party for Kunshan's Taiwan Investors." *EJI Insight*.

Chen, Jidong, Jennifer Pan, and Yiqing Xu. 2016. "Sources of Authoritarian Responsiveness: A Field Experiment in China." *American Journal of Political Science* 00(0): 1–18.

Chen, Weiguang. 2012. *You Yu Si: Sanshinian Gonghui Gongzuo Ganwu* [Concerns and thoughts: Realizations after thirty years of union work]. Beijing: China Social Sciences Press.

Chen, Xi. 2012. *Social Protest and Contentious Authoritarianism in China*. New York: Cambridge University Press.

2017. "Origins of Informal Coercion in China." *Politics & Society* 45(1): 67–89.

Chen, Xi, and Ping Xu. 2011. "From Resistance to Advocacy: Political Representation for Disabled People in China." *The China Quarterly* (207): 649–67.

Chen, Xiangming. 2007. "A Tale of Two Regions in China: Rapid Economic Development and Slow Industrial Upgrading in the Pearl River and the Yangtze River Deltas." *International Journal of Comparative Sociology* 48(2): 167–201.

Chenoweth, Erica, and Maria J. Stephan. 2011. *Why Civil Resistance Works: The Strategic Logic of Nonviolent Conflict*. New York: Columbia University Press.

Cheung, Peter T. Y. 1998. "Introduction: Provincial Leadership and Economic Reform in Post-Mao China." In *Provincial Strategies of Economic Reform in Post-Mao China: Leadership, Politics, and Implementation*, eds. Peter T. Y. Cheung, Jae Ho Chung, and Zhimin Lin. Armonk, NY: M. E. Sharpe.

Cheung, Tai Ming. 1996. "Guarding China's Domestic Front Line: The People's Armed Police and China's Stability." *The China Quarterly* 146: 525–47.

China Daily. 2015. "China-South Korea Cooperation Zone to Settle in Wuxi." *Wuxi New District*. www.chinadaily.com.cn/m/jiangsu/wuxinewdistrict/2015-08/31/content_21761226.htm (accessed September 17, 2020).

China Labor Crackdown Concern Group. 2019. "One Year, One Hundred Arrested, What You Need to Know About China's Labor Crackdown." *China Labor Crackdown Concern Group.* https://laoquan18.github.io/one-year-infographic/ (accessed February 14, 2020).

China Labor News Translations. 2009a. "Chinese Students Go Undercover to Investigate Coca Cola." *China Labor News Translations.* www.archives.truenorthperspective.com/Oct_09/Oct_23/chan.html (accessed September 18, 2020).

2009b. "Dagongzhe Migrant Workers' Centre Fights on Despite Violent Attack." *China Labor News Translations.* www.archives.truenorthperspective.com/Dec_09/Dec_18/migrant_workers.html (accessed September 18, 2020).

2009c. "The Bad and the Good of the Wal-Mart ACFTU Collective Agreement." *China Labor News Translations.* www.clntranslations.org/article/38/wal-mart-contract (accessed December 14, 2017).

2010. "Labor Lawyer Imprisoned in Xi'an for Organizing Against Corrupt Privatization of State Enterprises." *China Labor News Translations.* www.scribd.com/document/46789205/Zhao-Dongmin (accessed September 18, 2020).

China Labor Watch. 2015. "5,000-Worker Strike at Dongguan Stella Footwear Factory." *China Labor Watch.* www.chinalaborwatch.org/newscast/430 (accessed April 10, 2017).

China Labour Bulletin. 2005a. "Guangdong Labour Authorities Condemn 20 'Sweatshops.'" *China Labour Bulletin.* https://clb.org.hk/content/guangdong-labour-authorities-condemn-20-sweatshops (accessed September 18, 2020).

2005b. "Release and Sentence Reductions for Stella Shoe Factory Workers." *China Labour Bulletin.* https://clb.org.hk/content/release-and-sentence-reductions-stella-shoe-factory-workers (accessed September 18, 2020).

2007. "The Stella Shoe Workers' Protest." *China Labour Bulletin.* www.clb.org.hk/en/content/stella-shoe-workers-protest (accessed September 25, 2015).

2008. "Trade Union Official Says China Is Just One Step Away from the Right to Strike." *China Labour Bulletin.* www.clb.org.hk/en/node/100263 (accessed December 2, 2015).

2009a. *Protecting Workers' Rights or Serving the Party: The Way Forward for China's Trade Unions.* Hong Kong. https://clb.org.hk/sites/default/files/archive/en/share/File/research_reports/acftu_report.pdf (accessed September 18, 2020).

2009b. "In Handling of Taxi Strikes, Xining and Chongqing Provide Stark Contrasts." *China Labour Bulletin.* www.clb.org.hk/en/content/handling-taxi-strikes-xining-and-chongqing-provide-stark-contrasts (accessed September 18, 2020).

2016a. "An Introduction to China Labour Bulletin's Strike Map." *China Labour Bulletin.* https://clb.org.hk/content/introduction-china-labour-bulletin%E2%80%99s-strike-map (accessed September 18, 2020).

2016b. "What Happens When the Boss Actually Abides by the Law During a Factory Closure in China?" *China Labour Bulletin.* www.clb.org.hk/en/content/what-happens-when-boss-actually-abides-law-during-factory-closure-china (accessed April 10, 2017).

2017a. "Lu Yuyu and Li Tingyu, the Activists Who Put Non News in the News." *China Labour Bulletin.* https://clb.org.hk/content/lu-yuyu-and-li-tingyu-activists-who-put-non-news-news (accessed April 1, 2019).

2017b. "Strike Map Applies New Fixed Sampling Method in 2017." *China Labour Bulletin*. https://clb.org.hk/content/strike-map-applies-new-fixed-sampling-method-2017 (accessed April 1, 2019).

2018a. "China's Truck Drivers Strike over Stagnant Pay, High Fuel Costs and Arbitrary Fines." *China Labour Bulletin*. www.clb.org.hk/content/china%E2%80%99s-truck-drivers-strike-over-stagnant-pay-high-fuel-costs-and-arbitrary-fines (accessed June 11, 2018).

2018b. "Food Delivery Workers in China Strike over Pay Cuts and Unfair Work Practices." *China Labour Bulletin*. www.clb.org.hk/content/food-delivery-workers-china-strike-over-pay-cuts-and-unfair-work-practices (accessed June 11, 2018).

2018c. "Tower Crane Operators across China Organise Labour Day Strike over Low Pay." *China Labour Bulletin*. www.clb.org.hk/content/tower-crane-operators-across-china-organise-labour-day-strike-over-low-pay (accessed June 11, 2018).

2018d. "Jasic crackdown extends to trade union officials and lawyers." *China Labour Bulletin*. https://clb.org.hk/content/jasic-crackdown-extends-trade-union-officials-and-lawyers (accessed September 17, 2020).

2019. *CLB Strike Map*. Hong Kong. http://strikemap.clb.org.hk/strikes/en (accessed January 9, 2019).

2020. "Worker protests on the rise in June as wage arrears proliferate." *China Labour Bulletin*. https://clb.org.hk./content/worker-protests-rise-june-wage-arrears-prolifer ate (accessed September 16, 2020).

Chinese Characteristics Study Group of the China Police Studies Association Basic Theory Specialists Association. 1996. *Zhongguo Tese Jingcha Zhi Yanjiu*. Beijing: Qunzhong Chubanshe.

Cho, Mun Yong. 2013. *The Specter of "The People": Urban Poverty in Northeast China*. Ithaca, NY: Cornell University Press.

Chongqing Daily. 2007. "Wang Yang: Jixu Jiefang Sixiang, Jianchi Gaige Kaifang [Wang Yang: Continue to Liberate Thought, Persist in Reform and Opening]." www.cq.xinhuanet.com/cq/2007-11/14/content_11987609.htm.

CHRD. 2019. "Zhang Zhiru." *Chinese Human Rights Defenders*. www.nchrd.org/2019/07/zhang-zhiru/ (accessed February 14, 2020).

Chuang, Julia. 2015. "Urbanization Through Dispossession: Survival and Stratification in China's New Townships." *Journal of Peasant Studies* 42(2): 275–94.

Chung, Him, and Jonathan Unger. 2013. "The Guangdong Model of Urbanisation: Collective Village Land and the Making of a New Middle Class." *China Perspectives* 2013(3): 33.

Clarke, Simon. 2006. "The Changing Character of Strikes in Vietnam." *Post-Communist Economies* 18(3): 345–61.

Coalson, Robert. 2016. "Russian Truckers Resume Protests Against Controversial Toll System." www.rferl.org/a/russian-truckers-resume-protests-toll-system/28110513.html.

Collier, David, and Steven Levitsky. 1997. "Democracy with Adjectives: Conceptual Innovation in Comparative Research." *World Politics* 49(3): 430–51.

Cook, Scott J., and Nils B. Weidmann. 2019. "Lost in Aggregation: Improving Event Analysis with Report-Level Data." *American Journal of Political Science* 63(1): 250–64.

Cooke, Fang Lee. 2008. "The Changing Dynamics of Employment Relations in China: An Evaluation of the Rising Level of Labour Disputes." *Journal of Industrial Relations* 50(1): 111–38.

Cooney, Sean. 2007. "China's Labour Law, Compliance and Flaws in Implementing Institutions." *Journal of Industrial Relations* 9(5): 673–86.

Cooney, Sean, Sarah Biddulph, Kungang Li, and Zhu Ying. 2007. "China's New Labor Contract Law: Responding to the Growing Complexity of Labour Relations in the PRC." *University of New South Wales Law Journal* 30(3): 788–803.

CPJ. 2019. "Labor Rights Website Editor Wei Zhili Arrested in China; Another Is Missing." *Committee to Protect Journalists.* https://cpj.org/2019/03/labor-rights-website-editor-wei-zhili-arrested-in-.php (accessed April 5, 2019).

Crouch, Harold. 1996. *Government and Society in Malaysia.* Ithaca, NY, and London: Cornell University Press.

Cui, Zhikun, and Xin Cui. 2000. *Zhongguo Jingcha Yu Renquan Baohu.* Beijing: Jingguan Jiaoyu Chubanshe.

Cui, Zhiyuan. 2011. "Partial Intimations of the Coming Whole: The Chongqing Experiment in Light of the Theories of Henry George, James Meade, and Antonio Gramsci." *Modern China* 37(6): 646–60.

Davenport, Christian. 2015. *How Social Movements Die: Repression and Demobilization of the Republic of New Africa.* New York: Cambridge University Press.

Deng, Yanhua, and Kevin J. O'Brien. 2013. "Relational Repression in China: Using Social Ties to Demobilize Protesters." *The China Quarterly* 215: 533–52.

Diamond, Larry Jay. 2002. "Thinking About Hybrid Regimes." *Journal of Democracy* 13(2): 21–35.

Dickson, Bruce J. 2003. *Red Capitalists in China: The Party, Private Entrepreneurs, and Prospects for Political Change.* New York: Cambridge University Press.

2016. *The Dictator's Dilemma: The Chinese Communist Party's Strategy for Survival.* New York: Oxford University Press.

Dimitrov, Martin K. 2015. "Internal Government Assessments of the Quality of Governance in China." *Studies in Comparative International Development* 50(1): 50–72.

Distelhorst, Greg, and Diana Fu. 2019. "Performing Authoritarian Citizenship: Public Transcripts in China." *Perspectives on Politics* 17(1): 106–21.

Distelhorst, Greg, and Yue Hou. 2017. "Constituency Service under Nondemocratic Rule: Evidence from China." *The Journal of Politics* 79(3): 1024–40.

Dong, Guoqiang, and Andrew G. Walder. 2011a. "Factions in a Bureaucratic Setting: The Origins of Cultural Revolution Conflict in Nanjing." *China Journal* 15(65): 1–25.

2011b. "Nanjing's Failed 'January Revolution' of 1967: The Inner Politics of a Provincial Power Seizure." *The China Quarterly* 203: 675–92.

Dzirutwe, Macdonald. 2015. "Zimbabwe Union Says 20,000 Jobs Lost, Government to Amend Labor Law." *Reuters.* www.reuters.com/article/us-zimbabwe-employment-idUSKCN0QL0ID20150816.

Eckholm, Erik. 2002. "Corruption Protest in China Leads to Charges, Top and Bottom." *New York Times.*

2003. "2 Men Get Stiff Sentences in China Over Worker Protests." *New York Times.* www.nytimes.com/2003/05/09/international/asia/2-men-get-stiff-sentences-in-china-over-worker-protests.html (accessed June 5, 2017).

Eckstein, Harry. 1992. *Regarding Politics: Essays on Political Theory, Stability, and Change.* Berkeley and Los Angeles: University of California Press.

The Economist. 2012. "The Rise of State Capitalism." *The Economist*. www.economist
.com/node/21543160.

2016. "Deep in the Pit." *The Economist*. www.economist.com/news/china/21695091-large-
protests-miners-augur-ill-governments-reform-plans-deep-pit (accessed August 16, 2017).

2017. "Jewel in the Crown: What China Can Learn from the Pearl River Delta." www
.economist.com/special-report/2017/04/08/what-china-can-learn-from-the-pearl-river-
delta (accessed March 7, 2019).

Economy, Elizabeth C. 2018. *The Third Revolution: Xi Jinping and the New Chinese
State*. New York: Oxford University Press.

Eimer, David. 2008. "China's Toy Makers Face Bleak Christmas as Factories Shut
Down." *The Telegraph*. www.telegraph.co.uk/news/worldnews/asia/china/
3363293/Chinas-toy-makers-face-bleak-Christmas-as-factories-shut-down.html
(accessed January 8, 2016).

Ekiert, Grzegorz. 1996. *The State Against Society: Political Crises and Their Aftermath
in East Central Europe*. Princeton, NJ: Princeton University Press.

Elfstrom, Manfred. 2019a. "China's Contentious Cab Drivers." In *Handbook of Protest
and Resistance in China*, ed. Teresa Wright. Northampton, MA: Edward Elgar
Publishing Limited.

2019b. "Two Steps Forward, One Step Back: Chinese State Reactions to Labour
Unrest." *The China Quarterly* 240: 855–79.

2019c. "A Tale of Two Deltas: Labour Politics in Jiangsu and Guangdong." *British
Journal of Industrial Relations* 57(2): 247–74.

Elfstrom, Manfred, and Sarosh Kuruvilla. 2014. "The Changing Nature of Labor Unrest
in China." *Industrial and Labor Relations Review* 67(2): 453–80.

Elfstrom, Manfred, and Yao Li. 2019. "Contentious Politics in China: Causes,
Dynamics, and Consequences." *Brill Research Perspectives in Governance and
Public Policy in China* 4(1): 1–90.

Elmer, Keegan. 2019a. "At Least Five Labour Rights Activists Arrested across China |
South China Morning Post." *South China Morning Post*. www.scmp.com/news/
china/politics/article/2183209/least-five-labour-rights-activists-arrested-across-china
(accessed April 5, 2019).

2019b. "China police remove prominent labour activist in home raid." *South China
Morning Post*. www.scmp.com/news/china/politics/article/3042937/china-police-
remove-prominent-labour-activist-home-raid (accessed September 17, 2020).

Emerson, Robert M., Rachel I. Fretz, and Linda L. Shaw. 1995. *Writing Ethnographic
Fieldnotes*. Chicago: University of Chicago Press.

Erickson, Amanda. 2017. "Belarus Wanted to Tax Its Unemployed 'Parasites.' Then the
Protests Started." *Washington Post*. www.washingtonpost.com/news/worldviews/
wp/2017/03/10/belarus-wanted-to-tax-its-unemployed-as-parasites-then-the-pro
tests-started/ (accessed March 15, 2018).

Esping-Andersen, Gøsta. 1990. *The Three Worlds of Welfare Capitalism*. Princeton, NJ:
Princeton University Press.

Estlund, Cynthia. 2013. "Will Workers Have a Voice in China's 'Socialist Market
Economy'? The Curious Revival of the Workers Congress System." NYU School
of Law, Public Law Research Paper No. 13-80. https://papers.ssrn.com/sol3/papers
.cfm?abstract_id=2364552 (accessed September 18, 2020).

2017. *A New Deal for China's Workers*. Cambridge, MA: Harvard University Press.

Evans, Allison D. 2016. "Protest Patterns in Provincial Russia: A Paired Comparison of Company Towns." *Studies in Comparative International Development* 51(4): 456–81.

Fan, Shigang. 2018. *Striking to Survive: Workers' Resistnce to Factory Relocations in China*. Chicago: Haymarket Books.

Fauna. 2011. "Chongqing Migrant Workers Unpaid & Beaten, SWAT Deployed." *ChinaSmack*. www.chinasmack.com/2011/stories/chongqing-migrant-workers-unpaid-beaten-swat-deployed.html.

Feng, Emily. 2019. "GitHub Has Become a Haven for China's Censored Internet Users." *NPR.org*. www.npr.org/2019/04/10/709490855/github-has-become-a-haven-for-chinas-censored-internet-users (accessed April 12, 2019).

Feng, Tongqing. 2009. *Zhongguo Gongrende Mingyun: Gonghui Minzhu Xuanju Yu Gongren Gongmin Quanli Yansheng [The Fate of Chinese Workers: Union Democratic Elections and the Development of Civil Rights]*. Beijing: China Social Sciences Press.

2011. "Jiejue Laodong Shehui Shijiande Zhongguo Zhiduxing Ziyuan: Gonghuifa Tinggong, Daigong Tiaokuan Jiqi Shishide Jiedu [China's Institutional Resources for Resolving Labor Social Incidents: Interpreting and Implementing the Trade Union Law's Articles on Work." *Zhongguo Gongren* 10: 10–15.

Feng, Xiaojun. 2019. "Trapped in Precariousness: Migrant Agency Workers in China's State-Owned Enterprises." *The China Quarterly* 238: 396–417.

Fewsmith, Joseph. 2011. "The Elusive Search for Effective Sub-County Governance." In *Mao's Invisible Hand: The Political Foundations of Adaptive Governance in China*, eds. Sebastian Heilmann and Elizabeth J. Perry. Cambridge, MA: Harvard University Press.

2012. "Bo Xilai and Reform: What Will Be the Impact of His Removal?" *China Leadership Monitor* 38: 1–11. www.hoover.org/sites/default/files/uploads/docu ments/CLM38JF.pdf (accessed September 18, 2020).

2013. *The Logic and Limits of Political Reform in China*. New York: Cambridge University Press.

Fincher, Leta Hong. 2018. *Betraying Big Brother: The Feminist Awakening in China*. New York: Verso Books.

Finkel, Evgeny, Scott Gelbach, and Tricia Olsen. 2015. "Does Reform Prevent Rebellion? Evidence from Russia's Emancipation of the Serfs." *Comparative Political Studies* 48(8): 984–1019.

Fong, Tak-ho. 2007. "Wang Yang: A Rising Star in China." *Asia Times*. www.atimes.com/atimes/China/IE03Ado2.html.

Foucault, Michel. 1977. *Discipline and Punish*. New York: Vintage Books.

Franceschini, Ivan. 2012. "Another Guangdong Model: Labour NGOs and New State Corporatism." *The China Story*. www.thechinastory.org/2012/08/post-labour-ngos/.

2014. "Labour NGOs in China: A Real Force for Political Change?" *The China Quarterly* 218(May): 474–92.

2016. "Revisiting Chinese Labour NGOs: Some Grounds for Hope?" *Made in China: A Quarterly on Chinese Labour, Civil Society, and Rights* 1: 16–18.

2017. "Meet the State Security: Chinese Labour Activists and Their Controllers." *Made in China: A Quarterly on Chinese Labour, Civil Society, and Rights* 2(1): 34–37.

Franceschini, Ivan, and Kevin Lin. 2019. "Labour NGOs in China From Legal Mobilisation to Collective Struggle (and Back?)." *China Perspectives* 2019(1): 75–84.

Franceschini, Ivan, and Elisa Nesossi. 2018. "State Repression of Chinese Labor NGOs: A Chilling Effect?" *The China Journal* 80: 111–29.

Franzosi, Roberto. 1989. "One Hundred Years of Strike Statistics: Methodological and Theoretical Issues in Quantitative Strike Research." *Industrial and Labor Relations Review* 42(3): 348–62.

Frazier, Mark W., and Yimin Li. 2017. "Stemming the Tide of Demographic Transformation through Social Inclusion: Can Universal Pension Rights Help Finance an Ageing Population?" In *Handbook of Welfare in China, Handbooks of Research on Contemporary China*, eds. Beatriz Carrillo, Johanna Hood, and Paul Kadetz. Northampton, MA: Edward Elgar Publishing Limited.

Freedom House. 2018. "Freedom in the World 2018." https://freedomhouse.org/report/freedom-world/freedom-world-2018 (accessed March 19, 2018).

Freeman III, Charles W., and Jin Yuan Wen. 2011. "China's New Leftists and the China Model Debate after the Financial Crisis." Research Report of the CSIS Freeman Chair in China Studies.Washington, DC: Center for Strategic and International Studies.

Freeman, Richard B., and Xiaoying Li. 2013. "How Does China's New Labor Contract Law Affect Floating Workers?" www.nber.org/papers/w19254.

Frenkel, Stephen J., and Chongxin Yu. 2015. "Chinese Migrants' Experience and City Identification: Challenging the Underclass Thesis." *Human Relations* 68(2): 261–85.

Friedman, Eli. 2009. "External Pressure and Local Mobilization: Transnational Activism and the Emergence of the Chinese Labor Movement." *Mobilization: An International Journal* 14(2): 199–218.

2012. "Getting Through the Hard Times Together? Chinese Workers and Unions Respond to the Economic Crisis." *Journal of Industrial Relations* 54(4): 459–75.

2014a. "Economic Development and Sectoral Unions in China." *Industrial and Labor Relations Review* 67(2): 481–503.

2014b. *Insurgency Trap: Labor Politics in Postsocialist China*. Ithaca, NY: Cornell University Press.

2017. "Teachers' Work in China's Migrant Schools." *Modern China* 43(6): 559–89.

Friedman, Eli, and Ching Kwan Lee. 2010. "Remaking the World of Chinese Labour: A 30-Year Retrospective." *British Journal of Industrial Relations* 48(3): 507–33.

Friedman, John. 2005. *China's Urban Transition*. Minneapolis: University of Minnesota Press.

Froissart, Chloé. 2011. "'NGOs' Defending Migrant Workers' Rights: Semi-Union Organisations Contribute to the Regime's Dynamic Stability." *China Perspectives* 2011(2): 18–25.

2018. "Negotiating Authoritarianism and Its Limits: Worker-Led Collective Bargaining in Guangdong Province." *China Information* 32(1): 23–45.

Fu, Diana. 2016. "Disguised Collective Action in China." *Comparative Political Studies* 50(4): 499–527.

2018. *Mobilizing Without the Masses: Control and Contention in China*. New York: Cambridge University Press.

Fu, Diana, and Greg Distelhorst. 2018. "Grassroots Participation and Repression in Contemporary China." *The China Journal* 79: 100–22.

Fukuyama, Francis. 1992. *The End of History and the Last Man*. New York: Free Press.

Fuxin City Bureau of Human Resources and Social Security. 2017. "Fuxinshi Renli Ziyuan He Shehui Baozhangju Quntixing Shijian Yingji Yu'an [Fuxin City Bureau of Human Resources and Social Security Contingency Plan for Mass Incidents]." *Fuxin City Fuxin City Bureau of Human Resources and Social Security*. www.lnfx.lss.gov .cn/ecdomain/framework/fxrsw/aeigndmhfjhbbbogjkeklhfaopncalpc/aeijeemifjhbbbogj keklhfaopncalpc.do?isfloat=1&disp_template=glkjpnohdglcbbogimnmifhadhmogimc& fileid=20161101165023717&moduleIDPage=aeijeemifjhbbbogjkeklhfaopncalpc& siteIDPage=fxrsw&infoChecked=0 (accessed March 9, 2018).

Gallagher, Mary E. 2002. "'Reform and Openness': Why China's Economic Reforms Have Delayed Democracy." *World Politics* 54(3): 338–72.

2005. *Contagious Capitalism: Globalization and the Politics of Labor in China*. Princeton, NJ: Princeton University Press.

2006. "Mobilizing the Law in China: 'Informed Disenchantment' and the Development of Legal Consciousness." *Law & Society Review* 40(4): 783–816.

2015. "Transformation without Transition: China's Maoist Legacies in Comparative Perspective." In *Working Through History: Labor and Authoritarian Legacies in Comparative Perspective*, eds. Teri L. Caraway, Maria Lorena Cook, and Stephen Crowley. Ithaca, NY: Cornell University Press.

2017. *Authoritarian Legality in China: Law, Workers, and the State*. New York: Cambridge University Press.

Gallagher, Mary E., and Baohua Dong. 2011. "Legislating Harmony: Labor Law Reform in Contemporary China." In *From Iron Rice Bowl to Informalization: Markets, Workers, and the State in a Changing China*, eds. Sarosh Kuruvilla, Ching Kwan Lee, and Mary E Gallagher. Ithaca, NY: ILR Press.

Gallagher, Mary E., John Giles, Albert Park, and Meiyan Wang. 2014. "China's 2008 Labor Contract Law: Implementation and Implications for China's Workers." *Human Relations* OnlineFirs: 1–39.

Gallagher, Mary E., Ching Kwan Lee, and Sarosh Kuruvilla. 2011. "Introduction and Argument." In *From Iron Rice Bowl to Informalization: Markets, Workers, and the State in a Changing China*, eds. Mary E. Gallagher, Ching Kwan Lee, and Sarosh Kuruvilla. Ithaca, NY: ILR Press.

Gan, Nectar. 2019. "'Liberal' Policy Chief Unlikely to Mean a Softening on Xinjiang from China." *South China Morning Post*. www.scmp.com/news/china/politics/art icle/3019044/liberal-policy-chief-unlikely-mean-softening-xinjiang-china (accessed September 16, 2020).

Gandhi, Jennifer, and Adam Przeworski. 2007. "Authoritarian Institutions and the Survival of Autocrats." *Comparative Political Studies* 40(11): 1279–301.

Ganz, Marshall. 2009. *Why David Sometimes Wins: Leadership, Strategy and the Organization in the California Farm Worker Movement*. New York: Oxford University Press.

Gao, Qin, Sui Yang, and Fuhua Zhai. 2019. "Social Policy and Income Inequality during the Hu–Wen Era: A Progressive Legacy?" *The China Quarterly* 237: 82–107.

Garver, Paul. 2010. "Hong Kong Business Federations Derail Labor Law Reforms in Guangdong, China." *Talking Union*. https://talkingunion.wordpress.com/2010/09/30/hong-kong-business-federations-derail-labor-law-reforms-in-guangdong-china/.

Geddes, Barbara, Joseph Wright, and Erica Frantz. 2014. "Autocratic Breakdown and Regime Transitions: A New Data Set." *Perspectives on Politics* 12(02): 313–31.

Gehlbach, Scott, Konstantin Sonin, and Milan W. Svolik. 2016. "Formal Models of Nondemocratic Politics." *Annual Review of Political Science* 19(1): 565–84.

George, Alexander L., Andrew Bennett, and Andrew Bennet. 2004. *Case Studies and Theory Development in the Social Sciences*. Cambridge, MA: MIT Press.

Gerring, John. 2008. "Case Selection for Case Study Analysis: Qualitative and Quantitative Techniques." In *The Oxford Handbook of Political Methodology*, eds. Janet M. Box-Steffensmeier, Henry E. Brady, and David Collier. New York: Oxford University Press.

Ghosh, Arunabh. 2020. *Making It Count: Statistics and Statecraft in the Early People's Republic of China*. Princeton, NJ: Princeton University Press.

Gibson, Edward L. 2013. *Boundary Control: Subnational Authoritarianism in Federal Democracies*. New York: Cambridge University Press.

Gilboy, George J., and Eric Higenbotham. 2004. "The Latin Americanization of China?" *Current History* 103(674): 256–61.

Gilley, Bruce. 2004. *China's Democratic Future: How It Will Happen and Where It Will Lead*. New York: Columbia University Press.

Gillion, Daniel Q. 2013. *The Political Power of Protest: Minority Activism and Shifts in Public Policy*. Cambridge: Cambridge University Press.

Giugni, Marco. 2007. "Useless Protest? A Time-Series Analysis of the Policy Outcomes of Ecology, Antinuclear, and Peace Movements in the United States, 1977–1995." *Mobilization: An International Quarterly* 12(1): 53–77.

Giugni, Marco, Doug McAdam, and Charles Tilly, eds. 1999. *How Social Movements Work*. Minneapolis: University of Minnesota Press.

Giugni, Marco, and Sakura Yamasaki. 2009. "The Policy Impact of Social Movements: A Replication Through Qualitative Comparative Analysis." *Mobilization: An International . . .* 14(4): 467–84.

Gleiss, M. S. 2014. "How Chinese Labour NGOs Legitimize Their Identity and Voice." *China Information* 28(3): 362–81.

Global Labor Strategies. 2007. "Undue Influence: Corporations Gain Ground in Battle over China's New Labor Law – But Human Rights and Labor Advocates Are Pushing Back." *Global Labor Strategies*. https://laborstrategies.blogs.com/global_labor_strategies/files/undue_influence_global_labor_strategies.pdf (accessed September 18, 2020).

Goebel, Christian. 2019. "Social Unrest in China: A Bird's-Eye View." In *Handbook of Protest and Resistance in China*, ed. Teresa Wright. Northampton, MA: Edward Elgar Publishing.

Gold, Thomas B. 1986. *State and Society in the Taiwan Miracle*. Armonk, NY: M. E. Sharpe.

Goodman, David S. G. 2014. *Class in Contemporary China*. Malden, MA: Polity Press.

Gough, Neil. 2004. "Trouble on the Line." *Time Magazine*. http://content.time.com/time/magazine/article/0,9171,501050131-1019909,00.html (accessed April 10, 2017).

Grdešić, Marko. 2015. "Exceptionalism and Its Limits: The Legacy of Self-Management in the Former Yugoslavia." In *Working Through History: Labor and Authoritarian Legacies in Comparative Perspective*, eds. Teri L. Caraway, Maria Lorena Cook, and Stephen Crowley. Ithaca, NY: Cornell University Press.

Greitens, Sheena Chestnut. 2016. *Dictators and Their Secret Police.* New York: Cambridge University Press.

———. 2017. "Rethinking China's Coercive Capacity: An Examination of PRC Domestic Security Spending, 1992–2012." *The China Quarterly* 232: 1002–25.

Guo, Xuezhi. 2012. *China's Security State: Philosophy, Evolution, and Politics.* New York: Cambridge University Press.

Halegua, Aaron. 2008. "Getting Paid: Processing the Labor Disputes of China's Migrant Workers." *Berkeley Journal of International Law* 26(1): 254–322.

———. 2017. "Chinese Workers and the Legal System: Bridging the Gap in Representation." In *Made in China Yearbook 2016: Disturbances in Heaven*, eds. Ivan Franceschini, Kevin Lin, and Nicholas Loubere. Canberra: Australian National University Press.

Han, Dongfang. 2002. "CLB Press Release on Daqing Oilfield Workers' Protests." *China Labour Bulletin.* www.clb.org.hk/en/content/clb-press-release-daqing-oilfield-workers-protests.

———. 2016. "A Reply to the People's Daily Report on the Director of the Panyu Workers Service Centre, Zeng Feiyang." *China Labour Bulletin.* www.clb.org.hk/en/sites/default/files/File/letter to Peoples Daily.pdf (accessed January 14, 2015).

Hand, Keith J. 2006. "Using Law for a Righteous Purpose: The Sun Zhigang Incident and Evolving Forms of Citizen Action in the People's Republic of China." *Columbia Journal of Transnational Law* 45(1): 114–95.

Harney, Alexandra. 2015. "China Labor Activists Say Facing Unprecedented Intimidation." *Reuters.* www.reuters.com/article/2015/01/21/us-china-labour-idUSKBN0KU13V20150121.

Hartshorn, Ian M. 2018. *Labor Politics in North Africa: After the Uprisings in Egypt and Tunisia.* New York: Cambridge University Press.

Hassard, John et al. 2007. *China's State Enterprise Reform: From Marx to the Market.* New York: Routledge.

He, Baogang, and Mark E. Warren. 2011. "Authoritarian Deliberation: The Deliberative Turn in Chinese Political Development." *Perspectives on Politics* 9 (02): 269–89.

He, Qin. 2014. *Quntixing Laozi Chongtu Shijiande Yanhua Ji Yingdui [Evolution of and Responses to Mass Incidents Involving Labor-Capital Conflict].* Beijing: Social Sciences Academic Press.

He, Qinglian. 2012. "China's Stability Maintenance System Faces Financial Pressure." *Human Rights in China.* www.hrichina.org/en/crf/article/6415 (accessed September 18, 2020).

He, Weifang. 2011. "Weile Fazhi, Weile Women Xin Zhongde Na Yi Fen Lixiang [For Rule of Law, for That Ideal in Our Hearts]." *He Weifangde Boke.* www.rfi.fr/cn/%E9%A6%96%E9%A1%B5/20110412-%E8%B4%BA%E5%8D%AB%E6%96%B9%EF%BC%9A%E4%B8%BA%E4%BA%86%E6%B3%95%E6%B2%BB%EF%BC%8C%E4%B8%BA%E4%BA%86%E6%88%91%E4%BB%AC%E5%BF%83%E4%B8%AD%E7%9A

%84%E9%82%A3%E4%B8%80%E4%BB%BD%E7%90%86%E6%
83%B3 (accessed September 18, 2020).

Heilmann, Sebastian. 2008. "Policy Experimentation in China's Economic Rise." *Studies in Comparative International Development* 43(1): 1–26.

Heilmann, Sebastian, and Elizabeth J. Perry. 2011. "Embracing Uncertainty: Guerrilla Policy Style and Adaptive Governance in China." In *Mao's Invisible Hand: The Political Foundations of Adaptive Governance in China*, eds. Sebastian Heilmann and Elizabeth J. Perry. Cambridge, MA: Harvard University Asia Center.

Heurlin, Christopher. 2016. *Responsive Authoritarianism: Land, Protests, and Policy Making*. New York: Cambridge University Press.

Heydemann, Steven, and Reinoud Leenders. 2013. "Authoritarian Governance in Syria and Iran: Challenged, Reconfiguring, and Resilient." In *Middle East Authoritarianisms: Governance, Contestation, and Regime Resilience in Syria and Iran*, eds. Steven Heydemann and Reinoud Leenders. Stanford, CA: Stanford University Press.

Hildebrandt, Timothy. 2013. *Social Organizations and the Authoritarian State in China*. New York: Cambridge University Press.

Hillman, Ben. 2016. "Unrest in Tibet and the Limits of Regional Autonomy." In *Ethnic Conflict and Protest in Tibet and Xinjiang: Unrest in China's West*, eds. Ben Hillman and Gray Tuttle. New York: Columbia University Press.

HKTDC. 2014. "Jiangsu: Market Profile." *HKTDC Research*. http://china-trade-research.hktdc.com/business-news/article/Fast-Facts/Jiangsu-Market-Profile/ff/en/1/1X000000/1X06BV87.htm (accessed December 14, 2017).

2015. "PRD Economic Profile." *HKTDC Research*. http://china-trade-research.hktdc.com/business-news/article/Fast-Facts/PRD-Economic-Profile/ff/en/1/1X000000/1X06BW84.htm (accessed November 23, 2015).

2016. "Chongqing: Market Profile." *HKTDC Research*. http://china-trade-research.hktdc.com/business-news/article/Fast-Facts/Chongqing-Market-Profile/ff/en/1/1X000000/1X06BPV2.htm.

Howell, Jude. 1993. *China Opens Its Doors: The Politics of Economic Transition*. Boulder, CO: Lynne Rienner Publishers.

2008. "All-China Federation of Trades Unions Beyond Reform? The Slow March of Direct Elections." *The China Quarterly* 196: 845–63.

2015. "Shall We Dance? Welfarist Incorporation and the Politics of State-Labour NGO Relations in China." *The China Quarterly* 223: 702–23.

Howell, Jude, and Jane Duckett. 2019. "Reassessing the Hu–Wen Era: A Golden Age or Lost Decade for Social Policy in China?" *The China Quarterly* 237: 1–14.

Howell, Jude, and Tim Pringle. 2018. "Shades of Authoritarianism and State-Labour Relations in China: Shades of Authoritarianism and State-Labour Relations in China." *British Journal of Industrial Relations*. http://doi.wiley.com/10.1111/bjir.12436 (accessed November 1, 2018).

Hsu, Jennifer. 2012. "Layers of the Urban State: Migrant Organisations and the Chinese State." *Urban Studies* 49(16): 3513–30.

2017. *State of Exchange: Migrant NGOs and the Chinese Government*. Vancouver and Toronto: University of British Columbia Press.

Huang, Binhuan. 2014. "Shuangchong Tuoqian Yu Xinshengdai Nongmingongde Jieji Xingcheng [Double Disembeddedness and the Class Formation of a New Generation of Migrant Workers]." *Sociological Studies* 2(1): 170–88.

Huang, Joyce. 2016. "Unpaid Chinese Coal Miners in Heilongjiang Stage Protests." *Voice of America.* www.voanews.com/content/china-miners-protests/3234867 .html.

Hui, Elaine Sio-Ieng. 2018. *Hegemonic Transformation: The State, Laws, and Labour Relations in Post-Socialist China.* New York: Palgrave MacMillan.

Human Rights Watch. 2002. *Paying the Price: Worker Unrest in Northeast China.* Washington, DC: Human Rights Watch. www.hrw.org/reports/2002/chinalbro2/ chinalbro802.pdf

2009a. *Not Yet a Workers' Paradise: Vietnam's Suppression of the Independent Workers' Movement.* New York. www.hrw.org/report/2009/05/04/not-yet-workers-paradise/vietnams-suppression-independent-workers-movement.

2009b. *"We Are Afraid to Even Look for Them": Enforced Disappearances in the Wake of Xinjiang's Protests.* New York: Human Rights Watch.

2018. "'Eradicating Ideological Viruses': China's Campaign of Repression Against Xinjiang's Muslims." *Human Rights Watch.* www.hrw.org/report/2018/09/09/ eradicating-ideological-viruses/chinas-campaign-repression-against-xinjiangs#.

Hung, Ho-fung. 2011. *Protest with Chinese Characteristics: Demonstrations, Riots, and Petitions in the Mid-Qing Dynasty.* New York: Columbia University Press.

Huntington, Samuel P. 1991. "Democracy's Third Wave." *Journal of Democracy* 2(2): 12–34.

Hurst, William. 2009. *The Chinese Worker After Socialism.* New York: Cambridge University Press.

Hurst, William, and Kevin O'Brien. 2002. "China's Contentious Pensioners." *The China Quarterly* 170: 345–60.

Hyman, Richard. 1989. *Strikes.* 4th ed. London: The MacMillan Press Ltd.

ILO. 2018. "Number of Strikes and Lockouts by Economic Activity." *ILOSTAT.* www.ilo .org/ilostat/faces/oracle/webcenter/portalapp/pagehierarchy/Page27.jspx?subject=IR& indicator=STR_TSTR_ECO_NB&datasetCode=A&collectionCode=YI&_afrLoop= 978949287356033&_afrWindowMode=0&_afrWindowId=niffdzgoy_1#!%40% 40%3Findicator%3DSTR_TSTR_ECO_NB%26_afrWindowId%3Dniffdzgoy_1% 26subject%3DIR%26_afrLoop%3D978949287356033%26datasetCode%3DA% 26collectionCode%3DYI%26_afrWindowMode%3D0%26_adf.ctrl-state% 3Dniffdzgoy_74 (accessed March 4, 2019).

ITUC. 2015. "Zimbabwe: Trade Union Leaders Arrested Ahead of Planned Demonstration." *International Trade Union Confederation.* www.ituc-csi.org/zim babwe-trade-union-leaders-16406.

The Jamestown Foundation. 2006. "The 'Latin-Americanization' of China's Domestic Politics." *China Brief* 6(21). https://jamestown.org/program/the-latin-americaniza tion-of-chinas-domestic-politics-3/ (accessed September 18, 2020).

Javeline, Debra. 2003. *Protest and the Politics of Blame: The Russian Response to Unpaid Wages.* Ann Arbor: The University of Michigan Press.

Jick, Todd D. 1979. "Mixing Qualitative and Quantitative Methods: Triangulation in Action." *Administrative Science Quarterly* 24(4): 602–11.

Jin, Rong. 2007. "Wang Yang: Chongqing chengshiren nongcunren 2012nian hukou tongyang [Wang Yang: In 2012, Chongqing Urbanites and Rural People Will Have the Same Household Registration]." *Xinhua News.* www.cq.xinhuanet.com/news/ 2007-10/19/content_11443976.htm.

Johnson, Chalmers, ed. 1970a. *Change in Communist Systems*. Stanford, CA: Stanford University Press.

1970b. "Comparing Communist Nations." In *Change in Communist Systems*, ed. Chalmers Johnson. Stanford, CA: Stanford University Press.

Kerkvliet, Benedict J. Tria. 2010. "Governance, Development, and the Responsive–Repressive State in Vietnam." *Forum for Development Studies* 37(1): 33–59.

2011. "Workers' Protests in Contemporary Vietnam." In *Labour in Vietnam*, ed. Anita Chan. Singapore: ISEAS Publishing.

Kerr, Clark, and Abraham Siegel. 1954. "The Interindustry Propensity to Strike – An International Comparison." In *Industrial Conflict*, eds. Arthur Kornhauser, Robert Dubin, and Arthur Ross. New York: McGraw-Hill.

King, Gary, Robert O. Keohane, and Sidney Verba. 1994. *Designing Social Inquiry: Scientific Inference in Qualitative Research*. Princeton, NJ: Princeton University Press.

King, Gary, Jennifer Pan, and Margaret E. Roberts. 2013. "How Censorship in China Allows Government Criticism but Silences Collective Expression." *American Political Science Review* 107(02): 326–43.

Klare, Karl E. 1978. "Judicial Deradicalization of the Wagner Act and the Origins Modern Legal Consciousness, 1937–1941." *Minnesota Law Review* 62(3): 265–339.

Klein, Naomi. 2008. "The Olympics: Unveiling Police State 2.0." *Huffington Post*. www.huffingtonpost.com/naomi-klein/the-olympics-unveiling-po_b_117403.html.

Knowles, K. G. J. C. 1952. *Strikes – A Study in Industrial Conflict*. Oxford: Basil Blackwell.

Koesel, Karrie J. 2013. "The Rise of a Chinese House Church: The Organizational Weapon." *The China Quarterly* 215: 572–89.

Koesel, Karrie J., and Valerie J. Bunce. 2013. "Diffusion-Proofing: Russian and Chinese Responses to Waves of Popular Mobilizations against Authoritarian Rulers." *Perspectives on Politics* 11(03): 753–68.

Kohli, Atul. 2004. *State-Directed Development: Political Power and Industrialization in the Global Periphery*. New York: Cambridge University Press.

Koo, Hagen. 2001. *Korean Workers: The Culture and Politics of Class Formation*. Ithaca, NY: Cornell University Press.

Kornai, Janos. 1992. *The Socialist System: The Political Economy of Communism*. Princeton, NJ: Princeton University Press.

Korstad, Robert, and Nelson Lichtenstein. 1988. "Opportunities Found and Lost: Labor, Radicals, and the Early Civil Rights Movement." *The Journal of American History* 75(3): 786–811.

Kuruvilla, Sarosh. 2018. "Editorial Essay: From Cautious Optimism to Renewed Pessimism: Labor Voice and Labor Scholarship in China." *ILR Review* 71(5): 1013–28.

Lai, Hongyi Harry. 2002. "China's Western Development Program: Its Rationale, Implementation, and Prospects." *Modern China* 28(4): 432–66.

Lam, Willy. 2010. "Shaking Up China's Labor Movement." *The Wall Street Journal*. www.wsj.com/articles/SB10001424052748703389004575305712086031490.

Landry, Pierre F. 2008. *Decentralized Authoritarianism in China: The Communist Party's Control of Local Elites in the Post-Mao Era*. New York: Cambridge University Press.

Lau, Mimi. 2016a. "Guangdong Struggles to Keep Top Spot as China's Economic Powerhouse While Jiangsu Closes In." *South China Morning Post*. www.scmp .com/news/china/policies-politics/article/1904755/guangdong-struggles-keep-top-spot-chinas-economic.

———. 2016b. "The School of Hard Rocks: How Protests by China's Miners Shine a Light on an Industry in Decline." *South China Morning Post*. www.scmp.com/news/china/economy/article/1931641/school-hard-rocks-how-protests-chinas-miners-shine-light-industry (accessed March 27, 2019).

Lee, Ching Kwan. 1998. *Gender and the South China Miracle: Two Worlds of Factory Women*. Berkeley: University of California Press.

———. 2002. "From the Specter of Mao to the Spirit of the Law: Labor Insurgency in China." *Theory and Society* 31(2): 189–228.

———. 2007. *Against the Law: Labor Protests in China's Rustbelt and Sunbelt*. Berkeley: University of California Press.

———. 2016. "Precarization or Empowerment? Reflections on Recent Labor Unrest in China." *The Journal of Asian Studies* 75(2): 317–33.

Lee, Ching Kwan, and Yuan Shen. 2011. "The Anti-Solidarity Machine?: Labor Nongovernmental Organizations in China." In *From Iron Rice Bowl to Informalization: Markets, Workers, and the State in a Changing China*, eds. Sarosh Kuruvilla, Ching Kwan Lee, and Mary E Gallagher. Ithaca, NY: ILR Press.

Lee, Ching Kwan, and Yonghong Zhang. 2013. "The Power of Instability: Unraveling the Microfoundations of Bargained Authoritarianism in China." *American Journal of Sociology* 118(6): 1475–508.

Leung, Parry P. 2015. *Labor Activists and the New Working Class in China: Strike Leaders' Struggles*. New York: Palgrave MacMillan.

Levitsky, Steven, and Lucan Way. 2010. *Competitive Authoritarianism: Hybrid Regimes after the Cold War*. New York: Cambridge University Press.

Li, Guo. 2006. "Chongqing shiwei shuji Wang Yang: jiejue nongmingong kunnan gonghui da you kewei [Chongqing City Party Committee Secretary Wang Yang: the union has great prospects for resolving migrant workers' difficulties]." *People's Daily*. http://news .sina.com.cn/c/2006-02-20/01538250939s.shtml (accessed on September 17, 2020).

———. 2007. "Chongqingshi gonghui disanci daibiao dahui zhaokai [The third congress of the Chongqing City Union convened]." *Workers Daily*. http://news.sohu.com/20071128/n253609442.shtml (accessed September 17, 2020).

Li, Ju. 2012. "Fight Silently: Everyday Resistance in Surviving State Owned Enterprises in Contemporary China." *Global Labour Journal* 3(2): 194–216.

Li, Lianjiang, Mingxing Liu, and Kevin J. O'Brien. 2012. "Petitioning Beijing: The High Tide of 2003–2006." *The China Quarterly* 210(2012): 313–34.

Li, Yao. 2019a. "A Zero-Sum Game? Repression and Protest in China." *Government and Opposition* 54(2): 309–35.

———. 2019b. *Playing by the Informal Rules: Why the Chinese Regime Remains Stable despite Rising Protests*. New York: Cambridge University Press.

Li, Yao, and Manfred Elfstrom. 2020. "Does Greater Coercive Capacity Increase Overt Repression? Evidence from China." *Journal of Contemporary China*: 1–20.

Liasheva, Alona. 2017. "Belarus's Parasites." *Jacobin*. https://jacobinmag.com/2017/04/belarus-lukashenko-decree-three-social-dependency-parasites-tax-unemployment (accessed February 18, 2020).

Lichbach, Mark Irving. 1987. "Deterrence or Escalation? The Puzzle of Aggregate Studies of Repression and Dissent." *Journal of Conflict Resolution* 31(2): 266–97.

Liebman, Benjamin L. 2007. "China's Courts: Restricted Reform." *The China Quarterly* 191: 620–43.

Lim, Benjamin Kang, Matthew Miller, and David Stanway. 2016. "Exclusive: China to Lay Off Five to Six Million Workers, Earmarks at Least $23 Billion." *Reuters.* www .reuters.com/article/us-china-economy-layoffs-exclusive-idUSKCN0W33DS.

Lin, Kun-Chin. 2009. "Class Formation or Fragmentation? Allegiances and Divisions among Managers and Workers in State-Owned Enterprises." In *Laid-Off Workers in a Workers' State: Unemployment with Chinese Characteristics*, eds. Thomas B. Gold, William J. Hurst, Jaeyoun Won, and Qiang Li. New York: Palgrave MacMillan.

Lin, Xin. 2014. "China Closes 'Hazardous' Factories after Deadly Suzhou Blast." *Radio Free Asia.* www.rfa.org/english/news/china/blast-08072014115912.html (accessed December 3, 2015).

Linz, Juan J. 2000. *Totalitarian and Authoritarian Regimes.* Boulder, CO, and London: Lynne Rienner Publishers.

Liu, Junde. 2011. "Regional Cooperation in China's Administrative Region Economy: Its Links with Pan-Pearl River Delta Development." In *China's Pan-Pearl River Delta: Regional Cooperation and Development*, eds. Anthony G. O. Yeh and Jiang Xu. Hong Kong: Hong Kong University Press.

Liu, Kaiming. 2003. Shentide jiage: Zhongguo gongshang suopei yanjiu *[The Price of Bodies: Research on Chinese Work Injury Claims].* Beijing: Renminribao chubanshe.

Liu, Linping, Xin Yong, and Fenfen Shu. 2011. "Laodong Quanyide Diqu Chayi: Jiyu Dui Zhusanjiao He Changsanjiao Diqu Wailaigongde Wenjuan Diaocha [Regional Differences in Labor Rights: A Survey Investigation of the Pearl River Delta and Yangtze River Delta Regions' Migrant Workers]." *Zhongguo Shehui Kexue* 2: 107–24.

Liu, Mingwei. 2010. "Union Organizing in China: Still a Monolithic Labor Movement?" *Industrial and Labor Relations Review* 64(1): 30–52.

Liu, Mingwei, Chunyun Li, and Sunghoon Kim. 2011. "Chinese Trade Unions in Transition: A Three-Level Analysis." In *China's Changing Workplace: Dynamism, Diversity, and Disparity*, eds. Peter Sheldon, Sunghoon Kim, Yiqiong Li, and Malcolm Warner. New York: Routledge.

Liu, Mingxing, Linke Hou, and Ran Tao. 2013. "An Empirical Study on the Cadre Responsibility System of Local Government in China." *China Economist* 8(6): 82–98.

Liu, Yuanwen. 2014. "Gonghui Zuzhi Xingzhenghuade Shengcheng Jizhi Yu Gaige Qianjing [Mechanisms Generating Union Organization Bureaucratism and Prospects for Change]." *Gonghui lilun yanjiu* 4: 12–15.

Lorentzen, Peter. 2013. "Regularized Rioting: Permitting Public Protest in an Authoritarian Regime." *Quarterly Journal of Political Science* 8(2): 127–58.

2017. "Designing Contentious Politics in Post-1989 China." *Modern China* 43(5): 459–93.

Lorentzen, Peter, and Suzanne Scoggins. 2015. "Understanding China's Rising Rights Consciousness." *The China Quarterly* 223: 638–57.

Lu, Tu. 2012. *Zhongguo Xin Gongren: Mishi Yu Jueqi [China's New Workers: Lost and Rising]*. Beijing: Law Press.

Lü, Xiaobo, and Pierre F. Landry. 2014. "Show Me the Money: Interjurisdiction Political Competition and Fiscal Extraction in China." *American Political Science Review* 108(03): 706–22.

Lü, Xiaobo, and Elizabeth J. Perry. 1997. "Introduction: The Changing Chinese Workplace in Historical and Comparative Perspective." In *Danwei: The Changing Chinese Workplace in Historical and Comparative Perspective*, eds. Xiaobo Lü and Elizabeth J. Perry. Armonk, NY: M. E. Sharpe.

Lüthje, Boy. 2012. "Diverging Trajectories: Economic Rebalancing and Labor Policies in China."

Lyddon, Dave, Xuebing Cao, Quan Meng, and Jun Lu. 2015. "A Strike of 'Unorganised' Workers in a Chinese Car Factory: The Nanhai Honda Events of 2010." *Industrial Relations Journal* 46(2): 134–52.

MacFarquhar, Roderick, and Michael Schoenhals. 2006. *Mao's Last Revolution*. Cambridge, MA: Harvard University Press.

Magaloni, Beatriz. 2006. *Voting for Autocracy: Hegemonic Party Survival and Its Demise in Mexico*. New York: Cambridge University Press.

Mandel, Ernest. 1951. "The Theory of 'State Capitalism.'" *Ernest Mandel Internet Archive*. www.ernestmandel.org/en/works/txt/1951/theory_of_statecapitalism.htm (accessed February 2, 2018).

Manion, Melanie. 1985. "The Cadre Management System Post-Mao: The Appointment, Promotion, Transfer and Removal of Party and State Leaders." *The China Quarterly* 102(102): 203–33.

   1990. "Reluctant Duelists: The Logic of the 1989 Protests and Massacre." In *Beijing Spring, 1989: Confrontation and Conflict: The Basic Documents*, eds. Michael Oksenberg, Lawrence R. Sullivan, and Marc Lambert. Armonk, NY: M. E. Sharpe.

   2006. "Democracy, Community, Trust: The Impact of Elections in Rural China." *Comparative Political Studies* 39(3): 301–24.

Mantsios, Gregory. 2010. "Vietnam at the Crossroads: Labor in Transition." *New Labor Forum* 19(2): 66–76.

Marx, Karl. 1990. *Capital: Volume I*. New York: Penguin Classics.

Marx, Karl, and Frederick Engels. 1848. *The Communist Manifesto*. ed. Frederick Engels. New York: International Publishers.

Mattingly, Daniel C. 2020. *The Art of Political Control in China*. New York: Cambridge University Press.

McAdam, Doug. 1999. *Political Process and the Development of Black Insurgency, 1930–1970*. 2nd ed. Chicago and London: The University of Chicago Press.

McAdam, Doug, John D. McCarthy, and Mayer N. Zald. 1996. "Introduction: Opportunities, Mobilizing Structures, and Framing Processes – Toward a Synthetic, Comparative Perspective on Social Movements." In *Comparative Perspectives on Social Movements: Political Opportunities, Mobilizing Structures, and Cultural Framings*, eds. Doug McAdam, John D. McCarthy, and Mayer N. Zald. New York: Cambridge University Press.

McAdam, Doug, Sidney Tarrow, and Charles Tilly. 2001. *Dynamics of Contention*. New York: Cambridge University Press.

McLaughlin, Timothy. 2020. "Democracy Drives Labor in a Hyper-Capitalist City." *The Atlantic.* www.theatlantic.com/international/archive/2020/02/unions-hong-kong-protest-coronavirus/606136/ (accessed February 18, 2020).

Meng, Quan, and Jun Lu. 2013. "Political Space in the Achievement of Collective Labour Rights: Interaction between Regional Government and Workers' Protest." *The Journal of Comparative Asian Development* 12(3): 465–88.

Mertha, Andrew C. 2005. "China's 'Soft' Centralization: Shifting Tiao/Kuai Authority Relations." *The China Quarterly* 184: 791–810.

   2008. *China's Water Warriors: Citizen Action and Policy Change.* Ithaca, NY: Cornell University Press.

de Mesquita, Bruce Bueno, Alastair Smith, Randolph M. Siverson, and James D. Morrow. *The Logic of Political Survival.* Cambridge, MA: MIT Press, 2003.

Migdal, Joel. 2001. *State in Society: Studying How States and Societies Transform and Constitute One Another.* New York: Cambridge University Press.

Minzner, Carl F. 2006. "Xinfang: An Alternative to the Formal Chinese Legal System." *Stanford Journal of International Law* 42(1): 103–79.

   2018. *End of an Era: How China's Authoritarian Revival Is Undermining Its Rise.* New York: Oxford University Press.

Montesquieu, Charles de Secondant Baron de la Brede. 1990. *Selected Political Writings.* ed. Melvin Richter. Indianapolis, IN: Hackett Publishing Company.

Moore, Barrington. 1966. *Social Origins of Dictatorship and Democracy.* Boston: Beacon Press.

Mosley, Layna. 2011. *Labor Rights and Multinational Production.* New York: Cambridge University Press.

Mudie, Luisetta. 2012. "Steel, Beer Workers Strike." *Radio Free Asia.* www.rfa.org/english/news/china/strike-01062012173145.html (accessed February 26, 2018).

Nathan, Andrew J. 2003. "Authoritarian Resilience." *Journal of Democracy* 14(1): 6–17.

   2015. "The Problem with the China Model." *ChinaFile.* www.chinafile.com/reporting-opinion/viewpoint/problem-china-model (accessed March 17, 2016).

Naughton, Barry. 1995. *Growing Out of the Plan: Chinese Economic Reform, 1978–1993.* New York: Cambridge University Press.

   2007. *The Chinese Economy: Transitions and Growth.* Cambridge: MIT Press.

Nee, Victor, and Sonja Opper. 2012. *Capitalism from Below: Markets and Institutional Change in China.* Cambridge, MA: Harvard University Press.

NewsGD.com. 2006. "SZ to Crack Down on Unpaid Wages." *NewsGD.com.* www.newsgd.com/news/guangdong1/200608070004.htm (accessed January 16, 2016).

Ng, Sek Hong, and Malcolm Warner. 1998. *China's Trade Unions and Management.* London: Palgrave MacMillan.

O'Brien, Kevin J. 1996. "Rightful Resistance." *World Politics* 49(1): 31–55.

   2003. "Neither Transgressive nor Contained: Boundary-Spanning Contention in China." *Mobilization: An International Journal* 8(1): 51–64.

O'Brien, Kevin J., and Lianjiang Li. 1999. "Selective Policy Implementation in Rural China." *Comparative Politics* 31(2): 167–86.

   2006. *Rightful Resistance in Rural China.* New York: Cambridge University Press.

O'Donnell, Guillermo A., and Philippe C. Schmitter. 1986. *Transitions from Authoritarian Rule: Tentative Conclusions About Uncertain Democracies.* Baltimore and London: The Johns Hopkins University Press.

OECD. 2010. *OECD Territorial Reviews: Guangdong, China 2010*. Paris: OECD Publishing.

Ong, Lynette. 2018. "Thugs and Outsourcing of State Repression in China." *The China Journal* 80: 94–110.

Ong, Lynette, and Christian Goebel. 2012. *Social Unrest in China*. London: European China Research and Advice Network.

Paczynska, Agnieszka. 2006. "Globalization, Structural Adjustment , and Pressure to Conform: Contesting Labor Law Reform in Egypt." *New Political Science* 28(1): 45–64.

Paik, Wooyeal. 2014. "Local Village Workers, Foreign Factories and Village Politics in Coastal China: A Clientelist Clientelist Approach." *The China Quarterly* 220: 955–67.

Pan, Jennifer. 2020. *Welfare for Autocrats: How Social Assistance in China Cares for Its Rulers*. New York: Oxford University Press.

Pan, Jennifer, and Yiqing Xu. 2017. "China's Ideological Spectrum." *Journal of Politics* 80(1): 254–73.

Pan, Philip P. 2005. "Chinese Peasants Attacked in Land Dispute." *Washington Post*. www.washingtonpost.com/wp-dyn/content/article/2005/06/14/AR2005061401542.html (accessed January 29, 2018).

Pannekoek, Anton. 1936. "State Capitalism and Dictatorship." *Marxists.org*. www.marxists.org/archive/pannekoe/1936/dictatorship.htm (accessed February 5, 2018).

People's Daily. 2015. "Zhonggong Zhongyang Guowuyuan Guanyu Goujian Hexie Laodong Guanxide Yijian [Central Committee of the Chinese Communist Party and State Council Opinions on Building Harmonious Labor Relations]." *People's Daily Online* 1:1.

People's Government of Shaoyang. 2014. "Xian Renshi Ju Yufang He Chuzhi Quntixing Shijian Yingji Yu'an [County Personnel Bureau Contingency Plan for Preventing and Handling Mass Incidents]." *Shaoyang People's Government*. http://zwgk.syx.gov.cn/articles/126/2012-11/8314.html (accessed March 9, 2018).

Pepinsky, Thomas B. 2009. *Economic Crises and the Breakdown of Authoritarian Regimes: Indonesia and Malaysia in Comparative Perspective*. New York: Cambridge University Press.

Perry, Elizabeth J. 1993. *Shanghai on Strike: The Politics of Chinese Labor*. Stanford, CA: Stanford University Press.

   1994. "Shanghai's Strike Wave of 1957." *The China Quarterly* 137: 1–27.

   2002. *Challenging the Mandate of Heaven: Social Protest and State Power in China*. Armonk, NY: M. E. Sharpe.

   2008. "Permanent Rebellion? Continuities and Discontinuities in Chinese Protest." In *Popular Protest in China*, ed. Kevin J. O'Brien. Cambridge, MA: Harvard University Press.

   2010. "Popular Protest: Playing by the Rules." In *China Today, China Tomorrow: Domestic Politics, Economy, and Society*, ed. Joseph Fewsmith. Lanham, MD: Rowman & Littlefield Publishers, Inc.

   2012. *Anyuan: Mining China's Revolutionary Tradition*. Berkeley: University of California Press.

Perry, Elizabeth J., and Xun Li. 1997. *Proletarian Power: Shanghai in the Cultural Revolution*. Boulder, CO: Westview Press.

Pfaff, Steven. 2006. *Exit-Voice Dynamics and the Collapse of East Germany: The Crisis of Leninism and the Revolution of 1989*. Durham, NC: Duke University Press.

Piven, Frances Fox, and Richard Cloward. 1977. *Poor People's Movements: Why They Succeed, How They Fail*. New York: Vintage Books.

Posusney, Marsha Pripstein. 1997. *Labor and the State in Egypt: Workers, Unions, and Economic Restructuring*. New York: Columbia University Press.

Pringle, Tim. 2011. *Trade Unions in China: The Challenge of Labour Unrest*. Abingdon: Routledge.

2017. "A Class Against Capital: Class and Collective Bargaining in Guangdong." In *Chinese Labour in the Global Economy: Capitalist Exploitation and Strategies of Resistance*, eds. Andreas Bieler and Chun-Yi Lee. Abingdon: Routledge.

Pringle, Tim, and Simon Clarke. 2011. *The Challenge of Transition: Trade Unions in Russia, China and Vietnam*. New York: Palgrave MacMillan.

Pringle, Tim, and Quan Meng. 2018. "Taming Labor: Workers' Struggles, Workplace Unionism, and Collective Bargaining on a Chinese Waterfront." *Industrial and Labor Relations Review* 71(5): 1053–77.

Przeworski, Adam, and Henry Teune. 1970. *The Logic of Comparative Social Inquiry*. New York: Wiley-Interscience.

Pun, Ngai. 2005. *Made in China: Women Factory Workers in a Global Workplace*. Durham, NC: Duke University Press.

2016. *Migrant Labor in China*. Malden, MA: Polity Press.

Pun, Ngai, and Chris Smith. 2007. "Putting Transnational Labour Process in Its Place: The Dormitory Labour Regime in Post-Socialist China." *Work, Employment & Society* 21(1): 27–45.

Pun, Ngai, and Yi Xu. 2011. "Legal Activism or Class Action?" *China Perspectives* 2011(2): 9–17.

Qian, Yanfeng. 2010. "Workers Protest over Pay, Toxic Chemicals." *China Daily*. http://webcache.googleusercontent.com/search?q=cache:XoRsZtCYogIJ:www.chinadaily.com.cn/china/2010-01/18/content_9332793.htm&hl=en&gl=ca&strip=1&vwsrc=o (accessed January 8, 2016).

Ragin, Charles C. 2008. *Redesigning Social Inquiry: Fuzzy Sets and Beyond*. Chicago: University of Chicago Press.

Read, Benjamin L. 2012. *Roots of the State: Neighborhood Organization and Social Networks in Beijing and Taipei*. Stanford, CA: Stanford University Press.

Renmin University. 2015. "Chinese General Social Survey." *Cgiubese*. http://cgss.ruc.edu.cn/index.php?r=index/index.

Reuter, Ora John, and David Szakonyi. 2019. "Elite Defection under Autocracy: Evidence from Russia." *American Political Science Review* 113(2): 552–68.

Reuters. 2014. "China Sacks Officials for Factory Blast, 17 Dead in Latest Incident." *Reuters*. www.reuters.com/article/us-china-blast-punishment/china-sacks-senior-officials-for-deadly-factory-blast-idUSKBN0K903520141231 (accessed February 20, 2018).

RFA. 2019. "Wu ming Shenzhen laogong huodong huodong renshi bei jingfang zhuabu [Five Shenzhen Labor Activism Leaders Detained by Police]." *Radio Free Asia*. www.rfa

.org/mandarin/yataibaodao/renquanfazhi/yl-01222019100220.html (accessed February 14, 2020).

Ringen, Stein. 2016. *The Perfect Dictatorship: China in the 21st Century.* Hong Kong: Hong Kong University Press.

Rithmire, Meg. 2012. *The "Chongqing Model" and the Future of China.* Cambridge, MA: Harvard Business Review.

Roberts, Dexter. 2020. *The Myth of Chinese Capitalism: The Worker, the Factory, and the Future of the World.* New York: St. Martin's.

Roberts, Margaret E. 2018. *Censored: Distraction and Diversion Inside China's Great Firewall.* Princeton, NJ, and Oxford: Princeton University Press.

Robertson, Graeme B. 2011. *The Politics of Protest in Hybrid Regimes: Managing Dissent in Post-Communist Russia.* New York: Cambridge University Press.

Robertson, Graeme B., and Emmanuel Teitelbaum. 2011. "Foreign Direct Investment, Regime Type, and Labor Protest in Developing Countries." *American Journal of Political Science* 55(3): 665–77.

Rochlin, James. 2016. "The Political Economy of Impunity in Colombia: The Case of Colombian Labour." *Conflict, Security & Development* 16(2): 173–96.

Rosenman, Olivia. 2013. "Revealed: How Trade Unions Are Failing in Shenzhen's Factories." *South China Morning Post.* www.scmp.com/news/china-insider/article/1343678/revealed-how-trade-unions-are-failing-shenzhens-factories (accessed December 2, 2015).

Ross, Robert S. 2009. "China's Naval Nationalism: Sources, Prospects, and the U.S. Response." *International Security* 34(2): 46–81.

Sabea, Hanan. 2014. "Still Waiting: Labor, Revolution, and the Struggle for Social Justice in Egypt." *International Labor and Working-Class History* 86: 178–82.

Saich, Tony. 2015. *Governance and Politics of China.* 4th ed. New York: Palgrave MacMillan.

———. 2016. "State-Society Relations in the People's Republic of China Post-1949." *Brill Research Perspectives in Governance and Public Policy in China* 1(1): 1–57.

Saich, Tony, and Biliang Hu. 2012. *Chinese Village, Global Market.* New York: Palgrave MacMillan.

Sargeson, Sally. 1999. *Reworking China's Proletariat.* New York: St. Martin's.

Schiller, Bill. 2010. "Labour Strife Rolls across China." *The Toronto Star.* www.thestar.com/news/world/2010/06/08/labour_strife_rolls_across_china.html (accessed February 26, 2018).

Scoggins, Suzanne E., and Kevin J. O'Brien. 2015. "China's Unhappy Police." *Asian Survey* 56(2): 225–42.

Sheehan, Jackie. 1998. *Chinese Workers: A New History.* London and New York: Routledge.

Shih, Victor, Christopher Adolph, and Mingxing Liu. 2012. "Getting Ahead in the Communist Party: Explaining the Advancement of Central Committee Members in China." *American Political Science Review* 106(01): 166–87.

Shorter, Edward, and Charles Tilly. 1971. "The Shape of Strikes in France, 1830–1960." *Society for Comparative Studies in Society and History* 13(1): 60–86.

Shue, Vivienne. 1990. *The Reach of the State: Sketches of the Chinese Body Politic.* Stanford, CA: Stanford University Press.

Shue, Vivienne, and Patricia M. Thornton. 2017. "Introduction: Beyond Implicit Political Dichotomies and Linear Models of Change in China." In *To Govern*

China: Evolving Practices of Power, eds. Vivienne Shue and Patricia M. Thornton. New York: Cambridge University Press.

Silver, Beverly J. 2003. *Forces of Labor: Workers' Movements and Globalization Since 1870*. New York: Cambridge University Press.

Silver, Beverly J., and Lu Zhang. 2009. "China as an Emerging Epicenter of World Labor Unrest." In *China and the Transformation of Global Capitalism*, ed. Ho-fung Hung. Baltimore: The Johns Hopkins University Press, 174–87.

Simon, Karla W. 2011a. "Relaxing the Registration Rules for Civil Society Organizations in China." Alliance Magazine. www.alliancemagazine.org/blog/relaxing-the-registration-rules-for-civil-society-organizations-in-china/.

2011b. "The Regulation of Civil Society Organizations in China." *International Journal of Civil Society Law* 9(1): 55–84.

Siu, Kaxton. 2015. "Continuity and Change in the Everyday Lives of Chinese Migrant Factory Workers." *The China Journal* 74: 1–22.

Slater, Dan. 2010. *Ordering Power: Contentious Politics and Authoritarian Leviathans in Southeast Asia*. New York: Cambridge University Press.

Slater, Dan, and Nicholas Rush Smith. 2016. "The Power of Counterrevolution: Elitist Origins of Political Order in Postcolonial Asia and Africa." *American Journal of Sociology* 121(5): 1472–516.

Slater, Dan, and Daniel Ziblatt. 2013. "The Enduring Indispensability of the Controlled Comparison." *Comparative Political Studies* 46(10): 1301–27.

Solinger, Dorothy. 1999. *Contesting Citizenship in Urban China: Peasant Migrants, the State, and the Logic of the Market*. Oakland: University of California Press.

2004. "The New Crowd of the Dispossessed: The Shift of the Urban Proletariat from Master to Mendicant." In *State and Society in 21st Century China: Crisis, Contention and Legitimation*, eds. Peter Hays Gries and Stanley Rosen. New York: RoutledgeCurzon.

2009. *State's Gains, Labor's Losses: China, France, and Mexico Choose Global Liaisons, 1980–2000*. Ithaca, NY: Cornell University Press.

Spires, Anthony J., Lin Tao, and Kin-man Chan. 2014. "Societal Support for China's Grass-Roots NGOs: Evidence from Yunnan, Guangdong and Beijing." *The China Journal* 71: 65–90.

Statista. 2018. "Global Video Surveillance Market Size by Region 2009–2019 | Statistic." *Statista*. www.statista.com/statistics/484857/video-surveillance-market-size-worldwide-by-region/ (accessed January 9, 2018).

Steinhardt, H. Christoph. 2013. *How Rebellious Is Chinese Society? An Analysis of Official Figures and Survey Data*. Singapore: East Asian Institute, National University of Singapore.

Steinhardt, H. Christoph, and Fengshi Wu. 2016. "In the Name of the Public: Environmental Protest and the Changing Landscape of Popular Contention in China." *The China Journal* 75: 61–82.

Stern, Rachel E., and Kevin J. O'Brien. 2012. "Politics at the Boundary: Mixed Signals and the Chinese State." *Modern China* 38(2): 174–98.

Stockmann, Daniela, and Mary E. Gallagher. 2011. "Remote Control: How the Media Sustain Authoritarian Rule in China." *Comparative Political Studies* 44(4): 436–67.

Stone, Katherine Van Wezel. 1981. "The Post-War Paradigm in American Labor Law." *Yale Law Journal* 90(7): 1509–80.

Svartzman, Boris. 2013. "The Leap to the City: Resistance and Transition in a Chinese Village Facing Urbanisation." *China Perspectives* 2013(1): 41–52.

Svolik, Milan W. 2009. "Power Sharing and Leadership Dynamics in Authoritarian Regimes." *American Journal of Political Science* 53(2): 477–94.

2012. *The Politics of Authoritarian Rule.* New York: Cambridge University Press.

Swider, Sarah. 2015. *Building China: Informal Work and the New Precariat.* Ithaca, NY: Cornell University Press.

Taha, Mai. 2014. "The Egyptian Revolution in and out of the Juridical Space: An Inquiry into Labour Law and the Workers' Movement in Egypt." *International Journal of Law in Context* 10(02): 177–94.

Tang, Didi. 2015. "China's 168 Million Migrant Workers Are Discovering Their Labor Rights." *Business Insider.* www.businessinsider.com/chinas-168-million-migrant-workers-are-discovering-their-labor-rights-2015-4 (accessed April 10, 2017).

Tang, Jianguang. 2004. "Dongguan Xing'ang Xiechang Gongren Saoluan Diaocha [An Investigation of the Dongguan Xing'ang Shoe Factory Worker Disturbance]." *China Newsweek.* http://finance.sina.com.cn/roll/20041026/14151109647.shtml (accessed September 18, 2020).

Tanner, Murray Scott. 2004. "China Rethinks Unrest." *The Washington Quarterly* 27(3): 137–56.

2014. "The Impact of the 2009 People's Armed Police Law on the People's Armed Police Force." In *The Politics of Law and Stability in China*, eds. Susan Trevaskes, Elisa Nesossi, Flora Sapio, and Sarah Biddulph. Cheltenham: Edward Elgar Publishing Limited.

Tarrow, Sidney. 1998. *Power in Movement: Social Movements and Contentious Politics.* 2nd ed. New York: Cambridge University Press.

2008. "Prologue: The New Contentious Politics in China: Poor and Blank or Rich and Complex?" In *Popular Protest in China*, ed. Kevin J. O'Brien. Cambridge, MA: Harvard University Press.

2010. "Bridging the Quantitative-Qualitative Divide." In *Rethinking Social Inquiry: Diverse Tools, Shared Standards*, eds. Henry E. Brady and David Collier. New York: Rowman & Littlefield Publishers, Inc.

2011. *Power in Movement: Social Movements and Contentious Politics.* 3rd ed. New York: Cambridge University Press.

2012. *Strangers at the Gates: Movements and States in Contentious Politics.* New York: Cambridge University Press.

Taylor, Bill, Kai Chang, and Qi Li. 2003. *Industrial Relations in China.* Northampton, MA: Edward Elgar Publishing Limited.

Taylor, Brian D. 2011. *State Building in Putin's Russia: Policing and Coercion after Communism.* New York: Cambridge University Press.

Teets, Jessica C. 2014. *Civil Society under Authoritarianism: The China Model.* New York: Cambridge University Press.

Teitelbaum, Emmanuel. 2011. *Mobilizing Restraint: Democracy and Industrial Conflict in Postreform South Asia.* Ithaca, NY: Cornell University Press.

Tencent. 2015. "Guangzhou Gongbu Laodong Guanxi Hexie Qiye Bang 170 Ge Qiye Huo 3A [Guangzhou Announces That 170 of the Enterprises on the Honor Roll of Harmonious Labor Relations Enterprises Received a 3A Rating]." *Tencent Dayuewang.* http://gd.qq.com/a/20150519/048012.htm (accessed February 12, 2016).

Thaler, Richard H., and Cass R. Sunstein. 2008. *Nudge: Improving Decisions About Health, Wealth, and Happiness*. New Haven, CT: Yale University Press.

Tian, Robert G., and Yan Wu. 2007. "Crafting Self Identity in a Virtual Community: Chinese Internet Users and Their Political Sense Form." *Multicultural Education & Technology Journal* 1(4): 238–58.

Tilly, Charles. 1995. *Popular Contention in Great Britain: 1759–1834*. Cambridge, MA: Harvard University Press.

2006. *Regimes and Repertoires*. Chicago and London: University of Chicago Press.

Tomba, Luigi. 2014. *The Government Next Door: Neighborhood Politics in Urban China*. Ithaca, NY: Cornell University Press.

Tong, Yanqi, and Shaohua Lei. 2014. *Social Protest in Contemporary China, 2003–2010: Transitional Pains and Regime Legitimacy*. London and New York: Routledge.

Tracy, Joseph S. 1987. "An Empirical Test of an Asymmetric Information Model of Strikes." *Journal of Labor Economics* 5(2): 149–73.

Trade Union Law of the People's Republic of China. 2001. www.china.org.cn/english/DAT/214784.htm (accessed April 8, 2019).

Trần, Angie Ngọc. 2013. *Ties That Bind: Cultural Identity, Class, and Law in Vietnam's Labor Resistance*. Ithaca, NY: Cornell Southeast Asia Program Publications.

Trejo, Guillermo. 2012. *Popular Movements in Autocracies: Religion, Repression, and Indigenous Collective Action in Mexico*. New York: Cambridge University Press.

Trevaskes, Susan. 2010. *Policing Serious Crime in China: From "Strike Hard" to "Kill Fewer."* London and New York: Routledge.

Truex, Rory. 2016. *Making Autocracy Work: Representation and Responsiveness in Modern China*. New York: Cambridge University Press.

Tsai, Kellee S. 2006. "Adaptive Informal Institutions and Endogenous Change in China." *World Politics* 59(1): 116–41.

2007. *Capitalism without Democracy: The Private Sector in Contemporary China*. Ithaca, NY: Cornell University Press.

Tsai, Lily L. 2007. "Solidary Groups, Informal Accountability, and Local Public Goods Provision in Rural China." *The American Political Science Review* 101(2): 355–72.

Tsang, Steve. 2009. "Consultative Leninism: China's New Political Framework." *Journal of Contemporary China* 18(62): 865–80.

Unger, Jonathan, Diana Beaumont, and Anita Chan. 2011. "Did Unionization Make a Difference? Work Conditions and Trade Union Activities at Chinese Walmart Stores." In *Walmart in China*, ed. Anita Chan. Ithaca, NY: ILR Press.

Unger, Jonathan, and Anita Chan. 1995. "China, Corporatism, and the East Asian Model." *The Australian Journal of Chinese Affairs* 33: 29–53.

University of Cambridge Institute for Manufacturing. 2008. Understanding China's Manufacturing Value Chain: Opportunities for UK Enterprises in China. Cambridge, UK.

Vinogradova, Elena, Irina Kozina, and Linda Cook. 2012. "Russian Labor: Quiescence and Conflict." *Communist and Post-Communist Studies* 45(3–4): 219–31.

Vogel, Ezra. 1971. *Canton Under Communism: Programs and Politics in a Provincial Capital, 1949–1968*. New York: Harper & Row.

1989. *One Step Ahead in China: Guangdong Under Reform*. Cambridge, MA: Harvard University Press.

Walder, Andrew. 1988. *Communist Neo-Traditionalism: Work and Authority in Chinese Industry*. Berkeley: University of California Press.

Walder, Andrew, and Xiaoxia Gong. 1993. "Workers in the Tiananmen Protests: The Politics of the Beijing Workers' Autonomous Federation." *The Australian Journal of Chinese Affairs* 29: 1–29.

Wallace, Jeremy L. 2014. *Cities and Stability: Urbanization, Redistribution, and Regime Survival in China*. New York: Oxford University Press.

2016. "Juking the Stats? Authoritarian Information Problems in China." *British Journal of Political Science* 46(1): 11–29.

Wan, Xiangdong. 2005. Comparison between Migrant Workers in Pearl River Delta and Yangtze River Delta. Social Resources Institute. www.eu-china.net/upload/pdf/materialien/2011_Wan_Xiangdong-Comparison_Migrant_Workers_in_Pearl_and_Yangtze_River.pdf.

Wang, Chaohua, ed. 2003. *One China, Many Paths*. New York and London: Verso.

Wang, Juan. 2015. "Managing Social Stability: The Perspective of a Local Government in China." *Journal of East Asian Studies* 15(1): 1–25.

2017. *The Sinews of State Power: The Rise and Demise of the Cohesive Local State in Rural China*. New York: Oxford University Press.

Wang, Kan, and Manfred Elfstrom. 2017. "Worker Unrest and Institutional Change: Perceptions of Local Trade Union Leaders in China." *China Information* 31(1): 84–106.

Wang, Shaoguang. 2010. "China's Expenditure for the People's Armed Police and Militia." In *Chinese Civil-Military Relations: The Transformation of the People's Liberation Army*, ed. Nan Li. London: Routledge.

2011. "Tansu Zhongguoshi Shehuizhuyi 3.0: Chongqing Jingyan [Exploring Chinese-Style Socialism 3.0: The Chongqing Experience]." *Ai Sixiang*. www.aisixiang.com/data/38896.html (September 16, 2020).

Wang, Taiyuan. 1997. *Hu Zheng Yu Renkou Guanli: Lilun Yanjiu Zongshu [Household Registration and Population Management: Collected Theory and Research]*. Beijing: Qunzhong Chubanshe.

Wang, Yuhua. 2015. *Tying the Autocrat's Hands: The Rise of the Rule of Law in China*. New York: Cambridge University Press.

Wang, Yuhua, and Carl F. Minzner. 2013. "The Rise of the Chinese Security State." *The China Quarterly* 222: 339–59.

Wasow, Omar. 2020. "Agenda Seeding: How 1960s Black Protests Moved Elites, Public Opinion and Voting." *American Political Science Review* 114(3): 638–59.

Wedeman, Andrew. 2009. "Enemies of the State: Mass Incidents and Subversion in China." In *APSA Meeting Paper*, http://ssrn.com/abstract=1451828.

Weeks, Jessica L. 2012. "Strongmen and Straw Men: Authoritarian Regimes and the Initiation of International Conflict." *American Political Science Review* 106(02): 326–47.

Wemheuer, Felix. 2019. *A Social History of Maoist China: Conflict and Change, 1949–1976*. New York: Cambridge University Press.

Wen, Xiaoyi. 2015. "Employer-Initiated Collective Bargaining: A Case Study of the Chinese Sweater Industry." *Employee Relations* 38(2): 267–85.

Wen, Xiaoyi, and Kevin Lin. 2014. "Restructuring China's State Corporatist Industrial Relations System: The Wenling Experience." *Journal of Contemporary China* 24(94): 665–83.

Weston, Timothy B. 2004. "The Iron Man Weeps: Joblessness and Political Legitimacy in the Chinese Rust Belt." In *State and Society in 21st Century China: Crisis, Contention and Legitimation*, eds. Peter Hays Gries and Stanley Rosen. New York: RoutledgeCurzon.

Whiting, Susan H. 2001. *Power and Wealth in Rural China; The Political Economy of Institutional Change*. New York: Cambridge University Press.

———. 2017. "Authoritarian 'Rule of Law' and Regime Legitimacy." *Comparative Political Studies* 50(14): 1907–40.

Whyte, Martin King. 2010. *Myth of the Social Volcano: Perceptions of Inequality and Distributive Injustice in Contemporary China*. Stanford, CA: Stanford University Press.

WID – World Inequality Database. n.d. "WID – World Inequality Database." https://wid.world/ (accessed April 3, 2019).

Wines, Michael. 2009. "China Approves Law Governing Armed Police Force." *New York Times*. www.nytimes.com/2009/08/28/world/asia/28china.html?_r=0.

Wing Chan, Kam, and Will Buckingham. 2008. "Is China Abolishing the Hukou System?" *The China Quarterly* 195: 582–606.

Wintrobe, Ronald. 1998. *The Political Economy of Dictatorship*. New York: Cambridge University Press.

Wong, Catherine. 2018. "China's Military Veterans Ministry Opens after Pension Protests." *South China Morning Post*. www.scmp.com/news/china/diplomacy-defence/article/2141894/chinas-military-veterans-ministry-opens-after-pension (accessed April 18, 2019).

Wong, Chun Han. 2015. "China Factory Workers Strike Over Housing Benefits." *Wall Street Journal*. www.wsj.com/articles/china-factory-workers-strike-over-housing-benefits-1426054854#:~:text=Workers%20at%20Dongguan%20Stella%20Footwear,workers%20and%20labor%20activists%20said (accessed September 18, 2020).

Wong, Edward. 2014. "To Quell Unrest, Beijing Moves to Scatter Uighurs Across China." *New York Times*. www.nytimes.com/2014/11/07/world/asia/labor-program-in-china-moves-to-scatter-uighurs-across-han-territory.html (accessed May 12, 2017).

Wong, Kam C. 2012. *Police Reform in China*. Boca Raton, FL: CRC Press.

Wong, Sue-Lin. 2016. "Chongqing Blazes Economic Trail as Bo Scandal Recedes." *Reuters*. www.reuters.com/article/china-economy-chongqing-idUSKCN0W4053.

World Bank. 2017. "Doing Business: Measuring Business Regulations." *World Bank*. www.doingbusiness.org/rankings (accessed March 19, 2018).

World Footwear. 2018. "Stella Is Cutting Production Capacity in China." *World Footwear*. www.worldfootwear.com/news.asp?id=3445 (accessed April 2, 2019).

Wright, Teresa. 2010. *Accepting Authoritarianism: State-Society Relations in China's Reform Era*. Stanford, CA: Stanford University Press.

———. 2018. *Popular Protest in China*. Medford, MA: Polity Press.

Xie, Chuanjiao. 2017. "Facial Recognition IDs 25 Suspects at Qingdao Beer Fest." *China Daily*. www.chinadaily.com.cn/china/2017-09/01/content_31403703.htm (accessed February 16, 2018).

Xie, Yue. 2013. "Rising Central Spending on Public Security and the Dilemma Facing Grassroots Officials in China." *Journal of Current Chinese Affairs* 42(2): 79–109.

Xinhua. 2003. "Chinese Trade Unions to Strengthen Protection of Migrant Workers' Rights." *The Supreme People's Court of the People's Republic of China.* http://en .chinacourt.org/public/detail.php?id=3271 (accessed February 16, 2018).

——. 2005. "Leaders Greet Festival with Disadvantaged." *China Daily.* www.chinadaily .com.cn/english/doc/2005-02/09/content_416050.htm (accessed January 10, 2018).

——. 2008. "Premier Wen Visits Passengers Stranded in Guangzhou." *The State Council of the People's Republic of China.* www.gov.cn/english/2008-01/30/content_874968 .htm (accessed January 10, 2018).

——. 2010. "Party Officials Removed After Self-Immolation Protest." *China.org.cn.* www.china .org.cn/china/2010-10/11/content_21097539.htm (accessed September 18, 2020).

——. 2013. "Xi Jinping Meets Model Workers – People's Daily Online." *News of the Communist Party of China.* http://english.cpc.people.com.cn/206972/206976/ 207283/8229302.html (accessed January 10, 2018).

——. 2017. "Armed Police to Be Commanded by CPC Central Committee." *Xinhua News.* www.xinhuanet.com/english/2017-12/27/c_136855602.htm?utm_source=SupChina& utm_campaign=3ca076189a-20171227-448+People%27sArmedPolice&utm_medium =email&utm_term=0_caef3ab334-3ca076189a-162363033 (accessed January 11, 2018).

——. 2018. "China's Private Sector Contributes Greatly to Economic Growth: Federation Leade." www.xinhuanet.com/english/2018-03/06/c_137020127.htm (accessed April 8, 2019).

Xiong, Guangqing. 2008. *Zhongguo Liudong Renkou Zhongde Zhengzhi Paichi Wenti Yanjiu [Study on the Political Exclusion of China's Floating Population].* Beijing: Renmin University Press.

Xu, Hui, and Stefan Schmalz. 2017. "Socializing Labour Protest: New Forms of Coalition Building in South China." *Development and Change* 48(5): 1031–51.

Yan, Fei. 2015. "Rival Rebels: The Political Origins of Guangzhou's Mass Factions in 1967." *Modern China* 41(2): 168–96.

Yang, Baojun, and Dongxiao Jin. 2011. "Regionally Coordinated Development and Planning in the Pearl River Delta." In *China's Pan-Pearl River Delta: Regional Cooperation and Development,* eds. Anthony G. O. Yeh and Jiang Xu. Hong Kong: Hong Kong University Press.

Yang, Dali L. 2017. "China's Troubled Quest for Order: Leadership, Organization and the Contradictions of the Stability Maintenance Regime." *Journal of Contemporary China* 26(103): 35–53.

Yang, Yuan. 2019. "Inside China's Crackdown on Young Marxists." Financial Times. www.ft.com/content/fd087484-2f23-11e9-8744-e7016697f225 (accessed April 5, 2019).

Yang, Yujeong, and Wei Chen. 2019. "Different Demands, Varying Responses: Local Government Responses to Workers' Collective Actions in South China." *The China Quarterly*: 1–16.

Yin, Robert K. 2003. *Case Study Research: Design and Methods.* 3rd ed. Thousand Oaks, CA: Sage Publications.

Yu, Jianrong. 2010. *Kangzhengxing Zhengzhi: Zhongguo Zhengzhi Shehuixue Jiben Wenti [Contentious Politics: Fundamental Issues in Chinese Political Sociology]*. Beijing: People's Publishing House.

Zajak, Sabrina. 2017. *Transnational Activism, Global Labor Governance, and China*. New York: Palgrave MacMillan.

Zeng, Qingjie. 2016. "Democratic Procedures in the CCP's Cadre Selection Process: Implementation and Consequences." *The China Quarterly* 225: 73–99.

Zenz, Adrian. 2019. "'Thoroughly Reforming Them towards a Healthy Heart Attitude': China's Political Re-Education Campaign in Xinjiang." *Central Asian Survey* 38(1): 102–28.

Zenz, Adrian, and James Leibold. 2020. "Securitizing Xinjiang: Police Recruitment, Informal Policing and Ethnic Minority Co-Optation." *The China Quarterly* 242: 324–48.

Zhan, Shaohua. 2017. "Hukou Reform and Land Politics in China: Rise of a Tripartite Alliance." *The China Journal* 78(1): 25–49.

Zhang, Hao, and Eli Friedman. 2019. "Informality and Working Conditions in China's Sanitation Sector." *The China Quarterly* 238: 375–95.

Zhang, Lu. 2015. *Inside China's Automobile Factories: The Politics of Labor and Worker Resistance*. New York: Cambridge University Press.

Zhang, Yanlong. 2011. "Guangzhou Blames Zengcheng Riots on Neglect of Migrants, Fires Local Officials." Economic Observer. www.eeo.com.cn/ens/2011/0708/205614.shtml.

Zhang, Zhaorui. 2007. *Zhongguoshi Jingcha Guanli [Chinese-style police management]*. Beijing: Chinese People's Public Security University Press.

Zhao, Dagong. 2004. "Tantan Dongguan Xing'ang Xiechang Gongren 'Baoluan' Shijian [Talking about the Dongguan Xing'ang Shoe Factory Workers' 'Riot' Incident'." *Boxun*. https://boxun.com/news/gb/pubvp/2004/11/200411020222 .shtml (accessed September 18, 2020).

Zhao, Yuezhi. 2012. "The Struggle for Socialism in China: The Bo Xilai Saga and Beyond." *Monthly Review: An Independent Socialist Magazine* 64(5): 1–17.

Zheng, Siyao, and Tianguang Meng. 2020. "The Paradox of Responsiveness and Social Protest in China." *Journal of Contemporary China*: 1–21.E

Zhongguo Molihua Geming. 2012. "Shenzhen Saidaxin Keji Qian Ren Bagong Dulu [One Thousand People Strike at Shenzhen Saidaxin Technology and Block Road]." *Zhongguo Molihua Geming*. www.molihua.org/2012/12/20.html (accessed February 27, 2018).

Zhou, Changzheng. 2007. *Laodong Paiqiande Fazhan Yu Falu Guizhi [The Development and Laws of Labor Dispatch]*. Beijing: Zhongguo Laodong Shehui Baozhang Chubanshe.

Zhu, Xiaoyang, and Anita Chan. 2005. "Workplace Democracy or an Arena of Management-Labor Contestation: The Chinese Staff and Workers' Representative Congress." In *China's Experience: Workplace Governance and Workers Democratic Participation in Transitional Economy*, ed. Feng Tongqing. Beijing: Social Sciences Academic Press.

Zhu, Ying, Malcolm Warner, and Tongqing Feng. 2011. "Employment Relations 'with Chinese Characteristics': The Role of Trade Unions in China." *International Labour Review* 150(1–2): 127–43.

Zipp, Daniel Y., and Marc Blecher. 2015. "Migrants and Mobilization: Sectoral Patterns in China, 2010–2013." *Global Labour Journal* 6(1): 116–26.

Zuo, Mandy. 2016. "A Step Backwards? Chinese Cities' Harsh Draft Rules Against Taxi-Hailing Apps 'Hinder Innovation.'" *South China Morning Post*. www.scmp.com/news/china/policies-politics/article/2026832/step-backwards-chinese-cities-harsh-draft-rules-against.

Zwilling, Michael L. 2013. "Negative Binomial Regression." *The Mathematica Journal* 15: 1–18.

Index

accountability for labor resistance
  bureaucratic incentives and, 51–54
  jurisdictional boundaries in, 55–57
  regional differences in cadre turnover and,
    59–60
administrative punishments, for bureaucratic
    management of labor unrest, 52–53
African Americans
  great migration of, 41
  insider advocacy for civil rights by, 27
All-China Federation of Trade Unions (ACFTU)
  accountability for muddlers in, 53–54
  cadre promotion system and, 49
  cautious governance and, 80–81
  labor politics and, 23
  labor reforms and, 25, 114–116
  orthodoxy and risk-taking in, 68
  Party and state ties with, 22–23
  in Pearl River Delta, 88
  revival of, 143–145
  state- and post-state socialism and,
    161–162
  worker demands and, 34, 120–121
American Chamber of Commerce (Shanghai),
    155–156
apparel manufacturers, transgressive and
    boundary-spanning activism and, 38
arbitration
  claims and court cases in, 177–178
  responsive capacity of state and, 26, 114–118
Arellano-Bond Estimator, 185
  feedback effects of labor unrest and, 124–125
authoritarian legal citizenship, 28

authoritarian regime in China
  evolution of, 13–14
  international comparisons of, 159–160
  post-state socialist authoritarian typology of,
    160–163
authoritarian resilience, contentious politics
    scholarship and, 12–14
auto sector
  in Chongqing, 131–132
  contained activism in, 40–41
  in Pearl River Delta, 91

Baidu (Chinese search engine), censorship of
    labor coverage on, 2–3
Beijing, worker resistance in, 36
Belarus, labor politics in, 164–165
benchmarks, in cadre promotion system, 49–50
biometric data, state security use of, 111–112
bottom-up change
  bureaucratic incentives research and, 48–50
  labor politics and, 9–10, 129–130, 144–145
boundary-spanning resistance
  forms and causes of, 6–7, 27–29
  increases in, 158
  of migrant workers, 41–44
  organizations in Yangtze River Delta for,
    76–77
  in Pearl River Delta, 57, 91–92
  regional patterns in, 36
  repressive capacity of state and, 121–124
  responsive capacity and, 122–123
  sector-specific patterns of, 38
  tactics in worker resistance and, 31–32